# FIRE! FIRE!
# THE THEATRE'S ON FIRE!

# FIRE! FIRE!
# THE THEATRE'S ON FIRE!

*Rodney Hardcastle*

© Rodney Hardcastle, 2022

Published by Headfield Publishing

All rights reserved. No part of this book may be reproduced, adapted, stored in a retrieval system or transmitted by any means, electronic, mechanical, photocopying, or otherwise without the prior written permission of the author.

The rights of Rodney Hardcastle to be identified as the author of this work have been asserted in accordance with the Copyright, Designs and Patents Act 1988.

A CIP catalogue record for this book is available from the British Library.

ISBN 978-1-7398908-0-3

Book layout and cover design by Clare Brayshaw

Cover image © Wesleywalker81 | Dreamstime.com

Prepared and printed by:

York Publishing Services Ltd
64 Hallfield Road
Layerthorpe
York YO31 7ZQ

Tel: 01904 431213

Website: www.yps-publishing.co.uk

# CONTENTS

| | |
|---|---|
| Foreword | vii |
| Acknowledgements | viii |
| Prologue | xi |
| Ardwick Hippodrome | 1 |
| Bradford Empire | 13 |
| Brighton Grand | 28 |
| Cardiff Empire | 48 |
| Carlisle Her Majesty's | 67 |
| Chiswick Empire | 83 |
| Cleethorpes Pier Pavilion | 99 |
| Eccles Crown | 111 |
| Edinburgh Empire | 121 |
| Exeter Theatre Royal | 145 |
| Glasgow Coliseum | 163 |
| Huddersfield Palace | 177 |
| Kingston Empire | 190 |
| Rotherhithe Hippodrome | 212 |
| Sheffield Empire | 227 |
| Sheffield Theatre Royal | 249 |
| Southport Palladium | 267 |
| St Anne's On Sea Pier Pavilion | 284 |

# FOREWORD

Rodney Hardcastle is a man after my own heart. Struck by the theatre bug at an early age his enthusiasm turned from passion to obsession. For him it was the Dewsbury Empire aged 8, for me it was the Ardwick Hippodrome in Manchester at the age of 6.

Theatre was always a plush, warm, magical place filled with exciting possibilities and imagination. For me it became a place of work, for Rodney, a place of historic fascination and for both of us a place of important cultural, artistic and architectural heritage, never to be forgotten.

Rodney's contributions to the quarterly 'Old Theatres' magazine until its closure in 2018 were legendary. The magazine's publisher, Terry Kirtland, brought together many fine authors of live entertainment, but none finer in depth of research and detail than Rodney Hardcastle.

This man knows his subject, painstakingly scouring thousands of newspaper articles, features, programmes, archives and personal reminiscences. He brings all this meticulous research to bear in this wonderful book that will keep alive the memory these old hearts of our communities.

This is a glorious record of the greats, the ghosts, the gossip and the genesis of live theatre. Here's to Volume Two!!

Matthew Kelly

# ACKNOWLEDGEMENTS

Although my name is on the front of the book, and my photograph on the back cover, I cannot claim that it is 'all my own work'.

I am tremendously grateful and appreciative to the many people who have both inspired and helped me to record a little of the history of some of Britain's wonderful theatres.

The difficult part now, is knowing how to thank everyone, and in which order, without making it seem you are lower or higher on the list than anyone else! I can assure you all, there is no league table!

My immense appreciation goes to…

Duncan Beal and all others at York Publishing Services.

Our sons, Tim, Carl, Jonathan and James for their support and for their superb acting ability in managing to look interested, when I was repeating yet another theatre story they had probably heard me tell many times before.

To Matthew Kelly and his son Matt Rixon, both talented actors and performers who have inspired me on so many occasions with their tales about, and their tremendous enthusiasm of, their theatre and television experiences. Their superb acting ability has taken them to play so many parts in areas so immense we probably have so little knowledge of. Their careers would fill a book – maybe I just had an idea for my next one?

Another source of inspiration is Terry Kirtland, who was the Chairman of the Old Theatres magazine, until his poor health meant he had to lower the final curtain on the magazine.

Thank you to Jonathan Hardcastle, Olivia Hardcastle and our friend Mark Bolton for their photos. Thanks also to Beryl Johnson the partner of the late Duggie Chapman MBE, Theatre Impresario, who kindly gave me access to Duggie's vast collection of images from his theatre memorabilia.

*Duggie & Beryl*

A few years ago, we were chatting with some very close friends of ours, Mark and Vi Bolton, when I mentioned an article I was writing for the Old Theatres magazine. This led on to Mark saying there was a family story that his great grandfather had been 'on the stage' but he didn't know how true it was, or anything more about it. I was intrigued and that set me thinking! I did some research and was able to find that George Bolton was a famous entertainer of many years! He was top of the bill for all of his career only retiring in his 82nd year! George is mentioned in this book. Thank you George Bolton for firing my enthusiasm and for surprising your great grandson!

And finally, a huge thank you to my wife Margaret, who has declared war on my use of, (or lack of) commas and full stops! Her help, advice, proofreading, cups of tea and rescuing things I 'lost' on my computer have been very much appreciated.

*Throughout this book, reference is made to the various costs of things. Such as the building cost of a theatre, ticket prices or court fines, etc.*

*These amounts have been converted from pre-decimal currency (pounds, shillings and pennies) to decimal currency (pounds and pence).*

*However, the amounts have not been converted to the current day value. For instance something actually costing £20,000 in 1920 is shown as such, even though £20,000 would have a current value of £914,000.*

# PROLOGUE

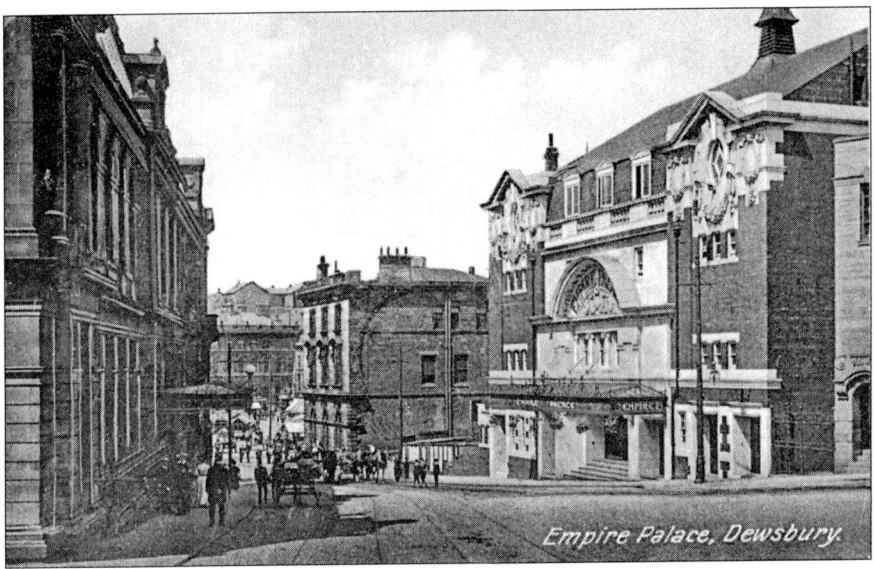

*The Dewsbury Empire Theatre*

**SCENE ONE**

At the age of eight years old in 1950, I was introduced to the amazing world of Theatres and Music Hall Variety. My mother treated myself and my older brother William (Bill) to a very regular Monday evening first house at the Empire Theatre in Dewsbury, Yorkshire. I think my father looked forward to his quiet Monday evenings at home alone!

    I was entranced by the whole experience and the excitement remains firm in my memory to this very day. There was everything to captivate the mind of a young child, glamour, music, dancing and acrobatics. I have been a fan of live entertainment ever since. Thank goodness the magic has never left me.

*Rodney Hardcastle as a child*

My one and only actual experience of appearing 'on stage', occurred on a damp cold Monday evening a few weeks later. My mother, my brother and I were entering the 'Gallery' known locally as the 'Gods', when my mother was approached by a gentleman. He said he was the manager of that week's star performer, the comedian and balloon modeller, Hal Monty, and would her younger son assist Hal Monty in his act later that evening?

After agreeing to this request I was asked to meet Hal Monty's manager during the interval, alongside the booking office. Full of apprehension and schoolboy nerves, I duly turned up and was taken, along with four other young boys, to the back stage area. It was a land of fantasy as far as I was concerned.

Hal Monty's manager gave me a schoolboy cap to wear and said whatever Hal did to me, for example, push me gently, then I had to do the same back to Hal, only much harder and fiercer! I had to clumsily drop things onto the stage floor, trip up etc.

Hal Monty came on stage and asked for five young 'volunteers'. We trooped onto the stage and he began his act. Each boy was introduced, but, being the only one wearing the schoolboy cap (and clearly being the stooge) I was totally and deliberately ignored, obviously gaining the sympathy of the audience.

Eventually, after the four other boys had left the stage, Hal acknowledged I was still there, standing alone, sad, forgotten and unwanted, and he then commenced my part of his hilarious act. I acted with gusto and sheer enthusiasm.

Hal was an expert at twisting the balloons into animals and my 'appearance money' was a huge swan shaped from balloons, but just as importantly, he gave me half a crown, worth £4 in todays money, but in those days it seemed a fortune to a little boy!

Walking home with my mother and brother after the show, when going across the bridge over Dewsbury's River Calder, a gust of wind blew my huge white swan out of my arms and into the fast flowing waters of the river. Fittingly, being a swan, it sailed majestically down the river, never to be seen again. Like a true Yorkshireman, I did hold on very tightly to my half crown though, my wife reminds me I have still got it!

Most Monday evenings the three of us visited the Empire. Each visit was eagerly anticipated and we had the privilege of seeing the leading stars of the day, as well as up and coming unknown ones such as Morecambe & Wise!

I remember clearly, Bill and I arriving home from school on Monday 28 March 1955 when I was twelve, to be told by my mother the devastating news that the Empire was to close after the following Saturday night's performance. The bill poster for the following week stated that the joint stars would be the singer Izzy Bonn and Ted Lune, probably my favourite comedian. That was not to be. It closed before they appeared.

These giant posters were displayed outside the theatre, but gradually deteriorated over the next five years in the wind, rain and snow, reminding us of what we were missing. The theatre was never re-opened. The Empire Theatre had opened on Monday 2 August 1909 and it was demolished in 1960 being replaced by a typical concrete monstrosity of an office block and retail units. Out of sympathy it was called 'Empire House'. Hardly a suitable comparison.

## SCENE TWO

After our marriage and whilst living in West Yorkshire in the 1970s, visiting many theatres became part of our lives for the next fifty years. We had two of the finest live variety entertainment venues on our doorstep, namely the Batley Variety Club and the Wakefield Theatre Club where we were royally entertained by both International and British stars of the day. Unfortunately these lost their popularity and closed down.

*The Dewsbury Empire Theatre's Last Ever Posters outside the Theatre*

Batley Variety Club is now a gym, and Wakefield Theatre Club a car park, after years of surviving as a ten-pin bowling alley.

My wife and I were able to attend the existing traditional local theatres in Leeds, Bradford, Wakefield and Huddersfield, and we made regular trips to London's West End theatres.

We then moved to East Yorkshire and were frequent visitors to Hull Truck Theatre and the Stephen Joseph Theatre in Scarborough. Being regular visitors to America we were able to see shows in New York on Broadway. The one that stands out was seeing the musical, '42nd Street' in a theatre actually located on 42nd Street, New York. Another wonderful experience was seeing the ballet Swan Lake in St Petersburg, Russia, and visiting theatres in the majority of the capital cities of Europe.

## SCENE THREE

My love of theatres never diminished over the years and after moving to live in York, North Yorkshire, for a while I became Chair of York Theatre Royal Citizens Trust in 2013.

My passion for writing also resurfaced and I was to be the author of features for the lovely magazine 'Old Theatres' from 2012 to 2018 when the ill health of the owner and publisher, Terry Kirtland, resulted in its immediate closure.

I had many articles about UK theatres in the pipeline for future magazine issues and I felt that a lot of the history of theatres was in danger of being forgotten. I wanted a record of their history to be retained and preserved for future generations. The majority of theatres had either been demolished or had a change of use. Hence this book!

By the early 1900s many theatres were destroyed or badly damaged by fires, therefore I decided that my theme for this book should be theatres who have been affected in some way by this destructive force of fire.

In addition to the life story of each theatre, I have added a little more information in a selection called 'Did you know…?' which, I hope, brings interesting true life incidents to the world outside and inside these theatres.

Happy reading!

Rodney Hardcastle

# ARDWICK HIPPODROME

*The Ardwick Empire Theatre*

## 1903 – THE EMPIRE

Mr Oswald Stoll, the famous theatre owner with a number of theatres in the UK, decided to build a new one on the corner of Hyde Road and Ardwick Green, a mere two miles from Manchester City centre. This piece of land which had been in use as a tennis court, formed part of the land fronting onto the old Ardwick Hall, which became a large lodging house.

On Thursday 9 June 1903, Stoll applied to the Manchester Watch Committee, chaired by Mr W. Trevor, to request a dramatic licence for his new theatre which was to be called the 'Ardwick Empire Theatre of Varieties'. Stoll said that the theatre would be extremely modern and able to seat an audience of 3,000. He anticipated it would cost £50,000 to build and was designed by the finest theatre architect, Mr Frank Matcham. The Stoll Empire Group was one of the largest in the UK, therefore they were in a position to attract the finest artistes available.

Stoll said that alcoholic beverages would not be sold in any part of the new theatre, nor had any facilities for them been included in Matcham's design. He also felt that the theatre would add value to the surrounding properties. A large number of local residents and businesses supported his application.

However, many people objected. The Rev J. Bennett of Hyde Road Methodist Free Church said that the theatre would be a temptation to the local youth. The owners of Ardwick Hall stated that 110 males and 46 females who lodged in Ardwick Hall said that it would be disadvantageous to have a music hall as a neighbour. Another objector, Mr Rylands said that two shows per evening in a theatre holding 3,000 could result in as many as 6,000 people visiting the locality daily, potentially causing social problems.

Another objector, the Rev J. B. McGovern, rector of St Stephen's, Chorlton-on-Medlock, feared that the Empire would attract "the riff raff and the rag tag and bobtail" to Ardwick and drive away the self respecting people of their neighbourhood. In addition, Councillor John Allison said that he felt the Empire would not be financially viable for Stoll as there was a theatre less than a mile away costing only 10p for the taxi fare to it. Two theatres so close together could not be justified.

The committee announced they would adjourn their decision for one week whilst they considered all the evidence. The following Thursday 16 June 1904, they announced that they had granted a dramatic licence to Mr Oswald Stoll for the Ardwick Empire Theatre of Varieties.

The theatre was one of the finest built, the imposing structure added finesse to the Ardwick area, classified as palatial and imposing by all concerned. The floor of the auditorium was covered with a thick pile, tan coloured carpet, the proscenium, boxes and entrances were hung with expensive drapes, also in matching shades of brown, the same as the covering of the seating.

The main entrance foyer at the corner of Ardwick Green and Hyde Road had an elaborate ceiling with three bays radiating from the central pay box. Two arched passages, one leading to the stalls, the other to the grand circle, had beautiful walls decorated with scenic paintings.

The auditorium, designed in a Renaissance style, had a large coved ceiling, with three arched panels featuring paintings representing Arts, Music and

Dancing. The proscenium was in marble, with semi circular corners. It had elaborately designed panelling, all decorated in a cream and light olive green tint, and relieved with shades of gold.

Matcham paid careful attention to all aspects of safety, for example, lighting and heating were by electricity. There were fourteen exits from all areas which would allow the theatre to be fully evacuated within two minutes. All stairwells were constructed of brick and concrete and were at least five feet wide.

## 1904 – THE OPENING

The official opening took place on Monday 18 July 1904 where, in front of invited guests, Stoll presented an excellent programme starring the famous Fred Karno's Company with Fred Kitchen and Miss Cassie Noel in the musical extravaganza, 'Saturday to Monday'. The other performers included Belle Davies and her singing entertainers; Seeley & West, music and comedy; Bros Phillips, acrobats; Ardel Company performing the playlet, 'A Zoological Comedy' and Hart & Leo in 'The American Professor'. Silent moving pictures were also shown.

*George Robey*

In the programme for this opening performance, the management stated that the Empire would present two shows per night, the first house commencing at 6.50pm and the second one at 9pm, each with a running time of two hours. This allowed only ten minutes for the theatre to be vacated and re-filled before the second house commenced, a very tight timescale. The programme was planned to change weekly. Stoll reconfirmed that all the leading stars of the day would be engaged including, for example, Marie Lloyd, George Robey, Little Tich, etc.

Admission on that first evening was 36p for a private box for four people; stalls cost 5p; grand circle cost 2.5p; the pit was 2p and the gallery (on cushioned seats) 2p with reductions to 1p for Tuesday, Wednesday and Thursday performances.

## 1904 to 1920

The Empire continued to attract huge audiences due to the high quality of stars it was able to attract. Between 1904 and 1920, performers such as W. C. Fields, Wee Georgie Wood, Will Hay, George Formby Senior, etc along with the ones promised in Stoll's opening speech, appeared at the Ardwick Empire.

## 1923

Audiences were beginning to decrease due to the economic situation of the time, and on Monday 18 May 1923, the management made a statement. They hoped this news would increase the number of audiences, especially families, attending the nightly shows. They were offering 2,000 seats either in the stalls, circle or even box seats all at a bargain price of 5p. The opening show for the new pricing strategy, effective from Monday 25 May 1923, starred Bert Cooke and Sybil Arundale in the revue, 'Here We Are'.

## 1930

The Stoll management shocked the community of Ardwick by announcing on Thursday 9 October 1930 that, after almost twenty-five years as a live theatre, with effect from Monday 27 October 1930, the Empire would become a cinema managed by Mr Bernard M. Woolley. An attempt to show films a few years previously had ended in disaster and they had quickly reverted back to live entertainment. However, over the past few years it had been used mainly as a repertory theatre with varying degrees of success,

A new ten piece band was recruited to augment the showing of silent films.

## 1934/35

Obviously a great deal of discussion was taking place at the Stoll headquarters concerning the future of the Empire but it would be part of more far reaching decisions which were being seriously considered.

Stoll had also built the Manchester Hippodrome in 1904, on Oxford Street in the city centre, again designed by Mr Frank Matcham. It used part of the site of the old Hangler's Grand Circus. That Hippodrome had opened on Monday 26 December 1904, with a circus presentation including performing animals, acrobats, high wire acts, clowns etc and continued with all types of live entertainment for many years. It had been equipped with the latest Western Electric sound system in early 1934 as it featured a small number of films.

Everything was to change, on Thursday 15 November 1934. The Stoll management announced that their Manchester Hippodrome had been sold to the Granada Theatre Circuit after only thirty years as a theatre. It would be demolished and a new art deco cinema built on the site. However, during construction it was sold yet again by Granada to the Gaumont British Theatre Group. Newly named the Gaumont Cinema, it opened in October 1935 and operated until Monday 28 January 1974. It had periods as various night clubs and was demolished in 1990. The site was neglected for many years and then developed as a multi storey car park.

The Manchester Hippodrome closed on Saturday 2 March 1935 with a strong variety bill including A. C. Astor, ventriloquist; Nora Williams, whistling singer; Nixon & Morrison, comedians; Three Bonos, acrobats; McDonald twins, dancers and a short pantomime performed by the Hartman Troupe.

The theatre finally closed the curtains as the audience, performers and theatre staff sang 'Auld Lang Syne'. Within days the theatre contents were cleared and the demolition men moved in.

Having made this decision to sell the Manchester Hippodrome, the Stoll management decided to move the whole Manchester theatre operation to the Ardwick Empire including Mr J. M. Early, theatre manager; Mr A. F. Wilby the stage manager, and Mr C. Windsor, the musical director, making the move seamless. More importantly, they also decided to transfer the name and, in future, the Ardwick Empire Theatre of Varieties would now be known as the 'Ardwick Hippodrome'.

It was obvious that the ageing Ardwick Empire had been neglected over recent years. In order to welcome its new status, the management agreed a total refurbishment plan, the feature being a large external neon lighting sign announcing its brand new name to all concerned. All the old seating was replaced by the most luxurious available on the market, new carpets and floor coverings and drapes were fitted in all areas and the whole theatre was totally re-decorated in delicate greens, browns and pinks.

The stage area was not neglected as it was obvious the ancient systems required immediate upgrading, especially the stage and house lighting. Additional modern sound systems and loudspeakers were installed to increase the enjoyment of the audiences. The two nightly programmes would be re-introduced, an alcohol licence had recently been obtained therefore new bar rooms were installed at all levels of the theatre.

## 1935 – THE OPENING OF THE ARDWICK HIPPODROME

On Monday 22 April 1935, Sir Oswald Stoll invited the local MP, Sir Edwin Stockton, JP to open the Hippodrome and he personally thanked Sir Oswald for transferring the business to Ardwick, calling him a 'pioneer of entertainment'. Sir Oswald said he had confidence in his decision to transfer the Manchester Hippodrome to Ardwick and they both wished the theatre every success in the future.

Mr Harry Welshman should have topped the bill, but was taken ill a few days earlier. He was replaced by Leslie A Hutchinson (Hutch), a singer and musician, who was supported by Arthur Prince and 'Jim', ventriloquist; Cole Bros, comedians; De Wolf, Metcalf & Ford, novelty dancers; Buck & Chic Company, rope manipulators and Blanche Collins, impersonator. They were accompanied by Charlie Windsor and his orchestra.

## 1940

*Norman Evans*

During the 1940s the top stars of the period appeared at the Hippodrome, such as George Robey, Jewel & Warriss, Norman Evans, Hylda Baker, Ted Ray, Henry Hall & his Band etc, The Hippodrome was very successful and thousands of people sat in the theatre's 3,000 seats over the years.

## 1950s

The success of the 1940s continued into the early 1950s and audiences were treated in their thousands to the popular stars appearing on its famous stage. 1950 saw Ted Heath & his Orchestra, the famous Will Fyffe, Jewel & Warriss with Tommy Fields starring in the annual pantomime 'Mother Goose'. The 1951 pantomime, 'Little Miss Muffet', starred Charlie Cairoli and Paul. During the year, stars such as Max Bygraves, Semprini, Max Wall, Ann Ziegler & Webster Booth graced the stage.

Audiences were beginning to fall, the management had Charlie Chester starring in Jack & Jill' in the 1954/55 pantomime.

During the year many stars appeared, including Albert Modley, Ken Dodd, Jimmy Clitheroe, Frankie Howard and the man with the Golden Trumpet, Eddie Calvert. Comedian Jimmy James was on the same bill commencing Monday 10 October 1955.

Audiences continued falling, and for week commencing Monday 5 August 1957 the management engaged Chas McDevitt and Nancy Whiskey following their hit recording of 'Freight Train'.

They were trying to attract younger audiences. They also followed this theme in week commencing Monday 16 June 1958 with a young Marty Wilde and the Wild Cats appearing, but good attendances were proving even more difficult.

The Hippodrome suffered from the lack of audiences as did all other theatres, due to the rapid increase in the ownership of television sets and other forms of entertainment being available which had a tendency to attract the younger people.

*Marty Wilde*

All theatres seemingly now had an 'ageing' audience who preferred the wider variety type of entertainment rather than the new skiffle and rock and roll craze. The management also criticised the shortage and ever increasing wages of existing talented variety acts, due to them being in demand at the newer theatre clubs who were paying more.

## 1960

As a last throw of the dice they engaged the talents of Gene Vincent and Eddie Cochran for week commencing Monday 28 March 1960.

On Monday 2 May 1960, Billy Cotton and his Band Show performed for one week but the situation was serious. The management felt they had no alternative but to close the Hippodrome for the whole of the 20 week summer holiday period, re-opening it on Monday 7 November 1960.

Bill Owen, who was later to star in 1973 in the long running BBC programme, 'Last of the Summer Wine', appeared with June Cunningham to reasonable audience numbers, in the farce, 'Love Locked Out'. Between November and the start of the pantomime, the Hippodrome was not in a financial position to attract 'big' names but hoped to continue presenting genuine family entertainment therefore prior to the 1960/1961 pantomime they presented shows aimed specifically at younger audiences.

Pantomimes performed annually to large audiences around December/January each year and their income probably funded a good proportion of the year's overheads. The last ever pantomime, performed in December 1960/January 1961 was 'Goody Two Shoes" starring Charlie Cairoli and Paul King as Lord Gorgeous of Glamour and the Mayor of the village. They were assisted by Henry Lytton as the Dame; Cox Twins as Late and Early; Miles Twins as Penelope the horse; Juel Morrell as the Saucy Maid; Bobby Bennett as Muddles and the famous Tiller Girls.

This was followed by the 'Max Wall Show'. Max was supported by Robert Earl, Jill Summers and McAndrews & Mills.

## 1961 – THE END

On Thursday 13 April 1961, a Stoll-Moss director stated that the Hippodrome was no longer a profitable enterprise and its future was in serious doubt, as was a large majority of their theatres.

The last ever show at the Ardwick Hippodrome was the revue 'Tokyo 1961' ending on Saturday 22 April.

The management announced that the theatre would be offered for sale, possibly being utilised for an alternative use such as a bowling alley or bingo. No interest was shown and the theatre remained 'dark'

At 11am on Wednesday 30 August 1961, F. S. Airey, Entwistle & Co auctioned the contents of the Hippodrome and these included all the stage equipment, fittings, floodlights, dressing room fixtures, spotlights, house tabs, scenery etc. In addition, all the ancilliary items were offered for auction such as floor coverings, office equipment, crockery, glassware, fire appliances, bar equipment and even the theatre vacuum cleaner.

## 1964 – THE FIRE

The Hippodrome sat in all its misery looking sad and neglected awaiting its fate when this was suddenly taken out of its hands. On Friday 21 February 1964, a fire was discovered on the premises which, despite the efforts of 60 firemen from Manchester City Fire Brigade, seriously damaged the Hippodrome. It was demolished the following August, and the area is now used as a car park and has never been re-developed, an identical fate to the Manchester Hippodrome!

What a sad end to a beautiful theatre.

## DID YOU KNOW…?

## 1904 – A THEATRE VERANDAH

Three months after the opening of the Ardwick Empire, the Highways Committee had conditionally sanctioned the erection of a shelter over a portion of the footpath at the corner of Hyde Road outside the Ardwick Empire Theatre.

Mr J. R. Wilson, Chairman of the Improvements Committee, asked the Highways Committee to "take this item back again so as to enable the Improvement Committee to come to better terms than now seemed probable with the owners of the theatre, for the purchase of ninety-three yards of land on the other side of the building for street purposes."

Mr J. Pitt Hardacre said it was utterly beneath the dignity of the Council that hundreds, perhaps thousands of people, should stand in the rain for want of shelter because of a dispute over the purchase of neighbouring land.

Alderman Tunstall, Deputy Chairman of the Highways Committee said he was quite willing that the subject should go back. Accordingly it was referred.

## 1906 – ARTHUR BAXTER

Signor Castini was billed as 'The Human Bullet' and was appearing at the Ardwick Green Empire Theatre of Varieties in week commencing Monday 2

April 1906. His act consisted of being fired out of a cannon and whilst flying through the air, grabbing hold of a trapeze above the auditorium.

Because this act was considered dangerous and liable to potentially cause injury, people were often auditioned to act as his understudy in case he was unable to perform. One such person was Arthur Baxter, a 23 year old gymnast who lived in Essex Street, Old Trafford, Manchester.

On one of the 'trial runs' of being shot from the cannon, young Arthur missed the trapeze and fell into the safety net underneath the trapeze. Unfortunately, he landed awkwardly and fractured his spine. He was taken to hospital where his condition was said to be critical. Sadly, he died two days later.

## 1909 – JOSEPH JOHNSON (ALIAS BIRTLES)

Joseph Johnson (alias Birtles) of no fixed address appeared at the City Police Court on 2 October 1909 before Mr R. J. Reynolds and Mr N. Meadows. He was charged with obtaining a pair of opera glasses by false pretences from Mr John Hay, the assistant manager of the Ardwick Empire Theatre.

On the previous Wednesday evening, Miss Nellie Sheerin, daughter of the licensee of the Sherwood Hotel in Chorlton-on-Medlock had visited the theatre and had left her opera glasses behind.

On returning home to the bar of the Sherwood Hotel, she mentioned this to some of her father's customers. The accused, Mr Johnson overheard this, left the Sherwood Hotel and went to the theatre telling them his wife had left her opera glasses there, and he had come to collect them.

He was afterwards arrested by Detective Sergeant McLelland and Detective Watson. Due to the fact that there were some previous convictions against Johnson, he was sent to prison for three months.

## 1914 – THE MANCHESTER ARTILLERY

In August of 1914, the Manchester Artillery were using the City Football Ground to put their hundreds of horses through their paces. Many of the horses were untrained and therefore there were quite a few spills but fortunately no injuries to the soldiers. The Ardwick Empire was used to 'house' the men at night and on both Saturday and Sunday night, 600 men slept in the theatre.

## 1915 – EMELIE HAYES

On Monday 27 December Emelie Hayes should have commenced her week's performance at the Ardwick Empire. Also appearing there that week was her husband, the singer G. H. Elliott.

However, she had contracted a bad cold during the previous week and decided she should rest. Emelie Hayes selected an artiste to take her place. Following the Monday matinee, that artiste also fell ill, and Miss Hayes was called by the theatre management at the last moment, to come to the theatre and deputise for her deputy!

## 1931 – A MOVING PLATFORM

'The Bioscope' a British Film Journal, reported in November 1931 that the stage carpenter of the Ardwick Empire Theatre had invented a mechanical, moving platform. It weighed three tons and could accommodate twelve musicians, moving them from the rear of the stage to the footlights and back again whilst still performing. The journal reported that *"the purpose of this innovation is to enable the orchestra to make a more intimate contact with the public and thus get their stuff over better"*.

## 1960 – EDDIE COCHRAN AND GENE VINCENT

Rock and Roll stars, Eddie Cochran and Gene Vincent were touring the UK between January and April in the spring of 1960. They appeared at the Ardwick Hippodrome on Monday 28 March 1960.

Their last performance of the tour was in Bristol just over two weeks later, on Saturday 16 April. Eddie Cochrane, Gene Vincent, Eddie's fiancé, Sharon Sheeley and their tour manager, Patrick Tompkins who was 29, were travelling towards London immediately after the show, to go to Heathrow airport to return home to America.

Whilst travelling through Chippenham, their taxi, a Ford Consul MK 2, driven by 19 year old George Martin, left the road just before midnight and hit a concrete lamp post. Eddie Cochran was thrown out of the taxi and suffered a traumatic brain injury. He never regained consciousness, and sadly died in hospital the following day, aged only 21.

Eddie's fiancé Sharon Sheeley who was 20 yrs old and a songwriter, suffered injuries to her back and thigh, Gene Vincent suffered a fractured collarbone

*Gene Vincent*  *Eddie Cochran*

and severe injuries to his legs, and Patrick Tompkins sustained facial injuries and a possible fracture to the base of his skull. The taxi driver, George Martin did not have any significant injuries. The enquiry later found the accident, which didn't involve any other vehicle, was the result of an excessive speed of 60 mph. The taxi driver was fined £50 and was banned from driving for fifteen years, but an appeal was made eight years later and the ban was lifted in 1968.

Gene Vincent and Sharon Sheeley returned to the United States after their hospital stays. Eddie Cochran's body was flown home, and after a funeral service, he was buried on April 25, at Forest Lawn Memorial Park in Cypress, California.

# BRADFORD EMPIRE

*Bradford Empire*

## 1898

In the late 1800s, hotels were being built to accommodate the many visitors to Bradford arising from its industrial growth. One of them, the Alexandra Hotel, erected in 1877 in Great Horton Road, was probably the most palatial and largest in Bradford. So what is the connection between this hotel and a potential theatre?

Mr H. E. Moss, who owned a number of Empire Theatres throughout the United Kingdom, decided that Bradford would be his next location. He appointed Mr W. G. R. Sprague, the eminent theatre architect, to design his new building. The 140 bedroomed Alexandra Hotel with its huge gardens was an ideal location being very near to the city centre. Sprague had a very unique plan, he would accommodate this theatre within parts of the hotel, and the hotel gardens.

The planning permission, submitted by Mr Neill of solicitors Neill and Holland, was approved by the local Council in January 1898. The alterations to the hotel and the erection of the new theatre structure commenced immediately with a view to opening the Empire in twelve months time. The design and planning was a major and complicated undertaking as many factors required detailed consideration, especially as the hotel would have to remain open to guests during its re-construction.

The Alexandra Hotel originally had 140 bedrooms but, with Sprague's intervention, this would be reduced to 70, with a third of the hotel's total floor space being utilised for the theatre. In return, the hotel would receive a total makeover including redecoration, refurbishment and the installation of electric lighting. It was emphasised at the very start that the hotel would have no connection with the theatre in any way as each would be managed as totally separate businesses. Many people questioned their compatibility and how it would work in practice. Very strange bed-fellows!

The gardens at the rear of the hotel would be the location of the large auditorium and stage, with the theatre entrance, reception rooms, booking office etc being situated within a third of the existing hotel building. There was seating for a total of 2,200 people within the ground floor, grand circle and balcony.

The decorations in the theatre's new entrance hall were in light blue, red and gold with the Arabesque style continuing into the auditorium. The ornate ceiling, designed around three hexagons each rising one above the other, culminated in a circular interior dome. It also had a sliding roof to improve the ventilation and a large Oriental electric lighting system illuminating the auditorium with an amber glow. Due to the clever design, there was an absence of pillars, thus ensuring that all patrons had a perfect view of the stage.

The building was constructed of concrete, brick and stone and included numerous fire-proof exits leading to street level from all areas of the theatre. A fire-proof curtain was fitted to the 30 feet wide proscenium and the new theatre had fourteen modern dressing rooms. The stage was 60 feet wide and 40 feet deep, fitted with the most modern equipment available at the time, including many traps to maximise the experience of the performance.

The main entrance of the original hotel was to be remodelled. The external aspects of the hotel received a considerable amount of attention, especially the new 100ft high corner towers, each one capped by miniature cupolas. Within these, were powerful searchlights with revolving coloured lenses, and could be seen for miles around. The total cost was £30,000. The contractors included Messrs Howe of West Hartlepool, builders; Messrs De Jong of London, decorations; Messrs Cranston & Elliot of Edinburgh. Furnishings, upholstery and electric lighting were supplied by Messrs Sax Slatter of London.

## 1899

The twelve month build target was met. The Empire opened on Monday 30 January 1899 when Mr Frank Allen, the general manager, thanked Moss and Sprague for commissioning and designing such a beautiful theatre which was welcomed with open arms into Bradford. These kind comments were acknowledged by a standing ovation for the two gentlemen from the sell-out audience, followed by further speeches from Alderman T. Speight, the ex-Mayor and Mr J. Lennon the acting theatre manager.

The opening bill was one of the finest that could be assembled and included Paul Sandon, ventriloquist; Musical Dale, musicians; Addie Conyers, comedienne; Bumbo Austin, acrobat; James & Marie Finney, specialist act; Syd May, impersonator; The Three Sisters Jonghmanns, vocalists; Austin Rudd, comedian; Hartley Milburn's Eight English Roses, vocalists & dancers; Lillian Lea, vocalist and Herr Grain, an animal act. They were accompanied by the Grand Empire Orchestra under the direction of Mr W. Forrest Hague.

## 1900 – 1916

In the early 1900s the Empire continued the theme of providing high quality entertainment featuring many of the top music hall acts including such major stars as both Stan Laurel and Charlie Chaplin who appeared together in a Fred Karno revue. Other iconic names such as Harry Houdini, W. C. Fields, Vesta Tilley, George Formby Snr., Marie Lloyd, and Mark Sheridan made regular appearances.

The healthy competition for audiences continued into the early 1900s, the Empire always attracting large audiences. However one planning proposal

*Marie Lloyd*       *W. C. Fields*

in 1913 caused great consternation for the management of the Empire as it could seriously affect its future. On the opposite side of the road, Mr Francis Laidler, another famous theatre impresario, planned to build a palatial Alhambra Theatre, capable of attracting people in their thousands, thus seriously affecting attendances at the Empire. The Alhambra building commenced in 1913, costing £20,000, and opened on Wednesday 18 March 1914 with a seating capacity of 1,400.

As expected, the Alhambra significantly reduced the Empire's attendance numbers. In 1916 a union was created between the two separate theatre owners, Laidler and Moss, but little progress was made leading to the continuing detriment of both parties. There could only be one survivor, and it was probably going to be the Alhambra, but, not to be defeated, the Empire closed down on Monday 1 May 1916 for refurbishment.

## 1916

The re-opening of the Empire took place on Monday 7 August 1916 when the audience appreciated the number of improvements made to it, especially the new colour scheme of gold and orange for the walls. The ceilings of the pit stalls, dress circle and upper circle were decorated with a new fibrous material, a rich green carpet covered all floors and new plush seating, covered in a tango coloured material, completed the startling effect.

The production and stage aspects were not neglected. Scenery of 24 feet high could now be used, the depth of the stage extended to 45 feet, new dressing rooms were built able to accommodate ninety people, making it very attractive for most touring companies. The electric theatre and stage lighting system had been significantly improved, with special emphasis placed on electrical dimmers for theatrical lighting effects. More importantly, all the facilities for the comfort of ladies were substantially improved!

Further discussions had taken place between the two theatre owners, Moss and Laidler, who agreed that the Empire would present once nightly plays, sketches and melodramas leaving the Alhambra as the venue for variety and music hall, offering two traditional performances each evening.

After the playing of the National Anthem, the opening presentation by Messrs Murray King & Charles Clark was Mr Edward Sheldon's play 'Romance' starring Miss Violet Fairbrother, Mr Nicholas Adams & Mr James R. Waters.

There was a degree of sadness during the week's run as Miss Fairbrother's brother, Captain Harcourt Fairbrother, who had been wounded in April 1915 in Mesopotamia, died on Tuesday 8 August 1916 after severe injuries which had caused him eighteen months of long term pain and suffering. He had been mentioned in despatches on three occasions, and awarded the Military Cross for his bravery.

## 1917 – CINEMA

On Monday 19 November 1917, Laidler and Moss decided that this business arrangement was no longer viable. The Empire management announced that the theatre had been leased to Bio-Colour, one of the UK's principle cinema houses. This group with numerous cinemas in London, Glasgow and Cardiff, announced that it had great plans for the Empire, confirming it would close at the end of the week for total refurbishment, and transforming it into a permanent cinema. Unfortunately, their plans had to be altered somewhat.

## 1917 – FIRE No 1

Two days later, on Wednesday 21 November 1917 at 7am, a man passing on his way to work, noticed smoke billowing from a side, upstairs window, and immediately notified the fire brigade. They attended within minutes with all available fire fighting equipment. Upon arrival they found the gallery and circle ablaze, full of smoke and fumes. The firemen tackled the fire and were able to extinguish it within one hour. The cause of the fire was never established, it was assumed that it had originated in the gallery, possibly from a dropped match or cigarette by a careless audience member when attending the theatre the previous evening.

The firemen, led by Chief Officer Scott, were able to confine the serious damage to the circle and gallery areas although a tremendous amount of superficial damage had also been caused in the auditorium due to smoke, fumes and water flowing from the fire stricken area. The fire-proof curtain proved its effectiveness by preserving the back stage area and preventing the fire from spreading. This could have potentially destroyed the whole theatre, and, possibly, the hotel. There was a touch of dark humour as the performance that week was entitled 'Ye Gods'. The area of the theatre known as the gallery, where the fire caused the most damage, had been nicknamed by the locals, for many years, as 'the Gods'.

The new lessees commenced the repair of the damaged areas, overhauling, re-equipping and finally converting the Empire into a cinema. A large entrance hall had been created as the Palm Court Cafe, with an all ladies orchestra, playing from 1pm to 10pm, under the conductorship of Miss Gabriel Hope, who claimed she could play ten different instruments. There was an additional orchestra in the auditorium, conducted by Mr Frank Wilson. The new owners stated that the maximum admission price would be 5p and the lowest 1p.

## 1918 – RE-OPENING

After this significant modification and refurbishment, the newly named Empire Cinema, opened on Monday 11 February 1918 to the showing of 'Sweetheart of the Doomed'. This 1917 silent film starred Miss Louise Glaum, the famous American actress who became internationally known for her characterisation of vampires. In this film, she played 'Honore' who hated all men and took revenge on every one she met after being betrayed. The advertisement included the phrases, 'Symphony Orchestra', 'Ladies Orchestra' and 'Moorish Tea Room' as enticements.

Miss Glaum, born in Baltimore, Maryland, USA, on Tuesday 4 September 1888, died on Wednesday 25 November 1970 in Los Angeles, California, USA, aged 82.

## 1926 – NEW OWNERS

Bio-Colour did not continue its ownership and it changed operators a number of times until, in November 1926, when it was obtained by the Gaumont British Picture Corporation for £15,000. This seemed to be a positive move for the Empire, as it brought it into the ownership of one of the major players in the cinema world. That was not going to be the case however, as further dark clouds were gathering on the horizon.

## 1929 – MORE COMPETITION

In 1929, a few hundred yards away, opposite both the Alhambra and the Empire, a 'super cine-variety theatre', the New Victoria was being commissioned by the Gaumont-British Picture Corporation making this 3,300 seater auditorium the third largest entertainment centre in the UK with a glamorous cinema being the central focus.

This would be the first ever cinema dedicated to 'talkies' built in the UK, at an amazing cost of £250,000. This huge complex also included a 200 seater restaurant, with a 420 square foot ballroom above it, and a sizeable cafe to complete this impressive building. The opening night of Monday 22 September 1930 was spectacular, the film 'Rookery Nook' starring Tom Walls, Robertson Hare and Mary Brough was shown. The evening concluded with an organ recital by Mr Leslie James and a live stage performance of the revue, 'The Follies of 1930'.

## 1937 – 1950

The Empire changed management again on Monday 3 May 1937, when it was acquired by the Buxton Circuit, who controlled a number of cinemas in Yorkshire and Lancashire. The owner, Mr Harry Buxton, assured customers that he would totally refurbish the cinema and carry out necessary improvements. His major initiative was the installation of the Mirrophonic sound system, costing £6,000, this being one of only three installations in the whole of England.

On Wednesday 4 April 1945, Harry Buxton made an announcement that twenty-three of his large number of cinemas would change in order to present live variety entertainment. There was a great deal of interest in this statement as thousands of Bradford residents were hoping for another live theatre in the city. Some of the cinemas changing over were The Pilot in Kings Lynn, the Scala and the Gaiety in Manchester, the Palace in Burnley and the Regal in Boston and Blackburn. After discussions with Laidler, from whom the Empire was sub-let, the Empire was removed from this list and continued as a cinema.

A far larger contract was negotiated on Monday 1 December 1947, for the whole Empire, Alexandra Hotel and a local garage site. This had been usually leased or sub-leased from Moss Empires by various people, and was now purchased outright by Hammonds United Breweries Ltd, Fountain Brewery, Manchester Road, Bradford. This was one of the many deals that had been concluded by Hammonds over the past year with its acquisitions of the Seth Senior Brewery in Shepley, near Bradford, the Tower Brewery in Tadcaster, and a number of individual large public houses. They also completed a merger with Bentley & Shaw Brewery, Huddersfield with its 192 tied houses. The Empire, leased by Horton Road Cinemas, was to continue as a cinema.

The lease for the Empire was then acquired by Mr L. Blond of Associated Companies, Liverpool on Monday 3 April 1950. They carried out a number of improvements including installing a new Western Electric sound system. The cinema re-opened for business the following Thursday.

## 1952 – FIRE No 2

Police Sergeant Harry Johnson, Constables A. J. Harris and V. Foulds were patrolling Bradford City centre, minutes after midnight on Friday 25 January 1952, when they smelled burning whilst patrolling in New Victoria Street.

Following their noses, they walked around local streets until they found the source of the burning smell. It was clearly coming from the Empire. On breaking open the stage door, they were met with smoke and flames burning in and around the cinema screen and stage area. Over 40 firemen and six appliances attended, under the direction of Chief Fire Officer W. Thomas, who found the seat of the fire raging in the basement boiler house, spreading to the stage, igniting the curtain and screen, and rapidly extending to the roof until reaching the magnificent dome in its centre.

Enormous amounts of water were poured into the Theatre from the turntable ladders whilst numerous firemen entered the auditorium and fought the stage fire from the ground floor. Unfortunately the ornate amber coloured glass in the roof dome cracked under the intense heat and was eventually washed away with the force of the water from the hoses.

Blazing timbers fell from the roof into the auditorium. The heat had been so intense that the hand rails in the circle were too hot to be touched for many hours. Unfortunately the auditorium, stage area and surrounding offices, workshops etc were destroyed and only a mass of debris remained in the smouldering wreck of the building. There were no injuries other than to fireman Mr William Huggan who injured his left knee whilst tackling the blaze.

Luckily, the Alexandra Hotel was undamaged. The manager, Mr Graham Chalk, as a safety precaution, advised the guests to dress and vacate the hotel until told to return. Among the forty-five guests staying at the hotel was the performer, Miss Kathleen West, coincidentally appearing as one of the Ugly Sisters in the pantomime 'Cinderella' at the nearby Alhambra.

## 1954 – 1993 – CLOSURE

The Management announced the following day that they had every intention to repair the Empire to an even higher standard, and that refurbishment work would be starting in a short while. Sadly this was a false promise as the Empire was never to reopen. However, the Alexandra Hotel continued to flourish as one of Bradford's leading hotels, as its near neighbour, the theatre, sat derelict, sad and unwanted. On Wednesday 7 July 1954 plans for the hotel were approved by the Bradford Planning Committee to install 23 additional bedrooms, a banqueting hall capable of seating 200 in the basement, a first class lounge, a dining room for 100 guests, a cocktail bar and a circular television lounge on the ground floor.

The owners, Hammonds United Breweries Ltd, planned to bring the hotel to the highest possible standard of any in Bradford. The chief architect for Hammonds, Mr G. S. Saunders, said that the refurbishment would commence within the next few weeks and should be completed by Christmas. The proposed plans would incorporate the majority of the old Empire Theatre back into the hotel, but there were no plans to include the original extension built in the gardens. In effect, the hotel would revert back to its pre 1899 original site plans.

This sad, old decaying Empire Theatre sat in its derelict state for many years until it was finally demolished in the early 1980s, becoming a college car park.

The Alexandra Hotel continued as a successful hotel until the mid 1970s when it became an extension to the nearby, rapidly expanding, Bradford College. It remained in educational use until 1989, when it was deemed unsafe for occupancy, and forced to close its doors until it was demolished in 1993. It is now also used as a city centre car park overlooking the Alhambra, which is still operating as one of the North of England's finest theatres.

## DID YOU KNOW…?

### 1902 – MR ROBERT WRIGHT

An inquest was held at the Bradford Town Hall on Tuesday 28 October 1902 to investigate the death of Mr Robert Wright, a long term employee at the Empire Theatre. He was found dead at his home, at 9.45am on Monday, 27 October 1902 by a neighbour and his estranged wife. He was last seen alive at the Theatre the previous Saturday evening, did not seem depressed in any way and had appeared to be in good spirits. Upon breaking into his house through a downstairs window, the couple found his body lying on the floor. Adjacent to his body was a length of rubber pipe leading from the gas supply, his head was covered by his coat and a strong smell of gas filled the room.

Mrs Martha Wright, his estranged wife, said they had parted some ten years previously, and were leading separate lives but she was aware that her husband had money problems as a result of gambling on horses. Another witness, Miss Clara Harker said she had heard Wright threatening to hang himself some days previously due to his on-going financial problems. The jury returned a verdict of 'suicide whilst temporarily insane'.

### 1902 – MISS ELLEN (NELLIE) GILHOOLEY

On Wednesday 9 July 1902, the Leeds City Coroner, Mr J. C. Malcolm, held an inquest in regard to the death of Miss Ellen (Nellie) Gilhooley who had been employed at the Empire as an usherette for a number of months, prior to terminating her employment, four weeks previously. She subsequently lodged with Miss Florence Burston, in Leeds, where she died from blood poisoning and septic peritonitis on Monday 30 June 1902, following what was assumed to be an 'illegal surgical operation'. Miss Burston was charged with aiding and abetting in that operation.

Dr W. J. Hainsworth, a local GP, said that he had examined Miss Gilhooley in April when she had complained of suffering from indigestion and pains in the stomach but denied she was pregnant. Other friends stated that she had been friendly with a married man during the past few months but had become depressed a few weeks ago by some issues they were unaware of.

The jury returned a verdict of 'wilful murder', by a person unknown.

## 1906 – MR ALBERT HALL

Mr Albert Hall, was well known in the music hall world, not as a performer, but as a prolific writer of popular songs for such stars as Dan Leno, Vesta Tilley, Marie Lloyd, Pat Rafferty, etc. He led a reclusive life, had no friends or relatives, no one was sure of his actual name although it was rumoured that he had played football for Preston North End, under the name of Riley, and had also served in the British Army, touring India.

Being so introverted and uncommunicative created numerous mental health problems for Hall, and for an unknown reason he decided to base himself in Bradford, rather than his native Ireland, but in the early 1900s he became an alcoholic as well as being destitute. In mid 1906 he entered the Bradford Workhouse, was taken ill in December 1906, removed to the Bradford Union Hospital where he died on Sunday 20 January 1907.

Mr Pat Rafferty, a famous Irish comedian/singer, and an artiste who had purchased songs from Hall over the past few years, was coincidentally starring at the Bradford Empire during week commencing Monday 21 January 1907.

During his act he sang Hall's songs 'He'll Ne'er Forget Ould Ireland', 'What Do You Think of the Irish Now' and 'Bravo Dublin Fusiliers', dedicating his whole performance to Hall's wonderful song writing talent.

As Hall had no real friends or relatives and was living in the Workhouse, he was to be given a paupers funeral by the Council and buried in an unmarked grave. Rafferty was not prepared to accept what he considered to be this insult in view of Hall's contribution to his, and other artiste's success. As a final gesture of kindness, he personally paid all the costs incurred in a dignified funeral, including the purchase of a private grave in a local churchyard.

The funeral was held on Friday 25 January 1907, Hall's actual age was unknown and very few people attended.

## 1907 – MR JAMES ROBINSON

On Monday 18 November 1907, Mr James Robinson, a Manchester based actor, was charged with obtaining sums of money by false pretences. He was accused of presenting a letter, allegedly signed by the manager of the Bradford Empire, regretting to announce that the theatre stage manager had died on Friday, 8 November 1907, and inviting people to make monetary donations for his funeral and dependants.

The judge said the letter was a complete untruth, it was one of the most dishonest ways of obtaining money through lying about someone's death. Robinson pleaded guilty to all charges. He had also been convicted of obtaining food by false pretences in other parts of the country. He was sent to jail for nine months, with hard labour.

## 1908 – THE SISTERS FREER

A hearing of the charges against Miss Almeda Freer and Miss Florence Freer of Yeadon, was heard in Bradford City Court on Saturday 2 May 1908 when they were accused of obtaining money by false pretences from twenty young women who had answered an advertisement for 'those interested in securing a career within the entertainment industry'.

The Freers had indicated at the interviews that they had had a contract for twelve years with Messrs Moss and Stoll, famous theatre owners, and were seeking young ladies to audition for a group of performers. Depending upon their standard of dancing and singing, the ladies would be invited to join a nationwide theatre revue tour paying them £1 per week.

The applicants were informed at the audition that the Freers were seeking at least sixteen ladies to appear in a revue, commencing at the Bradford Empire on Easter Monday 1908 followed by a year's UK tour.

Miss Elizabeth Ann Wilson, an applicant, visited the Freers auditions at the Prospect Hotel, Bradford, when, after auditioning, they confirmed her appointment and offered her £1 per week wages as set out in the advertisement. A number of other applicants were included in a total of nine cases brought against the Freers, however the Public Prosecutor, Mr H.R. Watling decided to hear only three of them, the one from Miss Wilson and two others from a Miss Fortune and a Miss French.

The Freers said that prior to the commencement of the tour, applicants would have to pay them 17p per week and make a contribution towards the stage costumes. No offers of work were forthcoming, in the meantime, Wilson had paid the Freers a total of £3.34p, Nellie Fortune paid £2.60p and Dinah French paid £3.03p

Mr Percival Craig, manager of the Empire said the Freers had no authority to make such statements as no arrangements or contracts had been made or even discussed. In their defence the Freers stated that they had never made such promises, they trained the ladies in song, dance and theatre techniques, and had genuinely attempted to secure work for them but they had never given any guarantees. The Freers were each sentenced to one month's imprisonment.

## 1951 – ANTISOCIAL BEHAVIOUR (CASE No 1)

There were some instances of antisocial behaviour at the Empire in the early 1950s. Following complaints, the Police made regular surveillance visits to the cinema. At Bradford Magistrates Court on Thursday 9 August 1951, Mr Willie Worth was charged with assaulting a policewoman who was keeping watch on the audience, on Monday 9 July 1951. He was found guilty of indecently assaulting PW Freda Nicholls, given a suspended sentence of one year and ordered to pay £15 towards the cost of the prosecution.

## 1951 – ANTISOCIAL BEHAVIOUR (CASE No 2)

In the same magistrates court on Thursday 9 August, 1951, Mr Alec Brian Price, a wool waste merchant of Bradford pleaded not guilty to indecently assaulting PW Louise Bormond. After hearing all the evidence the magistrates referred the matter to the Bradford Quarter Sessions.

At the Bradford Quarter Sessions on Monday 22 October 1951, the case was heard by the Recorder, Mr Frank Beverley. PW Bormond said that she visited the Empire on the afternoon of Monday 9 July 1951. Price had walked from the rear of the cinema, sat on her left, placed his right arm against her arm offering her a cigarette and attempted to enter into conversation with her. When cross questioned, PW Bormond agreed she was on duty, dressed in plain clothes and agreed she had been placed as 'bait'.

After hearing all the evidence, Recorder Beverley found Price not guilty of assaulting PW Bormond, dismissing the case.

## 1951 – ANTISOCIAL BEHAVIOUR (CASE No 3)

In the same magistrates court, on Thursday 9 August 1951, Mr Thomas Martin Connell was also referred to the Bradford Quarter Session for his case to be heard on Monday 22 October 1951, being accused of assaulting a sixteen year old girl at the Empire.

The Recorder, Mr Frank Beverley, heard the evidence, immediately quashed the order as depositions had not been properly taken, the girl had a mental age of less than ten and witness papers had not been signed. The case was dismissed.

## 1956 – MR CHARLIE CHAPLIN & MR STAN LAUREL

On Saturday 10 March 1956, at 5pm, a grey haired man of small stature walked steadily along the platform at Bradford's Forster Square Railway Station, almost unrecognisable to the hundreds of shoppers returning home.

This was the world famous comedian, actor, film-maker and composer Charlie Chaplin, who was making a nostalgic trip to where his show business career had started fifty or so years previously. He said it was a sentimental pilgrimage and he was disappointed that the Empire had been destroyed by fire.

In 1906, Chaplin appeared in the famous Fred Karno revues around the country, including the Bradford Empire, again starring in Karno's comedy 'Jimmy the Fearless' at the Empire during week commencing Monday 29 August 1910. Interestingly, Stan Laurel took the lead role in that revue at the Ealing Hippodrome on Monday 11 April 1910 for two weeks before being replaced by Chaplin. Laurel continued to appear in many different roles.

Chaplin's tour of 'Jimmy the Fearless' concluded at the Tottenham Palace, London on Saturday 17 September 1910. Three weeks later he emigrated to America on Monday 3 October 1910. He joined Mack Sennett and the Keystone Film Company where he achieved overnight, world wide, success.

Stan Laurel did actually appear again in Bradford, with his lifelong comic partner Oliver Hardy, on two occasions, during the weeks commencing Monday 28 July 1952 and Monday 3 May 1954 at the Alhambra. From his dressing room at the Alhambra, Laurel could see the burnt out ruins of the neighbouring Empire following its destructive fire on Friday 25 January 1952. Most likely, he shed a tear or two remembering the delightful times he spent on its stage in the early 1900s.

*Stan Laurel & Oliver Hardy*

# BRIGHTON GRAND

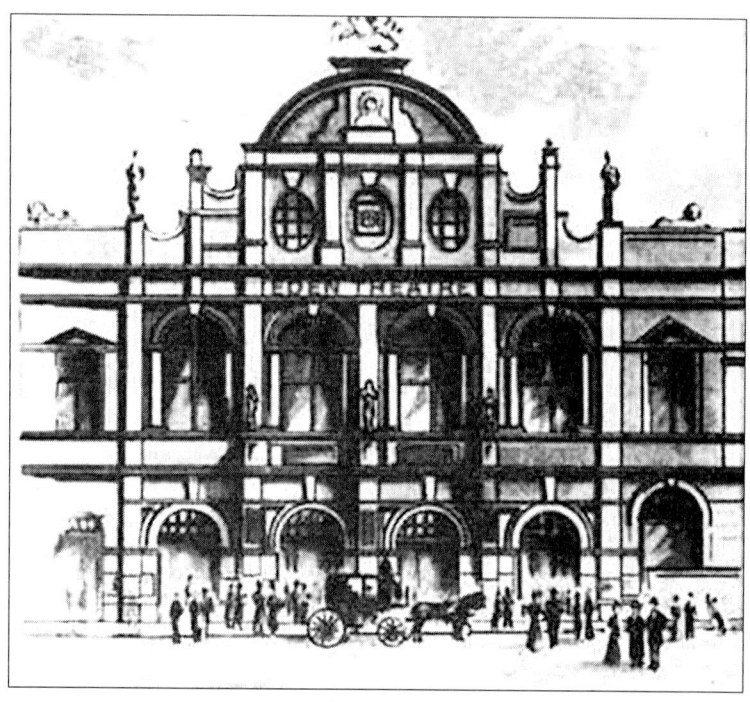

*The Brighton Grand Theatre*

## 1891 – GINNETT'S HIPPODROME CIRCUS

In the mid/late 1800s, Brighton's residents and many visiting tourists were hoping for live entertainment. One of the most popular live entertainments at that time was the world renowned 'Ginnett's Circus'. In 1891, Mr John Frederick (Fred) Ginnett, decided to open a circus in a purpose built structure on an area of land on North Street, near the corner of Queens's Road. He commenced building in January 1891 with a budget of £13,000, deciding to call it 'Ginnett's Hippodrome Circus'.

This large and lofty building measured 80 feet by 150 feet, and held a staggering 5,000 people. Ginnett insisted that all the nineteen doors would open outwards in case of an emergency evacuation. There were eight private boxes, a carpeted lounge measuring 70 feet, two 50 feet high traditional circus rings, one of 42 feet diameter and a larger one of 60 feet diameter.

## 1891 – THE OPENING

The opening date was chosen as Monday 19 October 1891, commemorating the Golden Jubilee of the actual founding of his father, Jean Pierre's Ginnett's Circus', in Nottingham in October 1841. Jean Pierre Ginnett died in Kensal Green, London in 1861 and was buried in the local cemetery.

Fred Ginnett was born in Lea, Essex in 1826, entering his father's circus world at the age of six as a tight rope dancer and horse rider, and billed as 'Infant Ginnett'.

Fred Ginnett addressed the audience welcoming everyone to this wonderful entertainment centre. He gave a brief history of 'Ginnett's Circus' from its early days in Nottingham, being seized by the bailiffs, re-starting again with only one act comprising of eight horses. It had been running successfully ever since those early, challenging days.

This opening speech was followed by a number of circus acts including Richard Hall, a bareback horse rider; Professor Frederick and his performing cats, rats, mice, canaries and monkeys; Billy & Toby, an amusing pair of clowns; The Rio Troupe of lady acrobats and Fred Ginnett's brother, Claude with his speciality horse riding act. Mr Bartlett acted as Ringmaster, with the circus manager being Mr Alfred Norton.

## 1892 – THE DEATH OF MR FRED GINNET

Three months after the opening, Fred Ginnett died suddenly from influenza, at his home in Wellington Road, Brighton on Tuesday 12 January 1892. He was aged 65.

*Fred Ginnet's Memorial*

Ginnett was married twice, had three sons with his first wife who followed him into the circus profession, and had five sons with his second wife. The last rites were performed at the Brighton Parochial Cemetery, Brighton, and he was buried in the family vault in Woodvale Cemetery and Crematorium, Brighton, which is marked by a magnificent mausoleum featuring a circus pony with its head lowered in sorrow.

## 1892 – WULFF'S CIRCUS

Upon the death of Fred Ginnett, Herr Edward Wulff acquired the Hippodrome Circus, continuing to present circus acts from 1892 but he regarded it as a temporary matter as he had considerable business interests elsewhere.

## 1894 – THE EDEN THEATRE

In mid 1894, the building was purchased by the Brighton Empire Company who decided to undertake a major internal re-construction to convert it from a circus into a theatre. In future it would be known as the Eden Theatre, and would have a much reduced seating capacity of 1,700. The whole of the interior was reconfigured. This involved a number of major structural alterations, for example the erection of a stage with adjacent dressing rooms in which had originally been the circus gallery.

The luxurious boxes were retained but re-upholstered, re-decorated and fully re-furbished. The theatre colour scheme was in shades of terracotta to match the new wall coverings, the seats were a crimson colour with matching curtains. To complete the interior decor, the carpets were dark blue.

Extra attention was paid to safety. All staircases were fireproof with brick and stone, electric lighting used rather than gas and all of the ample emergency exits were retained for ease of evacuation. The stage measured 30 feet deep by 32 feet wide, and was protected from the auditorium by a new fireproof asbestos safety curtain supplied by Bell's Asbestos Company.

The architects appointed were Messrs Clayton & Black, the building contractors Messrs V. P. Freeman & Co, the electrical work by Messrs Paine & Thompson, carpeting and furnishings were by Messrs Broadbridge & Sons, the seating by Deans of Birmingham and Mr James Henry supplied the stage fittings. A new back-drop and the proscenium columns were painted by Mr Leolyn Hart of London, the theatre iron work was provided by Messrs

Reed and all fire extinguishers were tested by Brighton's Fire Superintendent Lacroix for safe working.

## 1894 – THE OPENING

On Monday 10 July 1894, the newly named Eden Theatre was opened by Mr J. A. Botham, General Manager, who commenced the proceedings by welcoming everyone to the refurbished building and hoping it would be extremely successful for many years ahead. For the comfort of patrons, he stated that smoking would be allowed at all of the performances with the exception of the matinees! Mr Welbye Wallace, one of the performers, completed the opening ceremony by leading the audience in singing the National Anthem followed by Mr Rollo Balmain who presented two dramas 'Hoodman Blind' and 'Ben-My-Chree'.

The management decided to fix prices which would cater for (they said) 'all classes of people'. For the opening performance, they charged 52p for a box, 10p in the orchestra stalls, 12p in the pit stalls, 4p in the pit and 2p in the gallery.

## 1898 – NEW OWNER

Following the successful run of the pantomime Aladdin, on Saturday 12 March 1898, the Eden Theatre was sold by the Brighton Empire Company to two publicans, Mr George Evans and Mr Frederick George Dunkin who also owned a number of other businesses. They purchased both the Eden Theatre and the Brighton Empire Theatre of Varieties for £52,000, also renting the local Gaiety Theatre for seven years at £1,000 per annum, in effect they had acquired the majority of live theatre in Brighton.

On Saturday 1 October 1898, in view of local concerns, they issued a statement stating that the three theatres were not for sale and it was business as usual. In January 1899 they entered into an agreement to purchase the Alhambra Music Hall in Brighton for £52,000, paying a deposit of £4,000. These theatres were doomed to end in failure as Evans and Dunkin were declared bankrupt shortly afterwards. The Eden Theatre continued in business under new owners until a serious incident caused a great deal of concern.

## 1902 – FIRE No 1

At 12.30 am on Wednesday 15 October 1902 the alarm was raised at the Fire Station, based at the Town Hall, indicating that the Eden Theatre was on fire in the stage area, and in great danger of spreading to the remainder of the building. An hour earlier, at the close of the performance of the drama 'The King and Crime', the manager, Mr Charles Howard, had departed around 11.30pm, leaving the theatre's fireman and a stage hand on site.

Such were the problems of fighting the fire that hose reels had to be run through the auditorium, and some over the roof from the hydrants in North Road. In addition, a constant watch had to be kept to ensure the flames were not spreading to the theatre roof which would have been disastrous. Luckily the fireproof curtain had been lowered fully protecting the auditorium from destruction. In addition the firemen had to ensure that neighbouring property was safeguarded, however residents were advised to vacate their homes for the duration of the fire.

The following morning the extent of the damage could be seen. The auditorium had suffered enormous amounts of water sprayed into the theatre, all the stage equipment and scenery were ruined, the stage roof burned away and the orchestra pit full of water. Some of the helpers salvaging items had a wry smile when, in pulling the big drum out of orchestra pit, it spilled gallons of water over them. Scenery, in the process of being prepared for the Christmas Pantomime, was totally destroyed, and the 'The King of Crime' theatre team had to replace all their scenery as a matter of urgency. Whilst the stage was one mass of debris, the artistes dressing rooms remained untouched.

By 2pm, the fire had been fully extinguished, the estimate for the repairs could be fully established and luckily, the theatre was fully insured. Re-building work commenced immediately.

## RE-OPENING

On Christmas Eve 24 December 1902, the re-furbished and re-modelled Eden Theatre re-opened with the musical extravaganza, 'St George and the Dragon' and the 'Fair One with the Golden Locks'. This unusual presentation starred Miss Leonora Castello in the lead role, supported by Miss Constance Moxon, Mr Frank Gerald and Mr Harry Brayne.

## 1903 – AUCTION

Following the bankruptcy of Messrs Evans and Dunkin, three months later, the Eden and Empire Theatres were both offered for auction by Messrs Orgill, Marks and Lawrence at their Auction Mart on Tuesday 31 March 1903 at 1pm. The Eden was regarded as a highly valuable place of entertainment situated on North Road, Brighton, the equally palatial Empire on New Road, Brighton also included a modern restaurant, they would both be offered as one lot. The auctioneer received a bid of £19,000 for both of them but refused it. The theatres were then auctioned as separate items but no acceptable offers were made and they were withdrawn and left unsold. The auctioneer invited interested parties to discuss a possible purchase or lease outside of the auction.

## NEW OWNERS

On Thursday 11 June 1903, it was announced that the Eden lease had been obtained by Mr Wilfred Cotton, a well respected theatre agent, whose wife, Miss Ada Reeve, was a leading music hall comedienne and entertainer. They, with Mr A. G. Mackenzie, formed the Wilfred Cotton Ltd Company, obtaining a lease for three years at a rent of £1,500 per annum.

The Eden had deteriorated over the past year, the theatre was now requiring a major overhaul in the majority of areas, and in his first few days, Cotton planned a thorough and extensive modernisation of the theatre. His first priority was to replace the poor, basic seating with more modern, comfortable ones, furnished in a bright red plush fabric. Secondly, he partitioned off the refreshment bars from the main auditorium to create their own areas in order to decrease the level of noise and the negative effect it had on the performers and the audience. The whole theatre had a total redecoration in a crimson colour with doors painted in red, gold and white.

The walls were papered, new curtains fitted at all windows, again in a crimson colour to match the seating. New carpets were fitted to all areas including the original stone staircases. Finally, as his show piece, Cotton purchased a beautiful drop curtain from the Gaiety Theatre in London.

## REOPENING

Cotton, assisted by his wife, Miss Ada Reeve, opened the Eden for business on Monday 3 August 1903 with Forbes Robinson's performance of the melodrama, 'The Light That Failed' starring Mr Sydney Brough. In his introductory speech, Cotton said that his intention was to appeal to the wider population of Brighton with more attractive and professional productions available through his many London theatrical contacts.

## 1904

Unfortunately, Cotton's plans did not succeed. One year later on Thursday 21 July 1904, his company, Wilfred Cotton Ltd, was wound up due to bankruptcy. He accepted that the main reason for the failure was the fact that his wife contracted typhoid fever on a trip to Germany in October 1903 preventing her from appearing in their planned, sell out pantomime in the forthcoming December/January. The replacement entertainment resulted in a loss of £1,000 on the venture which created their financial difficulties.

## THE GRAND THEATRE

Mr Ernest Carpenter, already the owner of the Royal Theatre in Bristol, purchased the Eden in June 1904 and immediately renamed it 'The Grand Theatre'. After minor improvements it re-opened on Monday 18 July 1904. He explained to the audience that he had a great deal of experience in all matters relating to theatres and his intention was to implement a number of improvements especially around the standard and variety of shows.

The Mayor and Mayoress of Brighton, Alderman and Mrs E. M. Marx, together with the Ex-Mayor, Alderman J. C. Buckwell, other dignitaries, council officers etc were also invited. The comedienne, Miss Louise Freear, topped the bill and entertained the audience with her performance of 'Boy Bob', a three act comedy drama, accompanied by Miss Dora Rignold, Mr Edwin Sheppard, Mr Stephen Bond, and Mr William Birmingham.

## 1907 – A NEW OWNER

Carpenter continued to improve the quality of entertainment at the Grand, and fortunately the audiences increased quite significantly. However, he decided to sell it in March 1907 to Mr Ernest Gates, to help finance his purchase of the Lyceum Theatre in Wellington Street, London which was concluded on Saturday 30 March 1907.

The partnership of Mr & Mrs Carpenter, highly regarded for the high standard of pantomimes they presented in many theatres in and around London over the Christmas/New Year period, was to come to a sudden end. On Wednesday, 22 December 1909, Carpenter collapsed and died whilst his daughter performed in 'Aladdin' at the Lyceum.

## 1917/19

In July 1917, Gates, upon his bankruptcy, transferred his lease for the Grand to Mrs F. C. Kimberley a famous playwright and lessee of the Palace Theatre, Bordesley. On Thursday 8 May 1919 she purchased the freehold and committed to carry out a major refurbishment and redecoration programme.

## 1923/27

There was a further change of ownership in 1923 when Mr Andrew Melville acquired the Grand, continuing to present a wide variety of popular shows, especially his pantomimes, for a number of years. As with Carpenter, there was a sad event, the death of his wife at the age of 45, in a nursing home on Sunday 4 September 1927 after a major operation. His wife, known professionally as Rose Ralph, had appeared in many leading roles in all parts of the country, making her first stage appearance at the age of ten.

## 1930

There had been many rumours circulating in Brighton that the Grand may be available for lease or purchase. Melville, in early November 1930, announced that he was discussing a possible lease with Mr W. S. Robinson who had a number of cinema interests in the area. Robinson took control of the Grand on Monday 17 November 1930 but he agreed to continue with planned live entertainment until January 1931. The last live performance was the annual pantomime of 'Cinderella' with its usual lavish costumes, sets and special effects. The cast for the final pantomime included Madge White, Gilbert Payne and Johnson & Bert.

## 1931 – CINEMA

Robinson's intention was to 'provide the best films', making it one of the most popular cinemas in Brighton. It was the first cinema in the country to install the new Western Electric Co 'Westone' system providing more light and an improved sound, and costing £7,000. The opening film on Monday 28 January 1931 was 'Good News' starring Bessie Love and Cliff Edwards. It was an unusual film, as the majority of the scenes were in black and white but the final ones were in colour. Supporting it was the film 'The Ship From Shanghai' starring Louis Wolhelm and Kay Johnson.

During the 1930s the Grand offered films for the majority of the year but with their traditional pantomime continuing over the Christmas/New Year period.

In 1934/5, Andrew Melville presented 'The Sleeping Beauty' starring Miss Florrie Forde and Mr Harry Tate and in 1935/1936 'Dick Whittington starring Dick Tubb. The Grand continued to show films until a decision was made to revert back to live entertainment and the final film showing, on Saturday 12 October 1940, was Douglas Fairbanks Jnr and Madeleine Carroll starring in 'Safari' supported by Marlene Dietrich and Gary Cooper in 'Desire'.

## 1941 – THEATRE AGAIN

The theatre remained 'dark' for nine months, the new management under the direction of Mr Robert E. O'Brien, general manager, who had taken a three year lease on the Grand, refurbished it in a new colour scheme of green and silver and replaced the majority of the seating as well as upgrading many of the facilities.

On Monday 21 July 1941, Mr Robert E. O'Brien, who had promised a wide range of high quality entertainment, opened with a variety bill starring Miss Kate Carney, a comedienne, as top of the bill. There would be two performances each evening, 6pm and 8.15pm, prices ranging from 12p down to 2p. O'Brien committed to engaging only the top acts of the day, especially during the war years, in order to maintain high public spirits.

O'Brien followed with a period of leading music hall stars with the traditional pantomime of 'Dick Whittington' starring the comedian, Charles Austin as Sarah the Cook, for the Christmas/New Year break in 1941/2.

Unfortunately O'Brien only remained at the Grand for a few months.

## 1942 – ANOTHER NEW OWNER

The theatre was acquired by Southern Enterprises (1942) Ltd in March 1942. It was managed by Mr Albert Rose, remaining as a variety theatre under his control until 1951, offering twice nightly variety performances with a fourteen piece orchestra.

The new owners, Southern Enterprises (1942) Ltd re-opened the Grand on Monday 30 March 1942, with the Vaudeville programme, 'May We Entertain?' offering two shows per evening at 5.55pm and 7.55pm with admission prices between 4p and 12p. Many stars appeared on its famous stage over the years including Norman Wisdom, Alma Cogan, Petula Clark, Joseph Locke, Flanagan & Allen, Morecambe & Wise, Old Mother Riley, Terry Scott, Eddie Calvert, Albert Modley and Arthur English.

*Alma Cogan*

## 1950s

Audiences were no longer attracted to the Grand in the early 1950s. The management decided to feature different types of shows, especially 'girlie' ones. It was difficult to understand how these types of shows could attract family audiences back to the theatre who had been used to enjoying the talents of stars with their abundance of personality and skills. Hardly the place to take Grandma for her evening's entertainment where she had experienced the real 'stars'.

Famous for its pantomimes, the final one opened on Christmas Eve, Friday 24 December 1954 starring Leon Cortez, Doreen Harris, York & Brady, Billy Scott Coomber and included a beautiful Golden Coach and Ponies.

After taking their bows on their final show on Saturday 22 January 1955, the artistes packed all their personal effects, disappearing into the night onto their next engagement without giving the old theatre a second glance. There was hardly a murmur from the Brighton public that the Grand would be closing forever.

Probably seen as an insult to the famous stars who had performed on its famous stage over the years, the last ever show, one week later, on Saturday 29 January 1955 was 'Nudes in the News'. This was a typical girlie show, starring Beryl & Bobo, Sam Kerns & Pauline, Ava & Carol, Harry Gunn, Tommy & Sylvia Snapps, Max & Maxine and featuring the Glamorous Roma.

The Grand would have hosted, the following week, the famous Rosaires Travelling Circus, starring Joan Rosaire and her horse 'Goldy', but the theatre was now closed forever. Due to declining audiences at all theatres, with no future engagements, Rosaire's Circus closed down shortly afterwards.

The management said that they hoped to re-open the Grand in April 1955. It remained dark for another eighteen months with little hope that it would ever host live entertainment shows or films again, after almost seventy years.

## 1957 – CHANGE OF USE

It was announced on Thursday 15 August 1957 that the theatre would be converted into a furniture factory, the sound of music and laughter would never be heard again in this beloved theatre, only noisy machinery. Unfortunately it would not have a long term future for any use and would disappear forever.

## 1961 – FIRE No 2

On Thursday 1 June 1961, sixty firemen fought a blaze in this furniture factory which badly damaged this delightful old theatre building. In the early hours of the morning, a passer-by noticed flames from a window in the Grand, called the fire brigade, who dispatched ten pumps, some from nearby Lewes and Hove. Sadly, they were fighting a losing battle as flames leapt more than eighty feet into the night sky. The fire was aided by the amount of varnish, paint and other highly flammable materials stored on the premises. Amid these resulting explosions, many families had to be evacuated from their homes in local streets, as sparks and burning embers showered their homes.

The auditorium was totally destroyed when the roof collapsed, but firefighters were able to save some stocks of completed furniture which were being stored on the old stage, also rescuing many important business documents. The furniture factory was owned by Alderman Barry Funnell, who a few weeks earlier had been the Mayor of Hove, and was making a business visit to South Africa at the time the fire started. There were no casualties other than a fireman who suffered severe shock, and was taken to hospital but released home after treatment.

The remains were demolished, and the site used as a car park for a while.

## 1988

In 1988 a tower block was built on the site, being named Gresham House which changed its name to Tower Point in 2000.

Unfortunately it did not have the beauty nor the architectural prestige of the Grand Theatre. It was described as 'the existing Tower Point is a large brutalist building which is conspicuous within the city, but not engaging with the local environment'. What a sad replacement of a beautiful and delightful theatre.

*Gresham House, later Tower Point*

## DID YOU KNOW...?

## 1899 – MR GEORGE EVANS AND MR FREDERICK GEORGE DUNKIN

On Friday 7 July 1899, Mr George Evans and Mr Frederick George Dunkin, previous owners of the Grand Theatre, were declared bankrupt with debts totalling over £200,000. They attributed their failure to a loss of trading in their numerous public houses and failing to concentrate on their newly acquired theatre interests. Mr Hough, Senior Official Receiver asked for an adjournment due to the complexity of the situation, as it was effectively three bankruptcies in one, two individuals and one business.

To complicate matters, on Tuesday 24 April 1900, both Evans and Dunkin appeared at Bow Street Police Court to answer a charge of concealing a sum of £450, with intent to defraud, retained after issue of the bankruptcy proceedings. They stated they were innocent of such charges, were bailed on two securities, one for £50 and one for £100.

## 1902 – MISS ADA REEVE

Ada Reeve

Miss Ada Reeve, born Miss Adelaide Mary Reeves in London on Tuesday 3 March 1874, was an English actress who gained world wide fame as a music hall, variety and pantomime entertainer from the mid 1890s. She topped the bill at the majority of theatres in the UK, regularly touring the USA, South Africa, Australia and New Zealand with her entertaining skills and performing abilities.

In 1902, she married her second husband, Mr Wilfred Cotton, and as a wedding present for him, in June she leased the Eden, making major plans for its success especially as she would appear in the December 1903 Christmas pantomime. She was unable to do so due to a serious illness resulting in the venture ending in financial disaster. During her career she regularly 'appeared' in the witness box of various courts as she was continually either suing people or they were suing her.

Examples were on Tuesday 26 May 1903, she was sued by a Bond Street dressmaker for failing to pay £16 for garments supplied. This was followed on Thursday 28 February 1905 in an action by her for damages for libel and breach of contract against the Newspaper Syndicate Ltd in respect of an article in the 'Weekly Despatch'.

Many other court cases followed. One on Monday 19 February 1906, when she failed to appear at Broughton Theatre in the shows, 'Winnie Brooke, Widow' and 'The Adventures of Molly' as she had accepted an alternative engagement as principal boy in a Birmingham pantomime at a vastly improved financial offer, without giving the required notice.

Miss Reeve continued with court cases for the next ten years or so, her career continued to develop in the theatre world, before concentrating on making a total of nine films in the 1930s. She was the subject of the TV programme 'This Is Your Life' in 1956 and appeared in her last film. 'The Passionate Stranger' in 1957 when she was eighty-three. She died in London on Wednesday 5 October 1966, aged 92. What a life!

## 1905/06 – MR ERNEST CARPENTER

Mr Ernest Carpenter, the Managing Director of the Grand, on Friday 2 February 1906, appealed against a judgement made at Brighton County Court on Friday, 22 December 1905. It had been issued by the National Telephone Company for an outstanding payment of £24. He asked that this should be set aside as he had paid the invoice on Sunday 10 December 1905. Adverse publicity had been generated as the debt had been registered in the London Gazette, being especially damaging as he was well known and respected within the theatre world.

To make matters worse, on Saturday 20 January 1906, the National Telephone Company executed further proceedings for the non payment, but, after considerable discussions between them and Carpenter they realised they had made a serious error. It was proved that the money had been received by one department, they had not notified their finance department who automatically proceeded with the court case as it clearly showed on their records that it had not been paid.

The National Telephone Company offered their most sincere apologies to Carpenter for their error and fully agreed that the claim should be set aside. The Judge awarded costs to Carpenter.

## 1907 – PRINCE FEE LUNG

At Willesden Magistrates Court on Saturday 13 April 1907, Prince Fee Lung, Chinese by birth, and who had performed as a magician at Brighton and other music halls throughout the UK, was charged with deserting his wife.

Lung said that, his wife, acting as his stage assistant, was 'too stout' to perform a 'vanishing lady' trick with him. She was too large to disappear down a tube, situated under the stage, and she was 'replaced' on stage by a duck, as he required a more lightweight assistant.

The magistrate granted a separation order for Mrs Lung who received £1.50p per week. He also commented that marriages between Europeans and Asiatics would never work as the temperaments of the two people were so different!

## 1909 – MR ERNEST CARPENTER

On Wednesday 22 December 1909 Mr Ernest Carpenter, Managing Director of the Grand, was taken ill with an internal complaint, had an immediate operation, but passed away at the young age of 41. The funeral took place on Sunday 26 December 1909 at Harefield, Middlesex, attended by hundreds of performers including the full cast of Aladdin, famous stars including Fred Karno, plus representatives of the Brighton and Bristol Theatres that were once owned by him.

It was a particularly depressing time for Mrs Carpenter as she was with her husband in his final moments but she was fully aware that their 12 year old daughter, Marjory, was playing the part of Slave of the Lamp in 'Aladdin' at the Lyceum Theatre, London. As Marjory was acknowledging the cheers for her outstanding performance, her father lay dying, she was not told of his death by her mother until the following morning.

## 1912 – MR SYD BAKER

One of the most popular acts to visit the Grand was Miss Mabel Lowe's Company presenting 'The Cowboy King' and who where originally billed as 'Cowboys and Indians' displaying their skills of horse riding, lassoing, singing, etc. They commenced performing their revue on Monday 3 June 1912, for one week, attracting full audiences. One of the 'cowboys', Syd Baker, was starring with Bernard Whitcombe and Mabel Lowe.

On Thursday 6 June 1912, Baker was walking towards the theatre in readiness for the evening performance when a horse, owned by Messrs Fry & Co of Middle Street, Brighton, bolted from its stables. Baker stopped it, but the horse bolted again. He chased after it and using his well honed 'cowboy skills' grabbed it by its ears and pulled it to the ground before either it, or pedestrians, were seriously injured. He continued to calm the horse, before leading it back to the owners and its stable.

As a gesture of thanks for such a brave act, Messrs Fry & Co presented Baker with a gift during the interval.

## 1924 – MR ALFRED NIGHTINGALE

On Wednesday 19 November 1924, Mr Alfred Crittenden Walter Nightingale, the manager of the Grand, was charged with embezzling three sums of £1 belonging to the owner, Mr Andrew Melville. This was a complicated case as Nightingale had not embezzled money as such, but a case of wishing to be popular with the public.

He had also made loans to various people without keeping accurate records of payments or receipts, therefore making financial balances impossible to reconcile. In addition he had given away excessive complementary tickets to unknown people without any good reason, again not keeping adequate records. He had not paid invoices for goods and/or services supplied to the theatre, nor entered them into the financial accounts, resulting in potential court cases for non-payment, thus damaging Melville's reputation.

Nightingale had cost Melville a considerable amount of time and money to correct the situation, Melville did not wish to brand him a thief and was prepared to stand any financial loss as a result of this matter. As there was no proof of fraud the magistrates were duty bound to forward the court papers to the Public Prosecutor but agreed to suspend the case 'sine die'.

## 1925 – MR WILLIAM J. MILLER

The Grand had a reputation for presenting first rate pantomimes each year, and on Tuesday 27 January 1925 it was presenting 'Babes in the Wood'. During one of the comedy scenes, featuring cotton wool balls being fired from a cannon, one of the villains, comedian William J. Miller, was struck in the eye by a cotton wool ball, causing him great pain. However, he bravely continued with the remainder of the evening's performance.

After the show Miller was taken to the Sussex Eye Hospital, where he was found to be suffering from a haemorrhage at the back of his eye, and he remained in hospital for a number of days. The producer decided to withdraw the cannon scene with immediate effect from the pantomime.

## 1925 – MR MALCOLM SCOTT

The 'Babes in the Wood' pantomime had a further incident on Friday 30 January 1925 when Malcolm Scott, a well known comedian and female impersonator, was charged with failing to keep his dog under control. It was alleged it had bitten Miss Dorothy Youlder, one of the chorus girls, four times on her leg in addition to biting other performers. Scott said that the dog's trick was to burst a balloon during a school scene. It had apparently become confused, as the girls were wearing dresses of similar colour to the balloon. Scott was ordered to keep the dog under control and pay £2.10 costs.

This was not the end of the matter. On Friday 27 March 1925, Miss Youlder brought a further action against Scott for damages for on-going injuries caused by the bite from his dog in January. At that time, Miss Youlder was receiving £1.25p per week from the theatre, as since incurring the injury she has been unable to work and, for a considerable time, confined to her bed as the wound had become septic. The wound had not yet completely healed. The magistrates examined her leg during an adjournment, and after a twenty minute recess, they awarded her further damages of £67.75p against Scott.

## 1928 – MR GEORGE ERNEST GATES

On Wednesday 30 October 1928 one of the previous owners of the Grand between 1907 and 1917, Mr George Ernest Gates, appeared in the Bankruptcy Court confirming he had not been in employment since 1917 losing money by betting on horses and gambling on the Stock Exchange.

He had borrowed money from moneylenders and mortgaged his trust funds but could not give an approximate figure of his losses. The Registrar was highly critical of Gates and concluded the proceedings.

## 1929 – MISS GLADYS FRANCIS

The bad luck affecting the Grand continued, Miss Gladys Francis, aged 25, was playing the part of the principal boy in the pantomime 'The Forty Thieves' on Monday 7 January 1929. Upon leaving the stage during a matinee performance she, plus two other performers, were struck by some falling scenery, her injuries were not thought to be too serious, therefore she was taken to her hotel where she received medical attention.

She did not improve, and was removed to the Royal Sussex Hospital in Brighton two days later where an X-ray revealed an injury to her spine. Following an unsuccessful operation the next day, Miss Francis died in hospital, on Saturday 12 January 1929.

At the inquest on Wednesday 16 January 1929, the proprietor, Melville said that there were eight columns, 14 feet high, used in the Palace scene, made only of papier-mâché, canvas and wood. He believed that someone may have accidentally pushed against them causing their fall. There had been no complaints from anyone concerning the safety of the columns although Miss Francis's sister, the famous comedienne, Miss Maudie Francis, stated that she had said to her sister that she felt the scenery was not safe and that she had a premonition that something was 'going to happen'

Miss Itera McLean, aged 17, took over the role of principal boy at a few hours notice and she proved to be a success.

## 1942 – MR CARL DANE

Mr Carl Dane was a film star, music hall artiste, boxer, wrestler and strongman and was arrested between the two performances on Monday 26 January 1942. He was charged with stealing a chestnut mare, three horse blankets and a saddle valued at £61, the property of Miss Joan Makin, of Braintree, Essex, between 1 July 1940 and 13 November 1941.

Dane appeared at Brighton Magistrates Court confirming that he was not guilty. Miss Makin had sent the horse, called Ozone and other property, to him in August 1940 at his home in Harpenden, for the duration of the war. A few weeks later, Dane received two further horses from Miss Makin, called Rocker and Bitter Sweet, to stable them during the war, in line with the existing agreement.

In November 1941, Miss Makin received a letter from Dane explaining that he had moved house to Leicester and had taken the horses with him. Miss Makin said she wanted her three horses living nearer to her home in Braintree. Dane admitted he had sold Bitter Sweet for £40 without the permission of Miss Makin, and she collected the two remaining horses taking them back to Braintree.

The jury returned a verdict of guilty and that Miss Makin must be given the £40 sale figure that Dane had taken and to return the blankets and saddle.

The Chairman of the Bench said he would treat Dane more leniently than he deserved. He was placed on probation for three years and ordered to pay the costs of the prosecution.

## 1952 – MR AL MARSHALL

The comedy revue 'It's a Riot' was performing at the Grand during week commencing Monday 19 May 1952. Al Marshall, aged 50, a famous comedian, was topping the bill. On Friday 23 May 1952, at the end of the first house, he walked off the stage, complained of feeling unwell and was assisted to his dressing room by a stage hand.

The theatre manager said that Marshall looked very unwell, and everyone in the cast was naturally concerned. Shortly afterwards, an electrician was requested to attend Marshall's dressing room to ascertain Marshall's health. Upon arriving, Marshall collapsed into the electrician's arms, was rushed to hospital where he was reported as 'serious but improving', after suffering a severe stomach haemorrhage. He recovered sufficiently to return to 'It's a Riot' at the Grand Theatre, Byker, four weeks later.

## 1951/52 – MR RALPH SLATER

Mr Ralph Slater, the famous American hypnotist with family in Britain, decided to visit the UK and present his famous hypnosis act where audience members volunteered to be 'put under' becoming part of that evening's entertainment.

On Thursday 6 December 1951, Miss Dina Grace Rains-Bath, aged 19, went with her friend, Mrs Chessell, to the second house performance of Slater's show and volunteered, along with another fifteen people, to be a 'subject of hypnotism'. Miss Rains-Bath, daughter of Major J. G. Rains-Bath, was duly hypnotised, consequently conducted herself in a strange trance like manner. For example, she jumped out of her chair believing it was very hot; shouted out 'Peanuts' when Slater slammed his foot on the floor, cried and sobbed like a frightened little baby shouting out 'Mummy, Mummy' at the top of her voice etc.

After eliminating all effects of hypnotism, Slater sent her back to her seat, leaving the theatre at the end of his performance. One week later she woke from her sleep a different lady, couldn't concentrate, felt frightened, refused to leave the house and felt an emotional mess.

On Monday 24 March 1952 she appeared before Mr Justice Croom-Johnson at Lewes Assizes suing Slater for alleged negligence, breach of contract and assault. Slater decided to conduct his own defence. After a two day hearing when all the witnesses had presented their evidence, the Judge awarded Miss Rains-Bath a sum of £1,000 damages for negligence, £25 for assault and a further £107 for special damages. Slater said it was totally the wrong decision and he would certainly issue a notice of appeal.

Separately, on Wednesday 14 May 1952 Slater was refused a Ministry of Labour Work Permit and was ordered to leave the UK no later than Thursday 23 October 1952. Following an appeal, he was allowed to stay until Christmas, 1952 and continue with his theatre performances.

In the Appeal Court on Thursday 31 July, 1952, his appeal against the £1,000 damages was allowed but the £25 for assault and the £107 for special damages should stand. Slater said there was mis-direction by Mr Justice Croom-Johnson as he had failed to put the defence clearly before the jury. In summing up at the end of the hearing, Lord Justice Singleton said there was some legal misunderstandings plus Justice Croom-Johnson had also stated 'If anything happens, I shall not be asleep'. Hardly impartial.

A new trial was granted. However, on Friday 12 December 1952, Miss Rains-Bath's solicitor informed Slater's solicitor that his client had decided to take no further action. Slater welcomed the decision but said it had been a long and hard struggle and had affected him professionally and financially. Slater returned to the USA in late December 1952 a broken, bitter, penniless and disheartened entertainer.

## 1953 – MISS ANGELA HORSLEY

In the 1950s, 'girlie' type shows were regularly featured at the Grand and during week commencing Monday 19 October 1953, the revue 'Comic Strip' was being performed. However, eight girls were injured when the rostrum, on which they were posing, collapsed. Miss Angela Horsley, aged 18, and the other seven girls, who had recently completed their act, fell heavily onto the stage following its collapse. Miss Horsley receiving serious head injuries. The audience were unaware of the incident as the curtain had closed, stage hands and other performers rushed to the stricken girls, and made them comfortable until medical help arrived.

Miss Horsley was taken to the Royal Sussex County Hospital where she was detained for a number of days.

# CARDIFF EMPIRE

*The Cardiff Empire Theatre*

## 1886 – LEVINO'S HALL

Mr Dolph Levino, an American circus performer specialising in 'mesmerism', a type of hypnosis, submitted planning permission, on Thursday 11 November 1886, for a theatre in Queen Street. Simultaneously, two additional theatre developers submitted plans for theatres in Westgate Street and New Street. All three planning applications were granted and Levino immediately commenced building his theatre, Levino's Hall, with a planned opening date of April 1887, many people thinking this was an impossible target.

Costing £20,000, and seating 1,500, the end result was truly a magnificent building. The pit was 120 feet long, 48 feet wide and 50 feet high, with a proscenium arch measuring 28 feet high and 30 feet wide. The stage was 30 feet wide and 45 feet deep. Built by Mr Fredrick Martin, there would be six boxes, three on each side wall, the circle would be 15 feet above the pit and the gallery 15 feet above that. The auditorium lighting would be provided by a circular gas 'sun light' complete with eighty-seven burners, the balcony and boxes were illuminated by electricity supplied by the Anglo American Brush Electric Light Corporation Limited.

Numerous fire hydrants were provided by the local council and exits were installed at all levels to ensure evacuation in the case of an emergency, but this aspect of the building would be challenged shortly after its opening. The most striking feature would be the decorations as they would be carried out by the Levino Brothers.

## 1887 – OPENING

On the opening night of Monday 4 April 1887, the curtains opened at 8pm to the sight of Levino acknowledging the audience to tremendous applause and cheering. He apologised for the incomplete decorations, due to the speed of the build, but promised to have them completed by his brother and himself, as soon as possible.

Levino continued by indicating that there may be some unwelcome disturbances by people who were jealous of his project but he hoped the evening would proceed without interruption. After welcoming everyone to his unfinished new theatre, he introduced the acts which included Dusoni's trained dogs and monkeys; Mr & Madame Valjean, jugglers; The Pardos, trick-cyclists and Walter Stanton, farm yard impressionist. Levino concluded the evening's performance with a display of 'mesmeric' entertainment, magic tricks and audience participation antics which earned him a standing ovation.

## PROBLEMS

Levino was overjoyed at the success of his theatre and received many messages of congratulations for his efforts but his mood was to change drastically the following day. Mr Charles Rodney, manager of the New Street, Cardiff Philharmonic Music Hall, applied for a summons against

Levino, under a Cardiff Borough Act 1862. He accused Levino of opening his theatre without a licence for public entertainment as music had been played during the opening ceremony, especially when the audience sang the National Anthem, accompanied by the orchestra. In addition, the majority of the acts also required musical accompaniment. Levino argued that the music was subsidiary to the entertainment and had been played on many other unlicensed premises for years without objection or complaint. The meeting was adjourned for consideration.

There was a further Court case on Wednesday 4 May 1887 when Mr John Winstone was charged with being drunk and disorderly the previous evening at Levino's Hall. He argued that Levino's premises were not licensed for music therefore he had no case to answer and should have it dismissed. He also pointed out that there was regular trouble at the Hall as Levino had difficulty in controlling his audiences and, more seriously, he was using an unsafe building, insisting it should be closed down.

Levino said that the case was frivolous as it was rumoured that Rodney had organised the incident although Levino admitted that he had refused to sign the charge sheet against Winstone at the Police Station. The bench decided to dismiss the case against Winstone.

## LICENCE

Mr Harpur, the Borough Engineer, had been instructed by the Court to make a full structural and safety examination of the Hall and make his recommendations before a full licence could be considered. A further meeting was held on Thursday 22 September 1887 where Mr H. Morgan-Rees, on behalf of Levino, made a formal application for a licence for public dancing and music. Harpur had submitted his detailed report for consideration by the Bench which implied that the building was lacking in certain areas and needed immediate improvement before he was satisfied and could authorise a licence. After an hour and thirty minutes deliberation, the Mayor gave his decision of granting Levino a licence, conditional on his undertaking to carry out all the Borough Engineer's proposals, as soon as possible, especially, widening the exit stairwells from four to six feet wide. He also insisted that all the decorations and outstanding work should be completed. The Hall was closed immediately for the requirements of Harpur to be completed.

## RE-BUILD

Mr W. F. Gillett, appointed as Clerk of Works by Levino in late September 1887, was given total responsibility for the transformation of the Hall which must meet all the demands of Harpur. The balcony and gallery had been rounded, the seats were so arranged that there was a perfect view of the stage from every one of them. The exit stairwells had been increased from four feet to six feet wide, the exit doors would now open outwards, changes to the stage exit arrangements implemented, making the theatre one of the safest in the country.

The most impressive feature was the pure quality and quantity of the completed decorations which were outstanding works of art. The majority of these were painted by Mr Henri Levino, Dolph's brother. Every wall, from top to bottom, had been covered in his paintings. Amongst them were a life size portrait of the nobleman, Lord Bute, one picture of the 1886 Cardiff Mayor, Sir Morgan Morgan and views of Cardiff and Caerphilly Castles.

## REOPENING

Once the required changes had been made, Levino's Hall, often referred to as Levino's Museum of Varieties, was now ready for business. On Monday 7 November 1887 the grand re-opening saw a full capacity audience enjoy the vast improvements made by Gillett and the Levino brothers to the theatre. Everyone was impressed and waited for the show to begin. After a few brief words by Gillett who thanked the Levino brothers for their unbelievable efforts, over a very difficult time, he wished the theatre every success for the future. The opening performers that evening were Bros Martin, dancers & musicians; The Coco's, animal imitators; Captain Slingsby, ventriloquist; Miss de Launay, soprano; Miss Blanche Gerard, singer; Tom Leamore, comedian and Millie Zara, singer.

## 1888 – THE PAVILION

The Levinos were to experience a number of difficulties during their first few months of trading, their builder, Mr Frederick Martin, was declared bankrupt, blaming the building of the Hall to be the major cause. In addition, their water supply was declared insufficient to cope with an outbreak of fire. Their request for the renewal of their singing and dancing licence was refused. On

Saturday 7 January 1888, they dispensed with the Hall, the lease was taken over by Mr J. Morella who immediately changed its name to the Pavilion.

The Levinos issued a statement saying that all future contracts were cancelled and parted with the words "We have done our best". After completion of the sale, they eventually retired to America disillusioned and broke.

## 1888 – THE PAVILION

The Pavilion opened on Monday 2 April 1888 with a new image, the poor quality acts and initial problems associated with the opening would be replaced by a refurbished theatre and high quality acts. This proved not to be a success however, and the Pavilion was closed towards the end of 1888. Mr Isaac Morgan, the owner of the building offered it for sale, and many different parties carried out negotiations for its use.

## 1889 – THE EMPIRE PALACE OF VARIETIES

Mrs Adelaide McConnell Stoll, following the death of her husband, Mr John Stoll in 1880, continued to own the Parthenon Music Hall in Liverpool, immediately employing her son Oswald, at the age of fourteen, as her junior assistant helping out backstage until gradually taking more responsibilities.

Wishing to expand her theatre business interests, on Monday 24 June 1889, Mrs Stoll acquired the Cardiff Pavilion, plus some adjoining property, on a 999 year lease, to be managed by her two sons, Roderick and Oswald.

On Sunday 29 September 1889, the Stolls opened their new theatre. One of the first things was to rename it the Empire Palace of Varieties.

They had chosen to present two identical performances each evening, 7pm and 9pm. The theatre was tastefully decorated with evergreens and specimens of wild animals and birds, whilst all the seating, drapes and carpets had been replaced. The opening night's performers were Miss Marie Loftus, Walter Read, Tom Berrick, the Leclare Troupe, Pat Cashan, Will Vane and Griffin & Langan.

The theatre initially had great difficulty attracting audiences, in one week, their takings amounted to a mere £1.25p

Times were difficult for the Stolls, but in October 1889, they persuaded their close friend, Vesta Tilly, to appear at the Empire at a vastly reduced fee.

*Vesta Tilley*

Her appearance attracted large numbers and confirmed their decision that purchasing the Theatre was correct and their future looked rosy.

## 1894

By 1894, the success of the Empire was creating problems for Stoll as the theatre could not accommodate the huge demand for tickets therefore, in November 1894, he suspended performances, closed the theatre, contracted a local architect, Mr E. Webb of Quay Street, Cardiff to submit various designs. One was chosen, creating an additional 200 seats and increasing the standing areas, achieved largely by demolishing the large offices at the rear of the balcony.

The Empire continued to prosper, but Stoll quickly realised that this recent improvement could only be a short term measure and more drastic action must be taken. He approached Mr Frank Matcham and asked him to design a brand new theatre, an offer which was readily accepted. The last ever show in the 'old' theatre was 'A Merry Queen', performed on Saturday 28 December 1895 starring Kate Reeves and Edwin Keene.

The demolition and re-building commenced in January 1896, by a local contractor, Messrs J. E. Turner and Sons, at an estimated cost of £25,000. Turner moved quickly with the building project, and within four months the 'new' Empire would be ready for occupation and open for the presentation of entertainment.

Matcham had excelled himself in his design, the frontage had a red brick and stone elevation with an impressive central tower. The theatre entrance was illuminated with bright coloured glass lamps and all the entrances and exits were clearly marked. The interior was cleverly arranged, in that the galleries were constructed on a cantilever principle with an absence of columns to allow everyone a perfect view of the stage. The auditorium and circle consisted of luxurious tip-up seating, all the floors were covered by peacock blue Axminster carpeting, the decorations were in a French Renaissance style, and numerous mirrors for effect were provided. In every respect an impressive, but typical Matcham structure, clearly following his familiar style of theatre architecture for which he was renowned.

## 1896 – REOPENING

On Monday 4 May 1896, the curtain rose and the audience were transfixed at the outstanding set and sang the 'The March of the Men of Harlech'. They almost raised the roof when singing the 'National Anthem' with the Rhondda Glee Society. There were welcoming speeches, the one by Matcham received a standing ovation to applaud his efforts in designing such a beautiful building.

The performers on the bill were Miss Lizzie Valrose, vocalist; the Brothers Webb, musical comedians; Miss Ether Dove, vocalist; Abel & Welsh, gymnasts; Wallis & Langton, comedians; Mr Arthur Rosedon, comic vocalist and Mr Paul Langtry, vocalist.

In Edinburgh in 1899, a new company was formed resulting in the merger of theatres owned by Sir Edward Moss, Richard Thornton and Sir Oswald Stoll making it the largest chain of Variety Theatres and Music Halls in the United Kingdom with over 50 theatres under their ownership.

The Empire had tremendous success for the next three and a half years but disaster was waiting in the wings.

## 1899 – FIRE

At 10.30pm on Monday 30 October 1899, the audience vacated the theatre upon completion of the performance by Miss Lottie Collins, famed for her 'Ta-Ra-Ra-Boom-De-Ay' act. The theatre staff carried out a full check of all areas, found everything was in order, reporting this fact to Stoll sitting in his office, before locking the theatre. At 5.40am the following morning, Police Constable Knight was on patrol, when it became obvious that the Empire was on fire.

The fire brigade were immediately called, attended within minutes only to find the whole of the interior on fire with flames beginning to break through the roof. Further assistance was called, but the fire was now out of control. Consequently, the firemen concentrated on protecting the adjoining properties around Queen Street as there was very little hope of saving the now doomed Theatre. The majority of the roof over the auditorium collapsed as flames soared into the night sky, illuminating much of the surrounding area. The strength of the walls held firm or tremendous damage could have been caused by their collapse onto the theatre's neighbouring properties.

By 8am, all that remained was a burned out wreck, nothing flammable remained for the fire to destroy. The interior with its rich furnishings and beautiful decorations was totally destroyed. The walls were blackened by smoke and enclosed mangled, twisted ironwork.

Upon investigation the following morning, the amount of damage was obvious, the four outer walls remained, as did the ground floor office and the front entrance, but the sight of the desolation affected many people. The stairs to the circle were blackened and the fire, smoke and water damage was unbelievable. At least Stoll's office and all the important theatre documents and records were saved, therefore the business could continue.

The estimated cost of replacement was £25,000, thankfully covered by insurance. All the stage clothing, dresses and personal effects belonging to the artistes had also been destroyed and they were not covered by any form of insurance. One of the biggest financial casualties were the Sisters McNulty, an American troupe, who had collected together at least 40 specially designed dresses for their forthcoming USA tour, with an estimated loss of between £400 and £500. Lottie Collins also had many items destroyed as had the trick cyclist troupe, Lotto, Lilo & Otto who had to replace their specially manufactured cycles. In fact, everyone lost their personal possessions in the fire, especially the musicians, who lost the majority of their instruments. Sadly, one person had paid £400 for a harp the previous week.

Stoll came quickly to the rescue as the nearby Andrew's Hall, which he also owned, was made available for the Empire's show to continue, and, two evenings later, the show re-commenced whilst the old theatre was still smouldering. Using his contacts he was able to obtain sufficient clothes, scenery and music etc for the show to continue.

## NEW THEATRE

Within a few hours, Stoll had contacted Matcham instructing him to detail plans for the construction of the 'new' 1,750 seater Empire based on his original designs, which had proved very popular.

The budget for the build, carried out again by Messrs E. Turner & Son, would be £10,000, bearing in mind the original walls and frontage could be utilised, with a further £5,000 allowed for the new furnishings. Matcham's prime objective was to make the building as fireproof as possible with all structures being of concrete, steel, brick and stone with wood used only for furnishings. He also paid special attention to the stage area, iron doors replaced the old wooden ones, an easy rise and fall asbestos fire-proof curtain was fitted and fire hydrants, hoses and extinguishers were situated at all significant locations.

The stage itself received special attention. The proscenium had been positioned five feet nearer to the rear wall, the stage had been extended by 16 feet into the old rear second rehearsal stage. This resulted in a brand new, usable area 45 feet deep and 60 feet wide, much larger than the majority of the London stages. As with all Matcham's theatres, the decorations were outstanding, the carpets, upholstery and curtains were in shades of red, many plaster enrichments were evident with figures of famous people located in the arches and pilasters. The old sliding roof had been replaced by an impressive dome which significantly improved the visual aspect of the ceiling.

## 1900 – REOPENING

The opening night of Saturday 29 September 1900 was chosen by Stoll as it was eleven years to the day when his mother and himself had first opened the Cardiff Empire. It was also almost one year to the day since the fire. The star on that disastrous night, Marie Loftus was invited to return and repeat her humorous act in front of the opening audience, this time accompanied by her daughter, Cissie Loftus, a talented impersonator.

*Marie Loftus*

*Cissie Loftus*

It was a very emotional performance, Stoll was visibly shaken by the reception he was given by this appreciative audience. He introduced his new business partner, Sir Edward Moss, thanked the Mayor and Mayoress for their attendance and announced the Empire 'officially open'. The evening's proceedings began with the National Anthem, sung by the Canton Male Voice Choir, accompanied by the Cardiff Military Band. The artistes, who had been performing at the Andrew's Hall until the previous week, included Marie Loftus, Cissie Loftus, the Crawford brothers, the Florenz Troupe, the Brothers Onda and Ida Heath.

## 1913

Thirteen years later, In December 1913, the management announced the closure of the Empire from Saturday 3 January 1914, for a significant period of time to allow extensive alterations and improvements to take place. At the concluding performance the artistes and audience joined together to sing 'Auld Lang Syne'. The new building would cost £20,000 with a further £30,000 for fixtures and fittings, the audience capacity would be increased from 1,800 to over 2,800, achieved by purchasing the adjoining premises of the Molineux Shoe Company. The external aspects of the theatre would be reconfigured, and a new elevation on Queen Street would be built of Portland stone in a classical style. There would be a recess on the second floor for lighting effects faced with stone columns with Ionic capitals surmounted by a cornice and carved pediment.

A major feature of the interior would be an Italian marble staircase leading to the circle, complete with rubber paved steps for comfort, decorated with Corinthian columns and capitals. All the internal walls would be decorated in a Grecian style, coloured in grey. Carpets were to be of a light purple colour and woven by Messrs Morton. Only the finest materials, seating and drapes would be utilised.

The stage area was not neglected as all new machinery was installed, a new double covered asbestos curtain was fitted and also a velvet stage curtain. The new electric lighting was designed and installed by Mr H. W. Hawkins, chief engineer to Moss Empires Ltd., Messrs E. Turner & Sons were responsible for the rebuilding, the architects were Messrs William and T. R. Milburn of Sunderland.

## 1915 – RE-OPENING

The re-opening day was Boxing Day 26 December 1915 and Stoll decided to have four separate performances, 1.50pm, 4.00pm, 6.45pm and 9pm, with star artistes such as Ada Reeve, Ted Hopkin, Rinaldo, Joe & Willy, the Three Merrills and the Harlequinaders.

*Charles Coburn*

Many famous performers topped the bill over the years and attracted huge audiences including Sir Harry Lauder, George Robey, Charles Coburn, Marie Lloyd, Little Tich, Harry Tate and many other stars of the day.

## 1927

On Monday 5 December 1927, the management decided to change from twice nightly variety presentations to once per night plays. The opening performance, attended by the Lord and Lady Mayoress and the Aldermen of Cardiff City Council, saw the London Hippodrome's successful play of 'Sunny' starring Elsa Brown and Jack Melford. This play continued for two weeks followed by 'Cinderella' starring Ivy Luck as Cinderella and Elsie Denham as principal boy.

## 1931 – CINEMA

Rumours were circulating in Cardiff in March 1931 that Moss Empires were considering selling thirty-two of their theatres to a cinema chain, including the Empire Cardiff. It was announced on Wednesday 29 July 1931 that the Empire had been purchased by the Gaumont British Theatres Corporation and they commenced installing the most modern projection and sound equipment. It opened on Monday 7 September 1931 with the film 'Hell's Angels' starring Jean Harlow.

The Empire continued throughout the remainder of 1931, 1932 and early 1933 offering a mix of films and live entertainment.

## 1933

The Empire closed on Saturday 3 June 1933 for an extensive scheme of renovation, redecoration and alterations to convert it into one of the finest luxury cinemas in the country.

This changed the whole character of the building, the style and shape of the entrances were replaced by one large, elaborately decorated area to permit the quick entry and exit by patrons. All the seating, except in the gallery, was replaced by well sprung crimson plush tip-up seats, but the immediate effect was the removal of all the boxes at the rear of the circle and those positioned on the side walls, giving it a much more open feeling. The most notable feature was the installation of a new Compton organ in the old orchestra pit, capable of producing musical sounds varying from cathedral to dance band music, all created by the skill of the organist.

It reopened on Monday 7 August 1933 with the films 'The King of the Ritz' starring the comedian, Stanley Lupino supported by Betty Stockfield and 'Our Fighting Navy' with the organist Mr Fredric Bayco playing the magnificent organ.

## 1954 – THE GAUMONT CINEMA

The Empire Cinema changed its name to the Gaumont Cinema in 1954 as the films were then distributed through the parent company, The Rank Organisation. The famous and popular Compton organ was removed in 1955 and sold to a church in Bristol.

In addition to regular films, during the next twenty-five years or so, live entertainment was an occasional feature at the Gaumont, especially the Sunday evening musical shows which attracted the top names of the day including The Beatles, Cliff Richard, Eric Delaney & his Band, Gene Vincent and Eddie Cochran.

Cinema audiences dwindled over the years. Rank had three cinemas in Cardiff, one of them needed to close for economic reasons and the obvious choice was the Gaumont. In addition, only second release films were chosen for the Gaumont, ultimately affecting the size of audiences. The decision was made to finally close the Gaumont. The projector screened the last ever film on 30 December 1961. Any future stage shows were re-directed to the Capital Cinema which had less back stage facilities but could accommodate larger audiences.

## 1962

That was the end of the Gaumont and the demolition teams moved in during 1962 and reduced it to dust and rubble. Few tears were shed at its passing. A new retail building sprung up on the site and included the C&A fashion store with a large ballroom in the basement, which, in some way, continued the entertainment theme.

## 2001 – THE END

Almost forty years later, in 2001, the C&A store closed and the building was demolished once again, along with the ballroom. Another retail unit was built on the site and it is presently occupied by a national clothing company but they did not include any provision for dancing or entertainment.

# DID YOU KNOW...?

## 1899 – SIR OSWALD STOLL

Sir Oswald Stoll, born on Saturday 20 January 1866 in Melbourne, Australia, lived with his mother and father, Mr Oswald James Gray and Mrs Adelaide McConnell Gray until the death of his father when they returned to England. His mother remarried to Mr John G. Stoll the owner of the Parthenon Theatre in Liverpool and Oswald changed his surname to Stoll, the name of his stepfather. Mr John G. Stoll died in 1880 leaving the theatre to his wife who continued with the business.

*Oswald Stoll*

Mrs Stoll expanded her theatre business by purchasing the 999 year lease of the Cardiff Pavilion Theatre in June 1889, managed by her two sons Roderick and Oswald. Unfortunately Roderick died a year later on Saturday 14 June 1890 of consumption, which left Oswald in sole control of the Cardiff Empire. Roderick's funeral on Thursday 19 June 1890, was one of the largest seen in Liverpool attracting numerous famous music hall stars of the day including Vesta Tilley, Marie Loftus, Agnes Feeney etc.

Sir Oswald was the co-founder of the Stoll Moss Theatre Group. They owned Cricklewood Film Studios and founded the Royal Variety Performance annual charity show. Knighted in 1919, for his services to charity, Oswald died at his home in Putney, London in 1942,

## 1893 – MR THOMAS WILLIAMS

At a Cardiff Court hearing on Saturday 24 June 1893, Mr Thomas Williams was charged with stealing two watches and two chains from a dressing room at the Empire belonging to Mr James Fane, an acrobat performing at the theatre. Two days earlier, on Thursday evening, Williams, falsely entered the back stage area, stole the items around 8pm and the theft was discovered when Fane returned to his dressing room at 10.30pm. When charged, Williams admitted to stealing the items but stated that he had not eaten or slept in a bed for three days and was desperate. He also admitted entering the Newport and Swansea Empires intending to steal items before he was apprehended at Newport.

Fane said that he did not wish to press charges as the watches and chains had been returned to him, but the magistrates sent Williams to prison for 14 days with hard labour.

## 1894 – MR FREDERICK DODSON

A young man, Mr Frederick Dodson, was charged in Cardiff Court on Saturday 7 July 1894 of breaking and entering into the Empire Theatre the previous Wednesday night between the hours of 11.30pm and 1.30am with the intention of emptying the safe. It was alleged that on that same Wednesday afternoon, Dodson was overheard in a public house stating that he intended to break into the Empire later that night. Therefore two policemen positioned themselves in the theatre offices after the audience had left the theatre around 10.30pm.

At 1.30am they entered Stoll's office and found Dodson kneeling by the safe with a knife and a file in his hand, the safe had been opened and other burglary tools were lying on the floor. He was found guilty.

## 1904/05 – MR HARRY HOUDINI AND MR FRANK HILBERT (No 1)

In 1904, Houdini won a legal battle against the famous Moss and Thornton theatre circuit, and in revenge they hired an unknown magician, Frank Hilbert (The Handcuff King), to tour England's theatres and expose all Houdini's secrets. The pair were to meet in Cardiff in early April 1905, for a showdown! During week commencing Monday 10 April 1905, Mr Harry Houdini was appearing at the Kings Theatre and Mr Frank Hilbert at the Empire.

There would be fireworks.

On the evening of Tuesday 11 April 1905, Houdini disguised himself as an old man, wore a fake moustache, and was accompanied by a friend purchasing tickets for the stalls. Upon appearing on stage Hilbert announced he would perform his famous 'get out of these handcuffs trick', at which point Houdini began heckling him and accused him of being a fraud. Mr William Lea, the manager of the Empire, asked Houdini to leave quietly, which he refused to do. Houdini said he was then attacked by four Empire officials, three policemen and Lea who all threw him, violently, into the street.

Houdini brought a charge against Lea for assault as he had suffered a number of injuries to his leg, which was originally thought to have been broken, and which required lengthy treatment from a doctor.

After many hours of hearing witnesses, and statements from the policemen, the court decided there was no case to answer therefore the case against Lea was dismissed. From a business point of view, both the Empire and the King's Theatre were delighted as people flocked to each of the theatres to hopefully witness future incidents.

*Frank Hilbert*

*Harry Houdini*

## MR HARRY HOUDINI AND MR FRANK HILBERT (No 2)

The publicity between the stars continued the following week, just twelve miles away in Newport, where Houdini was appearing at the Lyceum and Hilbert at the Empire. The Chief Constable of Newport, Mr Sinclair, challenged both of them to escape from the Police Station on Tuesday 18 April 1905, through three locked doors. Houdini arrived at the police station, stripped off his clothes and was double locked into cell number 9.

Houdini re-appeared five minutes later, fully clothed having escaped from cell 9, opened the adjacent cell to retrieve his clothes and unlocked the door into the main corridor astonishing Sinclair.

Hilbert failed to appear for the challenge!

## MR HARRY HOUDINI

One of Houdini's closest friends in England, the magician, Mr Henry Evanion, born in 1832, and from whom he had purchased a number of amazing tricks, was taken ill and died a few days later, in London on Saturday 17 June 1905. Evanion died almost penniless. As a gesture of his friendship, Houndini paid for the funeral and financially supported his widow until her death some years later.

Houdini was born Erik Weisz, on Saturday 24 March 1874 in Hungary, the family emigrated to the USA in 1876 and settled in Milwaukee. At the age of nine, he developed an interest in magic and the rest is history. Houdini became, probably, the world's most famous magician and is still revered by all magicians to the present day. In 1926, Houdini died in strange circumstances, following a blow to his abdomen by a university student, Mr Jocelyn Gordon Whitehead.

At the conclusion of his performance at the Princess Theatre, Montreal on Friday 22 October 1926, Houdini invited Whitehead to punch him in his stomach, which he did quite severely, leaving him in severe pain, probably suffering from a ruptured appendix. For the next few days he continued to perform, always refusing medical help. On Sunday 24 October 1926, whilst travelling by overnight train to appear at the Garrick Theatre, Detroit, he collapsed. In Detroit, a doctor strongly advised him to visit the hospital, but he refused to do so. He insisted in carrying on with his act the following evening, although in great pain. He collapsed as he left the stage and was taken to hospital.

In hospital, the surgeons removed his appendix but the poison had spread to many other parts of his body. Houdini died of peritonitis on Sunday 31 October 1926 at the age of 52, with his wife, Bess and his two brothers by his bedside.

## 1911 – MR THOMAS SMITH

On Tuesday 19 September 1911, Mr Thomas Smith, aged 64, a commissionaire at the Empire, was notified that his brother, Mr Richard Smith, had died in Strathroy, Canada and he was asked to travel to Canada in order to settle the estate. Richard had emigrated over sixty years previously and whilst in search of water for his new home had instead struck oil, which proved to be the richest well in Canada. Thomas had no idea of Richard's wealth, he only remembered Richard stating that he would leave £1,000 to each of his brothers and sisters. No other discussions were ever made concerning money or business matters although they kept in regular contact.

Thomas, upon arriving in Canada, was staggered to learn that Richard had left over £2 million and he would receive one-fifth as his share. Upon returning to Cardiff a very rich man he said that he would retire and live in the countryside!

## 1915 – MR GEORGE ROWLAND WILLIAMS AND MR LOUIS COREL

On Monday 15 March 1915, Mr George Rowland Williams and Mr Louis Corel were charged in the Cardiff Magistrates Court of assaulting Mr William Rowland Brinson, an attendant at the Empire, on Saturday 13 March 1915.

Both of the accused were causing a disturbance by shouting when the acts were performing and Brinson requested them to leave the premises. They verbally abused and threatened Brinson who called a policeman to eject them. As they were descending a staircase, Williams struck Brinson a violent blow to the head which caused him to fall, both of the accused continued with the attack while he lay on the floor.

Williams was found not guilty by the court as it was felt there had been some provocation, however, Corel was found guilty and fined 25p for assaulting Brinson and 35p for assaulting the constable.

## 1930 – MR STANLEY ARTHUR

This was a most unfortunate incident. On Monday 1 September 1930, a touring company was visiting the Empire, presenting 'Rose Marie' for the week. The twenty strong cast decided to take a day of relaxation on Thursday 4 September at Lavernock, a small seaside town seven miles south of Cardiff.

One of the cast, Stanley Arthur, who had only joined the cast two weeks previously, was very popular and enjoyed playing practical jokes. However, it was noticed he was missing in the middle of the afternoon and they assumed it was another of his jokes.

The organiser of the troupe, Bernard Leslie, worried about Arthur, questioned the cast, and one of the girls reported that she thought she saw him fall backwards into the water, but had taken no action as they assumed he was 'fooling around'. His body was recovered at 8pm that evening, the cause of death was recorded as a heart attack.

## 1959 – MR JOHN MILLS AND MISS HAYLEY MILLS

In 1959, the Gaumont was suffering from declining audiences and, as a last hope, it hosted the premiere of 'Tiger Bay', a film shot in the Tiger Bay district of Cardiff. The film concerned a murder. The police superintendent was played by the famous actor, John Mills.

*John Mills*

John Mills' twelve year old daughter, Hayley was the witness to the murder. This film was highly acclaimed and regarded as one of the finest produced and filmed in Wales.

In April, 1959, John and Hayley Mills were proud to attend the premiere of 'Tiger Bay' which attracted thousands of filmgoers, but this was short lived as the following films over the next year or so did not attract audiences to the Gaumont and the end was inevitable.

Mr John Mills, born Saturday 22 February 1908 became one of England's finest film actors and starred in over 120 films in the following seven decades. He died on Friday 23 April 2005, His daughter, Hayley, born Tuesday 18 April 1946, won, at the age of 13, the Award for the Most Promising Newcomer for her part in Tiger Bay.

# CARLISLE HER MAJESTY'S THEATRE

*Her Majesty's Theatre, Carlisle*

## 1874 – VICTORIA HALL

A number of public halls had been opened in the city in the early/mid 1800s. Many of these were no longer viable as they had been gradually converted into other uses or were not sufficiently large enough for entertainment purposes. The local Council committed to building two halls on a 2,600 sq yd plot between Chapel Street and Lowther Street, appointing Messrs Habeshon & Brock to create suitable designs. Eventually the Council agreed on two separate designs. The Albert Hall, a smaller 500 seater building for meetings, sale rooms and entertainment on a small scale, opening in June 1874. The second, the Victoria Hall, a much larger building, took a further five months to complete.

The Victoria Hall, could accommodate 1,350 in the auditorium and 650 in the gallery totalling 2,000. The gallery, supported on wooden pillars, continued around three sides of the hall. The dome shaped ceiling had three gas burner lighting units suspended above the auditorium, which, along with matching wall fittings, ensured first class lighting for the whole theatre.

The stage measured 38ft wide by 32ft deep, and beneath it was a large room suitable for rehearsals with adjoining smaller dressing rooms for the visiting artistes. For the convenience of patrons, the designers provided a large refreshment room, albeit unlicensed, but many patrons complained at the shortage of cloakroom and toilet facilities.

Although the opening show did not commence until 7.30pm on Monday 26 October 1874, the Hall was full to capacity by 7.00pm, with a recorded attendance of 2,500, well above the authorised figure, and which was further increased by 230 performers.

The guest list was very impressive and included the Lord Bishop of Carlisle, the local MPs and their families, Sir Richard and Lady Musgrave, Mr P. H. Howard of Corby and many other local dignitaries. The performers appearing on that first night were a local combined choir composed of the members of the Carlisle, Wigton, Penrith, Cockermouth and Langholm Choral Societies. The sizeable orchestra included a number of guest musicians including Mr J. Smith of Kendal known for his brilliant trumpet playing abilities. The solo artistes were Miss Edith Wynne, soprano; Madame Patey, contralto; Mr Cummings, tenor and Mr Patey, bass. An excellent opening evening for this new entertainment centre specifically erected for the residents of Carlisle and surrounding districts.

## 1889 – REFURBISHMENT

In June 1889, the theatre closed for extensive alterations, re-decorating and replacement of all seating, re-opening on Monday 19 August 1889 with many distinguished guests invited. These included the Mayor, Mr J. R. Creighton, Colonel Bellamy and Officers of the Border Regiment, Colonel Binning and Officers of the 1st Volunteer Battalion Border Regiment and the Chairman and Directors of the Public Hall Company. The opening attraction was Miss Gladys Heathcote's Comic Opera Company presenting 'La Mascotte'. The prices of admission were dress circle 15p; side boxes and orchestra stalls 10p; pit 5p and gallery 2p. The performance began at 7.45pm and carriages were to be booked for 10.30pm.

## 1904 – HER MAJESTY'S THEATRE

In spring 1904, the theatre, now re-named Her Majesty's Theatre, closed for alterations and refurbishment to improve its appearance and be more attractive to the local residents and visiting performers. Mr J. F. H. Harriman from Carlisle, was appointed as architect and the construction was under the management of Messrs Gorden & Logan.

Safety was extremely important. A fully automatic rise and fall fireproof curtain was installed by Messrs Oldroyd and Co of Leeds for mandatory use during every interval period and when the theatre was not in use. The curtain completely cut off the stage from the auditorium in the event of a fire or other emergency. The height of the stage roof was increased to enable the scenery, especially from the national touring companies, to be used which was not possible in the old, cramped theatre.

Following complaints from artistes, new, modern and fully furnished dressing rooms were built and in addition, a fireproof band room with fully automatic closing fire doors replacing the old wooden ones. A new proscenium was installed, designed and painted by Mr Bookbinder, the well known theatre decorator, bringing the total cost of the refurbishment to £800.

The theatre re-opened on Monday 1 August 1904 with Mr F. A. Scudamore's sentimental drama, 'Because I Love You', performed in front of a maximum audience. The bookings for the remainder of 1904 were very encouraging and included the D'Oyly Carte Opera Company in 'Kitty Grey' and the Philharmonic Society in the 'Belle of New York'.

## 1904 – FIRE No 1

A few weeks later, on Monday 12 September 1904, Mr George Dance's company commenced a week long contract, presenting 'Country Girl'. On Wednesday evening 14 September, the sell-out performance was concluded at 10pm.

In line with standard procedure, the theatre manager carried out his detailed inspection of the building once the audience had vacated the premises, found all in order, locked the doors and left around 11pm.

At 3am the following morning, a passing policeman noticed smoke was visible around the main entrance and he notified the local fire brigade. The firefighters from the West Walls and Spring Gardens stations quickly arrived, assisted by soldiers from the Castle and local policemen, who commenced fighting the fire but they soon established that the whole building was in great danger of being destroyed.

The fire spread to the roof which collapsed in flames into the auditorium. This ignited two oxygen cylinders stored at the side of the stage which exploded with a loud bang, causing even more damage. To make matters worse, a large portion of the north-eastern wall collapsed with a number of policemen, soldiers and firemen having a very narrow escape. The fire continued to rage in spite of the valiant efforts of all concerned and by 7am it had burned itself out. All that remained of the theatre was a mass of smouldering rubble, brick and iron girders. Due to the heroic efforts of the firemen, they prevented the flames from spreading to adjoining properties, such as the Carlisle Dispensary, the Scottish National Church and a large Council school.

All Dance's scenery and stage dressings for 'Country Girl' were totally destroyed but a small number of their costumes were undamaged. The cause of the fire was unknown but it was assumed that it started in the auditorium when an audience member may have discarded a cigarette or cigar which smouldered for some time, before igniting the carpet. The damage was estimated between £5,000 and £6,000, and fortunately, the building was fully insured by the London and Atlas Insurance Company A commitment was made by the owners, the Carlisle Public Hall Company, that the theatre would be rebuilt in the quickest possible time.

Three soldiers assisting the firemen and police were injured, Corporal Dent was knocked down by a fire engine, Corporal Manley suffered an ankle injury and Corporal Bash damaged his hand when it was a struck by a falling beam.

## RE-BUILD

Designed by the architects, Beadle & Hope, the external appearance had been altered very little as most of the remaining walls were found to be in a sound condition. The interior changed significantly as there were many improvements from the old theatre's original design, the dress and upper circles and gallery were now supported on a semi-cantilever principle. Only two pillars of a small diameter were used to support these from the auditorium, therefore ensuring every seat had an uninterrupted view of the stage.

A large number of exits were provided for safe evacuation should an emergency arise. The interior decorations were magnificent, a colour scheme of cream and gold emphasised by crimson upholstery impacted upon the audience when entering the building. Axminster carpets covered all the floors and the most modern type of tip-up seats were provided.

Behind the patented fireproof safety curtain and its 31ft proscenium opening, an enlarged stage was evident together with nine roomy, well ventilated and upholstered dressing rooms for the comfort of visiting performers. An interesting improvement was the raising of the orchestra floor by nine inches as the performers had complained that they could not see or hear the orchestra.

In view of the disastrous fire twelve months earlier, the building throughout was of a fire proof construction with steel, brick and concrete used at every opportunity.

## 1905 – RE-OPENING

Her Majesty's Theatre, was formally re-opened by the Mayor of Carlisle on Friday 15 September 1905. The Mayor made an inspiring speech to the specially invited audience and introduced Mr Stanley Rodgers, theatre manager, who thanked everyone for their support and outlined the forthcoming attractions. The show was opened with the singing of the National Anthem, led by Miss Lily Shalders, sister of the lessee, followed by a musical programme presented by both professional and amateur performers.

The following Monday 18 September 1905, Her Majesty's Theatre opened to the general public who witnessed a performance of 'San Toy', presented by Mr Geo Edwards' Company, with Mr Clifford Seyler, Mr G. Edward Hall, Mr George Partie, Miss Clarence Lockstone and Miss Mabel Carr in the leading parts.

## 1924/1932

Her Majesty's Theatre struggled during the next twenty years or so, introducing films, staging live entertainment including their famous pantomime, plays, musicals, variety etc. On Wednesday 3 December 1924, the theatre was offered for sale and Mr Sidney Bacon, a local theatre/cinema owner, acquired the building and leased it to Mr Ernest Stevens.

Stevens continued presenting shows until Saturday 20 May 1932 when he announced that he was closing the theatre that evening after the final performance of 'London Wall' as it was operating at a loss. Bacon re-advertised the theatre many times in June and July and leased it to Mr A Stewart on Tuesday 13 September 1932 who re-opened it the following month.

## 1935

Mr Thomas Ferguson, better known under his stage name of A. C. Astor, 'the Globe Trotting Ventriloquist' had taken America by storm in the 1920s.

In August 1935, he bought the struggling theatre for his wife due to sentimental reasons. He was born, educated and had his first job in Carlisle as a trainee pharmacist. Astor became quite a character as the name of Her Majesty's Theatre, Carlisle, was rarely out of the news until he closed it down in 1958.

## 1937 – FIRE No 2

Astor redecorated the theatre, carried out a number of improvements prior to opening in September 1937, but he had to overcome the difficulties of a fire a few weeks later on Sunday 24 October 1937. Theatre staff were posting bills around the outside of the theatre, artistes were rehearsing on the stage, when a passer-by noticed that smoke was rising from the roof.

Upon immediate investigation, the fire was located in the upstairs gallery bar and was extinguished by the theatre firemen prior to the arrival of the Carlisle Fire Brigade leaving only a small amount of damage. The Carlisle Operatic Society who were rehearsing a production of 'Rio Rita', their thirteenth in succession, were able to continue. The show went ahead as planned the following evening. Damage was estimated at £500.

## 1954 – DIFFICULT TIMES

Through Astor's vast contacts, he was able to attract the leading music hall stars over the years, probably the most famous were Stan Laurel and Oliver Hardy who starred during week commencing Monday 19 April 1954. They were supported by Jill, Jill & Jill, Jimmie Elliot, Ursula & Gus, Bobbie Kimber, Derek Rosaire & Tony-the Wonder Horse, Lorraine, Dorothy Reil & Mack and Betty Kaye's Pekinese.

During an interview with the local press, Stan Laurel stated that he had never appeared at Her Majesty's Theatre even though he was born in that area. His memory must have failed him as he did appear on its stage, aged seventeen, with H. B. Levy & J. E. Cardwell's Juvenile Pantomime Company in 'The Sleeping Beauty" during week commencing Monday 23 March 1908. The cast was headed by the famous comedian Wee Georgie Wood and Stan Laurel played a small supporting role as Ebenezer.

Over the years many leading music hall stars appeared at the theatre including Jack Anthony, Harry Lauder, Jose Collins, Ella Shields, Frank Randle, Ralph Reader & His Gang Show and Tommy Trafford. There was rumour of an underground tunnel linking the theatre with the public house across the road, The Howard Arms, where performers could secretly have a drink during the show!

*Wee Georgie Wood*

The trading situation of the theatre began to suffer in the 1950s due to the attraction of new forms of entertainment, principally television, and on Thursday 22 May 1958, Astor, the owner of the theatre, announced he had no alternative but to close it at the end of the summer repertory season. He blamed the inability to attract suitable touring shows and quality performers to rural locations. He said they were reluctant to travel such distances as other, more rewarding appearances nearer to their homes, were being offered to the detriment of theatregoers in Carlisle.

In June 1958, a local business man Mr Frank Lett, organised a petition urging the City Council to purchase the theatre for community use as well as continue with live entertainment. In order to increase awareness of the drastic situation, during week commencing Monday 28 July 1958, Tessie O'Shea, the famous music hall artiste, starred with the Fraser Neal Company in the revue, 'Sailor Beware', playing to large numbers. She joined the thousands of residents signing the petition wishing to keep the theatre open. This was presented to the Mayor in September 1958 who promised to involve the Council in some way if an independent buyer could not to be found.

Her Majesty's Theatre struggled on throughout 1958 hoping that a buyer would be found. The future of the theatre was again in doubt when no offers were forthcoming. It finally closed again in late 1958. Numerous meetings were held with the Council during the spring and summer of 1959/1960.

## 1960 – A MUNICIPAL SAVIOUR

In August 1960, it was announced that the Council had taken a three year lease on the building, a committee of trustees being appointed to manage the theatre, hoping to make a profit within the first twelve months. Mr John Sullivan, the previous Manager, agreed to take the role of General Manager.

The Mayor of Carlisle, Alderman Tom Souness, in his opening speech on Monday 3 October, 1960, hoped that the newly formed company would make a success of the venture. It would now be known as the Municipal Theatre.

## 1960 – THE MUNICIPAL THEATRE

There was a slight hiccup a week later on Monday 10 October 1960 as the performance of Elroy Flacker's play 'Hassan' was cancelled due to an unreasonable demand by the Musicians Union. The producer, Mr Basil Dean, had organised a special recording of the Delius music score but the Union insisted on a minimum of six musicians at every performance. Due to these financial implications, the theatre management cancelled the contract and the previous week's performers were asked to extend their performance by one further week.

The Council's hopes and dreams were dashed as the theatre closed down, once again, on Saturday 19 January 1963, the final night of the pantomime 'Red Riding Hood' after a very successful four week run. However, losses exceeding £34,000 had been experienced during the previous three years whilst under Council control and these could not be sustained. The final pantomime was an emotional event for Eddie Morrell, who usually concentrated on his 'Starlights' summer show at the Central Pier in Morecambe, but agreed to produce the final ever show. The performers were Janita Morrell, (Eddie's daughter) as Red Riding Hood; Billy Strutt as Simple Simon; Tommy Trafford as the Dame; Carole Maudie and Marilyn Wildman as principal boy and girl; Jacqueline Toye as Fairy Hyacinth; Bert Gunnel as the Baron and Alex Charles as the Palace Butler.

## 1963 – 1978

On Thursday 15 August 1963, it was announced that the theatre's lease had been taken over by Mr John Moody, the owner of the nearby Regal Cinema which had recently changed to Bingo. In 1976, he sold the theatre to the EMI Group who spent £45,000 on refurbishment converting it into a social/multi purpose theatre by lowering the stage roof, installing a new heating system, total redecoration and retaining the stage for the occasional live entertainment use. Due to the poor state of the theatre they did this by creating a 'building within a building' at the level of the stalls. The remainder of the space was unused. In December 1978 the EMI Group decided that they could no longer continue with the building due to its poor condition, moved elsewhere, and the theatre was put up for sale yet again.

## 1979 – THE LAST DAYS

On Thursday 1 March 1979, a Whitehaven businessman stated his intention to re-open the theatre, spend over £100,000 on its refurbishment, remove the 'building within a building' and utilise the whole space. He had visions of creating a nightclub and attracting the leading cabaret acts and pop groups of the day. Unfortunately this project did not materialise.

In August 1979, furniture giants Daniel Johnston paid £40,000 for the three tiered theatre and immediately announced that they had no alternative but to demolish it as 'if we don't pull it down, it's going to fall down' they said. It was duly demolished within days, originally used as a 2,000 sq ft car park before the land was developed into a large department store.

That was the end of such a beautiful theatre with quite a unique history, and it is still remembered with great fondness by the residents of Carlisle.

## DID YOU KNOW…?

## 1907 – MR CHARLES R. STONE

On Wednesday 10 July 1907, the comedian and stage manager, Mr Charles R. Stone, had an unfortunate accident whilst performing Myles in the play, 'The Colleen Bawn'. A gun had to be fired by Stone in one of the scenes. Forgetting the gun was loaded, he pulled the trigger, as a result two fingers on his left hand were badly injured.

Bravely, although in severe pain, he completed his performance, was then rushed to hospital where one finger was amputated. The other finger was saved but required extensive treatment. He was able to appear on stage for the remainder of the week.

## 1909 – MR ISAAC LOWTHER

On Saturday 16 October 1909, in the Carlisle Police Court, Mr Isaac Lowther was accused of wounding Miss Mary Elizabeth Clark at the theatre, with intent to cause grievous bodily harm. Lowther and Miss Clark had been in a relationship but Miss Clark had caught him with another woman, they had separated and argued at length over the matter. The previous evening, Miss Clark entered the theatre bar after the performance, where Lowther was already seated, he grabbed her by the neck, pulled a knife out of his pocket and tried to cut her throat. They struggled, fell to the floor and she was cut on the face three times, one of the wounds being very deep and serious.

Lowther denied using a knife and could not explain the cause of Miss Clark's injuries. The jury found Lowther guilty, the Recorder sentenced him to fifteen months imprisonment with hard labour.

## 1909/10 – MR JOHN GOWANCOCK AND MR WILLIAM LOWDEN

Early on Sunday morning 14 November 1909, Mr John Gowancock and Mr William Lowden were accused of breaking into the theatre, removing the safe from the manager's office, and dragging it through the theatre into the joiners' shop situated adjacent to the stage. Once they were in that sound proof room, they were able to use pick axes to break into it and had stolen a cheque for £4, £7 in gold, £7 in silver and £1 in copper. The first hearing was adjourned and at a second one heard on Thursday 6 January 1910, the jury could not agree on a verdict as the evidence was inconclusive. They were discharged by the Magistrates.

At the Carlisle Quarter Sessions on Wednesday 6 April 1910, both Gowancock and Lowden, had been re-arrested as additional evidence had been obtained. After a further hearing, the jury again found them not guilty and they were discharged.

## 1933 – MISS MARGARET TWEDDLE

This was a particularly sad case involving Miss Margaret Tweddle, aged 22, who disappeared after attending the theatre with her mother, on the afternoon of Thursday 12 January 1933. Upon leaving, they were separated by the crowd, Miss Tweddle did not return home and was reported missing. The police of two counties carried out a massive search, the local radio was involved. Miss Tweddle was said be of a nervous disposition and it was feared she may have had a memory loss. Her father reported that she suffered from rheumatic fever which had affected her mentally.

Miss Tweddle's body was later found in the River Irthing, and had been held under water by a submerged tree for several days. At the inquest on Friday 12 May 1933, an open verdict of 'found drowned' was recorded. There was no evidence of any foul play but no-one could explain how, why, or where, she entered the water.

## 1935 – MISS FRANCELYN HAMPSON

Commencing Monday 21 March 1935, Mr Carroll Levis presented his famous 'Discoveries Show' at Her Majesty's Theatre. It was a unique form of entertainment where Carroll Levis, who had earlier auditioned amateur performers, chose the successful ones for a variety show in theatres around the country. On Friday 25 March 1935, the show was in full flow and Miss Francelyn Hampson, one of the acts, was in the middle of her quick fire comedy act when the compere, Carroll's brother, Cyril Levis entered the stage.

Miss Hampson looked utterly confused. He ordered the orchestra to play the 'Wedding March', presented her with flowers, congratulated her and announced to the audience that she had married her childhood sweetheart, Mr Archibald Galbraith, at Gretna Green the previous day! She received a standing ovation.

## 1937/38 – TOMMY FRANCIS

In December 1937 and January 1938, Mr Tommy Francis, the famous London comedian, was playing the Dame in the pantomime 'Babes in the Wood' commencing on Boxing Day Sunday 26 December 1937. After his performance he complained of feeling unwell, was examined by a doctor and taken to the Cumberland Infirmary the following day. His wife travelled from

Keighley where she was staying with their daughter, Elva, who was principal boy in 'Aladdin' at the Keighley Hippodrome.

Mrs Francis stayed at her husbands bedside for a day and a night. It was announced that Mr Tommy Francis had passed away at the time of the final curtain the following Wednesday evening 29 December 1937. The theatre management and cast agreed to give a concert on Sunday 2 January 1938 with all proceeds given to his wife. His part of the Dame was taken by the producer of the pantomime, Mr Charles Denville.

## 1939 – MISS HANNAH WATT AND MR A. C. ASTOR (Part 1)

On Tuesday 23 January 1939, Mr A. C. Astor, the proprietor of the theatre brought an action for alleged slander against Miss Hannah Watt, an actress, and her mother, Mrs Dorothy Ruth Watt, both residents of Carlisle. Astor said Miss Watt had approached him in August 1937 concerning an engagement at his theatre. She asked for a salary of £50 per week. He felt that Miss Watt was rather inexperienced and suggested a guaranteed payment of £25 plus 50% of the profits after deducting expenses and Miss Watt had agreed to this proposal. During her performance Astor had to leave the theatre for a while as he was managing Sir Harry Lauder's company for a UK tour.

On the following Saturday, Miss Watt was given a statement by the theatre manager, Mr Williams, that the profit was £64.17p, therefore with her guarantee of £25, less the expenses, she would receive £52.82p which was less than she expected as she believed other expenses had been deducted. Miss Watt and her mother, vigorously denied calling Astor a 'twister' and commented that she had become almost unemployable due to the bad publicity she had received as a result of bringing this case. She was presently appearing, as principal boy, in 'Babes in the Wood' at the Belfast Opera House.

The Judge, Mr Justice Croom-Johnson dismissed the case.

## 1939 – MR DAVE MORRIS

On Monday 16 October 1939, Mr Dave Morris a London based comedian, was accused of assaulting Mr Arthur C. Crosby, manager of the theatre on Saturday 23 September 1939. Morris was the lead comedian and touring manager for the revue 'Too Funny For Words' which was performing at the theatre from Monday 18 September to Saturday 23 September. At the completion of the booking, Morris and Crosby were seated in an office discussing income and expenditure for the week, when Morris suddenly attacked Crosby who was injured by the blows. In addition, his spectacles were broken, he was temporarily blinded by the amount of blood pouring from his wounds, knocked to the floor and also received a broken bone in his forehead.

Morris stated that Crosby was the aggressor as he had punched him in the stomach, knocked the pipe out of his mouth and they both fell onto the floor. Morris was found guilty, fined £5 and costs which were capped at £5.

## 1940 – EVE-OH, THE NAUGHTY GIRL REVUE

Her Majesty's Theatre continued presenting a variety of shows for many years and gained a reputation as a solid, reliable theatre but this was to drastically change when its wrong-doings hit the national press headlines as a result of its show on Tuesday 12 March 1940. The offending show, 'Eve, Oh, The Naughty Girl Revue', included one act where a young lady, Miss Melville Glen, clad only in her 'panties', was accused of being 'lewd, unchaste and immoral' as she allegedly stood in the nude, facing the audience for a few seconds as the lights were gradually dimmed and the curtains lowered.

Miss Glen and three men, Mr Harry Bennett theatre producer from London, Mr Arthur Charles Crosby, the theatre manager and Mr Francis Pinney Adey, an actor from London appeared in front of Carlisle magistrates on Friday 3 May 1940 charged with various offences.

Bennett argued that it was an artistic and unobjectionable show therefore did not require the Lord Chamberlain to pre-authorise the script hence no offence had been committed. After a lengthy hearing the magistrates fined Bennett £21 with £5 costs, Crosby, £1 with £1 costs and they dismissed the cases against the actor and actress, Adey and Miss Glen as they were merely following instructions.

## 1940 – MISS HANNAH WATT AND MR A. C. ASTOR (Part 2)

On Wednesday 19 June 1940, Mr Astor brought a libel action against Oldham's Press Ltd, Northern Counties Conservative Newspaper Co Ltd and the Daily Herald (1928) Ltd following his unsuccessful slander action against Miss Hannah Watt in January, 1939. It was alleged that Astor had been called a 'twister' and the Judge was not convinced those words had been used by Miss Watt, hence his decision.

Astor said that there was a suspicion in peoples minds that his honesty and integrity had now been brought into question and the reports in the papers had been unfair and had given the wrong impression. Mr Justice Atkinson found the newspapers guilty, assessed damages of £150 in respect of the Daily Herald and £75 regarding the Newcastle Journal report.

## 1941 – MR A. C. ASTOR

At the Magistrates Court on Saturday 29 March 1941, Mr Astor was charged with keeping two dogs without a licence, at his residence in Heads Nook, near Carlisle. Astor said that the matter had been overlooked as he had been bombed out of his London office, lost a significant amount of documents and no attempt had been made to avoid payment.

Astor wrote a letter to the Court and said that with all the troubles at the present time, the Court should not waste the time of two policemen on such a trivial matter and a reminder would have been sufficient. He continued by stating that the Court should set an example and not waste their time in dealing with trivialities such as dog licences! The Chairman fined Astor £1 and payment of costs.

## 1944 – Mr CHARLES DENVILLE & Mr A. C. ASTOR

On Monday 7 February 1944, Mr Justice Cohen in the Chancery Division heard the case of a dispute between Mr Charles Denville and Mr A. C. Astor, arising out of the production of a pantomime at the theatre from Friday 24 December 1943 to Saturday 22 January 1944. There had been an agreement between the two parties where Denville would produce the 'Babes in the Wood' pantomime, Astor would provide the theatre, the two would share the profits. However, there had been a loss of £823 and Denville claimed that Astor should share this figure which he had refused to do.

Astor denied liability and alleged that the loss on the production was due to Denville's breach of duty in failing to attend rehearsals, drunkenness, drinking with dancing girls, assaulting the manager and using bad language to the cast.

Denville denied these allegations and said that he was never drunk as, if so, he could not have played the 'giant' due to the heavy boots he had to wear and also carry his fifteen year old son on his shoulders. He agreed he had been taking medicine to cure a bad cold, had fallen down some steps but this was accidental and not because of drink.

The pantomime was regarded as 'poor' by both the public and press which seriously affected attendances, hence the loss. On Saturday 19 February 1944, Mr Justice Cohen decided that the loss and costs of the action should be borne in the proportion of two-thirds by Denville and one-third by Astor.

## 1957 – MISS BERTHA RICARDO & MR JACK ANTHONY

On Saturday evening 23 February 1957, Miss Bertha Ricardo and Mr Jack Anthony were travelling in a car from a theatre performance to their home in Roxburghshire when it skidded on an icy road and hit the parapet of a bridge with some force. They were pulled out of their car by the emergency services but despite deep cuts, sprains and severe bruising they were able to perform in a charity concert at Her Majesty's Theatre the following evening. Upon entering the stage they were greeted with a standing ovation.

## 1960 – MR DAVE WILLIS

Mr Dave Willis, at the age of 65, the famous Scottish comedian, was appearing in 'Robinson Crusoe' at the theatre during the pantomime when he had to spring into action on Wednesday 13 January 1960. During the afternoon matinee, Dave Willis and his fellow comedian Pete Martin were on stage, when Martin's two year old daughter wandered into the path of the ship's half ton mast, a stage prop, which was about to crash onto the stage.

Willis, risking serious injury, saw the impending disaster, rushed forward, grabbed the girl as the mast fell, pulling her to safety. Martin said afterwards "it was a miracle and he would be eternally grateful to Willis"

## 1980 – MR ELLIOT WILLIAMS

Mr Elliot 'Barnstormer' Williams of Annan, had appeared in pantomimes at Her Majesty's Theatre for over three decades. On Sunday afternoon 2 March 1980 he became the last ever actor to speak on the stage. His programme, on

Radio Carlisle, was broadcast from the actual stage with him reminiscing on his many experiences and performances at the old theatre. One could hear the noise of the actual demolition being carried on all around him which led to an emotional broadcast.

In this farewell he criticised the public of Carlisle for allowing such a beautiful theatre to fail. His final words were 'I blame the theatre-going public of Carlisle who have allowed over 100 years of tradition to fall by the wayside'. It is a sad refection on the whole city's population that this wonderful old theatre has to be razed to the ground'.

# CHISWICK EMPIRE

*The Chiswick Empire Theatre*

## 1910/11

In 1910, Mr Oswald Stoll, (who was later knighted in 1919), decided to add a further addition to his company's ever increasing number of Empire Theatres. He commissioned one in Chiswick, six miles from the centre of London.

This proposal caused consternation in Chiswick. Stoll announced that he planned to open the Empire Palace Theatre at 414 Chiswick High Road, in an exclusive and select part of West London, opposite Turnham Green and Christ Church. He anticipated some antagonism from residents, and at a heated public meeting held in the Town Hall, the residents were unrelenting in their objections.

One objector stated that *'people who attended music halls did not have sufficient food, clothing or accommodation'*. Another stated that it would *'lower the tone of the area and drive away the better class inhabitants'* with another resident saying *'We don't want to become another Shepherds Bush'*.

Those in favour of the theatre signed a petition totalling 2,000 names, claiming that the theatre would bring healthy entertainment and provide employment in the area. In spite of the many objections, Stoll succeeded in obtaining planning permission, and the building of the theatre went ahead in 1911 at 414 High Road, replacing numerous shops and a blacksmith's premises.

As with many of his new theatres, Stoll appointed Mr Frank Matcham as the architect, and agreed a budget of £50,000 to create a superb theatre able to accommodate 4,000 people. No expense was spared, only the best luxurious seating, brilliant lighting, quality fixtures and fittings, perfect ventilation and excellent decorations were used.

It would have the usual ground floor seating areas, circles, and balcony. The colour scheme of terracotta, electric blue, shades of old gold and white for the ceiling and matching coloured walls. Matcham introduced a new concept in comfortable seating. In the balcony, each individual seat was separated from its neighbour, gone were the long uncomfortable wooden benches. Every seat in the house had an uninterrupted view of the 44 feet wide stage. For added comfort, a sliding roof was installed however, it eventually proved highly uncomfortable, as each time it opened it showered the audience with dust!

Stoll was correct in his presumption that Chiswick was becoming more popular as a residential area and the population was increasing. Evidence of this was when the District Railway opened a new railway station, coincidentally only a short walk from the theatre.

## 1912 – OPENING

The Chiswick Empire opened for business on Monday 2 September 1912 with a quality variety show featuring a number of top music hall stars. Perhaps the most intriguing was a demonstration by Mr Raymond Phillips, an electrical engineer and inventor, who demonstrated his ground-breaking wireless controlled airship, flying it wirelessly of course, around the auditorium. This was previously thought impossible. However, the military departments of the Government were also taking a serious interest in Phillips' invention, in view of the worsening political situation.

Many more stars performed that evening including Miss Ella Shields, a male impersonator, singer & dancer; Rameses, a magician; Mr Yorke Stephens, an American actor; Miss Margaret Moffatt, an actor and Thora, a ventriloquist.

Further stars included Mr Billy Merson, comedian; Cornalla & Eddie, tumbling comedians; My Fancy, dancers and Mr Harry Ellis & Mr Tom McKenna, comedians. As a finale, a film of the Chiswick Horse Show was shown to the enthralled audience on the new cinema projection system, but without any sound,

## 1913 – FIRE

On the evening of Tuesday 19 August 1913, the 'Le Petit Cabaret', presented by Toby Calude & Co. had completed their evening performance around 10.30pm. The audience vacated the theatre whilst some artistes agreed to stay behind to rehearse the following week's production of 'The Devil's Dream'. At midnight, all the artistes left the theatre, leaving behind a few workmen carrying out maintenance work. These and the duty fireman were the only people left in the theatre. The workmen completed their duties and left around 12.30am leaving the fireman on his own.

Four hours later, at 4.30am, on the Wednesday morning, during his regular patrol, the fireman discovered flames at the rear of the stage, quickly spreading to the scenery, drapes, stage fittings etc and immediately telephoned the local fire brigade. He valiantly attempted to extinguish the flames using the theatre's own fire fighting equipment but the hosepipes provided were far too small to have any effect on the ever-increasing flames.

The Chiswick Fire Brigade, with a crew of twenty, arrived on scene within five minutes. Captain Eydmann, the Chief Fire Officer, realised the situation was extremely serious as flames were now bursting through the stage roof to a height of twenty feet. He requested all local fire brigades to immediately attend the Empire. Numerous fire engines and crew arrived from Acton, Richmond, Barnes, Ealing, Brentford, Hounslow and Southall stations within a short time.

Efforts were made to lower the safety curtain to protect the remainder of the theatre but unfortunately it stopped half way down, allowing the flames in the stage area to sweep into the auditorium. One theory for its failure to descend was that the heat had distorted its tracks, whilst another theory attached the blame to the operating track being obstructed by a temporary cable leading from the stage to the auditorium, which was in use during the rehearsals.

The rear of the theatre was now a mass of flames rapidly spreading through the half open safety curtain into the auditorium, igniting the seats in the first few rows. The flames also spread upwards to the ceiling decorations which, in turn, caused the roof to ignite and eventually collapse sending flames, slates, decorations, lighting etc onto the stage. The original iron roof supports, many of them four or five feet wide, thirty feet long and two feet deep, also collapsed and lay twisted and bent on the stage making the task of fighting the fire from the interior almost impossible.

The neighbouring shopkeepers and residents were concerned for the safety of their properties. Thankfully, their fears were unfounded as the firemen successfully prevented the flames from spreading beyond the fabric of the Empire Theatre. In the meantime, they were able to obtain temporary shelter in nearby houses. By 8.30am, the fire was under control and the majority of the district fire brigades were stood down.

The sight greeting the management at 9.00am that morning from the front entrance in Chiswick High Road, was that little damage had been caused to the exterior, but the interior revealed a very different picture. On the remaining parts of the wooden stage that were not badly burned, were several feet of bricks, charred scenery, roof tiles and the twisted remains of the roof girders. The orchestra pit was severely damaged, the metal rails separating the stalls seating was twisted and burned beyond recognition. The whole of the stalls seating were just long rows of blackened frames whilst all other seating and decorations in the theatre were either scorched, burned or severely damaged by water. Luckily, the below-stage dressing rooms escaped serious damage and the white and gold decorations of the ceiling were only heavily smoke damaged.

The rear stage wall was declared unsafe and the management ordered that heavy ropes be attached to these dangerously leaning walls and employees were instructed to pull them down before they collapsed and injured passers-by.

There would be a tremendous amount of work needed at the rear of the theatre before it could be re-opened. Stoll insisted that all the work must be completed within eight to ten weeks and the theatre open for business by the end of the year, at the very latest. The cause of the fire was shrouded in mystery but it was believed it started either under, or on the stage, as the rear of the theatre was severely damaged. The total damage was estimated at around £12,000, but as the theatre was insured, rebuilding could begin immediately.

Curiously, 'Old Moore's Psychic Predictions' stated that 'a theatre or music hall would be destroyed, by fire, within two years!'.

## BENEVOLENT SHOW

A large number of artistes, musicians, and staff suffered significant financial losses as a result of the fire at the Empire damaging their personal possessions. Their fellow music hall artistes quickly gathered to arrange a benevolent concert at the famous London Palladium on Thursday 18 September 1913 commencing at 2pm. The organising committee were overwhelmed at the response, the capacity audience had the pleasure of fifty-eight performers on the programme, finally closing the curtains at 6pm. This list included many 'stars' of the day including Hetty King, George Robey, Fred Emney, Dusty Rhodes etc.

No announcement as to the actual amount raised was published, but a considerable sum must have been raised to assist the many who lost personal items, instruments, private possessions, clothing etc as a result of the fire.

## RE-OPENING

True to his intention and down to the dedication of the many contractors, Stoll re-opened the Empire Theatre three months after the fire, on Saturday 15 November 1913. The theatre had been fully re-decorated, restored to its former grandeur with the decor now in pale cream and old gold. There was new seating in bottle green upholstery and new murals added to the corridors.

It reopened with the aptly named play 'The Miracle' by Rev John Maclaren and Mr Alfred Denville as its first production. 'The Miracle' was presented in two acts of eleven magnificent scenes with the number of performers totalling over 250. To accommodate such a large production, the stage was extended and the orchestra was temporarily re-located into the balcony area.

Prices of admission for the opening show were 90p for a box, 7p in the circle, 5p in the first circle & orchestra stalls, 4p in the second circle & pit stalls and 2p in the pit stalls and balcony.

# 1929

The Chiswick Empire continued as a very successful theatre and became one of the most prominent music halls in the suburbs of London during the stewardship of Stoll. He was well known as a very strict disciplinarian who insisted that he personally vetted artistes scripts for any unsuitable material. All staff were issued with a clear policy of acceptable behaviour and customer service to be adhered to at all times. Stoll was a man of high standards and felt that everyone of any age should be able to enjoy a visit to any of his dozens of theatres throughout the United Kingdom without fear of embarrassment.

Stoll's business motto was 'variety is the spice of life'. He was at the forefront of entertainment by presenting opera, circus, and mystery plays. He also announced the introduction of 'talkie' cinema, in addition to variety, at the Empire with effect from Monday 5 August 1929.

*Al Jolson 'The Jazz Singer' Poster*

The theatre was equipped with the most modern projection and sound equipment, the initial attraction would be Al Jolson in 'The Singing Fool', his follow up to 'The Jazz Singer'.

The film was typical Jolson, but a little boy, three year old Davey Lee, took the acting honours and appeared in a number of films over the following years. An additional attraction was the sound from British Movietone News, a shock for many people who had only seen the silent version!

The Chiswick Empire played to full houses in the 1920s and 1930s with the occasional film being shown but the priority was definitely variety. Among the artistes appearing around this time were, Albert Whelan, Sybil Thorndike, Tommy Handley, etc. Stoll also presented a series of Shakespeare's plays performed by the actor, Mr Andrew McMaster and an opera performed by the Carla Rose Opera and the D'Oyly Carte Company. Unfortunately these were not too well supported as the Chiswick patrons preferred 'good old variety'.

The famous annual pantomimes were greatly supported over the years as numerous stars of the day appeared including George Formby Snr, Gladys Cooper, Vesta Tilley, Marie Lloyd etc.

## 1932

In 1932, the new theatre manager announced, in view of his successful background in cinema management, that there would be no further live shows at the Empire and it would now be dedicated to the showing of films, having undergone the installation of a high quality Western Electric sound system. This change failed, and, by October 1933, the Empire had reverted back to permanent live entertainment with films relegated to Sundays only, when live shows were not permitted.

## 1939

Following the Declaration of War between England and Germany, on Sunday 3 September 1939, the Government ordered the immediate closure of all theatres, cinemas, dance halls and places of public entertainment but the anticipated air raids failed to materialise. As a result of a change in Government policy the Empire re-opened in November 1939 to a full programme of performances.

The Empire closed yet again at the height of the blitz in September 1940 but reopened again in May 1941. It continued to present variety throughout the rest of the war and beyond, to enormous and enthusiastic audiences. The Empire attracted the top music hall stars of the day including Vera Lynn, Old Mother Riley, Chico Marx, Max Wall, Jimmy James, Donald Peers, Max Miller plus Jewel & Warriss in their revue 'Black Vanities'.

*Vera Lynn*

**1947**

The Empire was undamaged during the blitz of the second world war, in spite of the heavy bombing of the capital and the destruction of dozens of theatres.

On Monday 15 September 1947, Dermot McDermot and his orchestra were playing their opening number at the commencement of the second house when there was an almighty crash. Part of the ornamental ceiling collapsed. Plaster shattered against the circle rails causing many people sitting in the vicinity of the circle and stalls to be struck with falling debris. The circle rails and the seats immediately underneath were severely damaged. When the dust had cleared away, Mr Bill Burke, the duty manager, asked the audience to evacuate the theatre in an orderly fashion whilst the orchestra played the National Anthem.

Five ambulances, doctors, police cars and fire engines rushed to the scene and eleven injured people were taken to hospital for treatment. Some were taken to the West London Hospital where two were detained, Mr E. Hosking and Mrs D. Goodman, both with head injuries. Another four were taken to the West Middlesex Hospital and two people were detained. Others who had been injured were allowed home after treatment. The Empire was closed until the following Saturday and by then the theatre ceiling damage had been fully repaired.

**1950s – POST WAR**

The 1950s arrived, together with the newer brand of stars including Ken Dodd, Ronnie Carroll, Terry Thomas, Joan Regan, Norman Evans, Dickie Valentine etc. There were many other productions including stars from the TV show, Six-Five Special including Lonnie Donegan, Wee Willie Harris and Terry Dene.

Audiences were falling alarmingly in all theatres as people now had the choice of different forms of entertainment such as television, night clubs etc.

The management attempted to offer other forms of live entertainment such as 'Strip Stars of 1957' featuring, (according to their play bill), 'June' (42-20-36) and 'Iris' (40-22-36) who appeared during week commencing Monday 5 August 1957.

Another show, entitled 'Festival of Striptease' during week commencing Monday 25 February 1959 featured the famous strip-tease artiste 'Jane' together with a selection of relatively unknown music hall acts. These type of presentations would never have been permitted by Sir Oswald Stoll, who had died, aged 76, on Tuesday 9 January 1942, having been knighted by King George V in 1919.

A performer who was more than able to fill the Empire was Cliff Richard, for week commencing Monday 27 April 1959 supported by the group The Five Dallas Boys; Des O'Connor, comedian; Ray Alan & Lord Charles, ventriloquist; Jean & Peter Barbour, puppeteers; Tommy Wallis & Beryl, musicians and Kim & Kimberley, dancers.

However, these were in the minority, the net was closing as thousands of long established music hall audiences were no longer attracted to the predominantly nude, low quality variety shows being presented and they voted with their feet.

## 1959 – CLOSURE

On Monday 16 March 1959, the management of the Empire Theatre announced its closure. The last remaining London music hall on the Stoll circuit, and the nineteenth to close down in Greater London since the end of the war.

Middlesex County Council approved plans for the demolition of the Empire, replacing it with a concrete commercial building, following its purchase by Town and City Properties. Costing £250,000, it was an eleven storey concrete office block rising 120ft above the ground, containing fifteen shops and nine maisonettes with the provision for the parking of one hundred cars. Quite the opposite of the beautiful Empire building.

Stoll would have been proud of the sell-out final performance at the Empire on Saturday 20 June 1959 when the flamboyant virtuoso pianist Liberace brought colour, glamour, genuine entertainment and charm to the Theatre, very reminiscent of the 1920s, 30s and 40s.

Liberace was in London defending a court case regarding an earlier article in the Daily Mirror for libel. He was successful, and awarded £8,000 for damages and costs. As the curtain closed for the last time there were loud cheers and thunderous standing applause for both Liberace and the Chiswick Empire. The theatre died with the utmost dignity and went out in a blaze of entertainment glory which helped to cushion the sadness of the occasion, albeit with a newly decorated and refurbished dressing room carried out on Liberace's instructions!

Liberace disappeared into the night leaving hundreds of fans waving goodbye, not only to Liberace but to the Chiswick Empire.

*Liberace*

Demolition commenced immediately, some internal fittings were disposed of to other remaining theatres, whilst old play bills and programmes were purchased by theatrical historians.

Unfortunately, the majority of the fixtures and fittings were scrapped. Every famous variety artist had performed in person and all of them were proud to do so, the famous George Robey having appeared there at the ripe old age of 77 in 1945.

How sad it should close so suddenly, but at least the name of the Chiswick Empire would not be forgotten as the new building would be called Empire House. This, as a permanent reminder of the wonderful theatre which stood on that site for almost fifty years. It had withstood two world wars, including heavy bombing and also flying bombs. The 'new' Empire commercial building continued for the next fifty years, when in November 2020 it was announced that the building had been purchased by Great Marlborough Estates and their plan was to convert it into housing, still a great epitaph for the good old Empire.

# DID YOU KNOW…?

## 1913 – MR ARTHUR PRINCE

One of the greatest ventriloquists of the early 1900s, was Mr Arthur Prince, who with his ventriloquist dummy, Sailor Jim, topped the bill at the majority of theatres in the United Kingdom. He was engaged to appear at the Chiswick Empire in week commencing Monday 7 April 1913, Prince explained that, whilst in the middle of his act the previous week, a fire engine raced past the outside of the building. The audience began to panic until Sailor Jim said 'eight bells, change of watch' quickly calming the situation down.

Prince was travelling to Chiswick by train, and Sailor Jim's head was in a small wicker basket placed on his knee. The train ticket collector entered the compartment and Prince using his skill as a ventriloquist, made a barking noise as though it was emanating from the basket. The ticket collector was suspicious, thought Prince was defrauding the railway company, and demanded that the basket be opened. Prince refused. More senior railway officials were summoned. Prince finally relented, the ticket collector opened the basket to see Sailor Jim's head peering at him and he almost fainted, This was made worse when Prince picked up the head from the basket and Sailor Jim said, 'why did you disturb me?'. The railway people were not amused.

Prince was born on Thursday 17 November 1881, famous as the first ventriloquist to perform whilst drinking a glass of water, and he appeared in the first ever Royal Command Performance at the Palace Theatre, London in 1912 followed by a world tour. He died in Hampstead, London on Sunday 14 April 1946.

## 1941 – MR MARTIN VERGLIO

Mr Martin Verglio, a music hall artiste, was a member of a company playing at the Empire during week commencing Monday 8 September 1941. He appeared in Court accused of assaulting Mr William Henshall, a revue producer, after the final show at the theatre. Verglio said Henshall had previously kicked his wife and he had visited the theatre office seeking an apology. Once again they started fighting, each one was accused of kicking and punching the other, both instigating the assault. Witnesses were called from the theatre, and, after hearing all the evidence, the bench dismissed the summons.

## 1945 – FIELD MARSHALL MONTGOMERY

On Saturday 4 August 1945, Field Marshall Sir Bernard Montgomery KG, GCB, DSO, PC, DL was given an enthusiastic reception by the people of Chiswick as he made his way, in an open car, to the Empire Theatre to receive the Freedom of the Borough from the Mayor, Alderman T. W. Stroud.

*Sir Bernard Montgomery*

In the theatre over 2,000 people representing every organisation in the borough, along with 600 school children, were present to hear a fanfare of trumpets by the band of the Irish Guards, as 'Monty' entered the stage to receive the well deserved award for his outstanding war efforts.

When the theatre closed in 1959, many people said that the presentation to 'Monty' was the proudest day ever at the Empire and will remain in people's memories for a long time.

## 1947 – MASTER ADRIAN HAMMOND

On Easter Monday 7 April 1947, Adrian Hammond, aged four, sat in the balcony at the Empire with his 'big' sister, seventeen year old Lily, when he decided to visit the toilet, by himself, during the interval. He found himself locked in the toilet, so opened a window, climbed outside onto a nineteen inch ledge which was fifty feet above the pavement. Passers-by raised the alarm and told him to sit down, not to move until help arrived. Lily heard the commotion, did not realise it involved Adrian and patiently waited for him to return to his seat.

Alerted to the danger, Mr Gerald Russell, the theatre's fireman, climbed out of the toilet window, dropped onto the outside ledge, even though it was raining heavily, he reached for Adrian and pushed him back through the window. The assistant electrician, Mr Carter, inside the toilet, pulled Adrian to safety and put him into the hands of his sobbing sister who by now, had realised he was missing. The fire brigade attended with a fifty foot ladder but were not required thanks to Russell's quick thinking and bravery.

In the aftermath, Adrain and Lily were immediately relocated into the stalls where they would be much safer. Russell was later nominated for a bravery award.

## 1947 – MR STAN LAUREL & MR OLIVER HARDY

On Monday 22 September 1947, during their UK tour, Laurel & Hardy were contracted by Bernard Delfont to appear at the Finsbury Park Empire, London. However, Delfont had experienced contractual problems with The Inkspots, an American jazz vocal group, who refused at short notice to appear at the Chiswick Empire the same week.

Urgently needing a top of the bill act, the ever-obliging Laurel & Hardy, although at the end of an exhausting UK tour, agreed to 'double-up' by changing the running orders at each of the theatres in order to allow this to happen. There would be different supporting acts.

This was an enormous challenge for both the elderly men, four shows per evening over six nights were required, travelling fifteen miles each way, made worse by an accident, on stage, to Stan.

Laurel & Hardy were performing their famous 'Driving Licence' sketch when Stan should have flicked a ruler thirty feet away from him but he made a mistake and flicked it into his own face causing blood to stream from a deep cut under his left eye. He continued manfully with the sketch to its conclusion, by holding a handkerchief against the cut to stem the bleeding until a Red Cross nurse treated and dressed his wound during the interval.

## 1949 – MONKEY BUSINESS

On Sunday 20 February 1949, a monkey escaped from a local pet shop, climbed onto the front of the theatre roof and caused great amusement as he ran along the frontage. Offers of food hoping to tempt him down had no effect and then he proceeded to enter the theatre through an upstairs open window. The monkey, once inside, made his way to the upper circle, and was chased for half an hour by members of the theatre and pet shop staff. He was finally caught by the pet shop owner's wife and returned to his cage in the shop.

## 1951/52 – MISS CHARLOTTE NEUMAIER

A very unusual act appeared at the Empire from Monday 10 December 1951 involving a snake dancer from a touring company. Miss Charlotte Neumaier's act involved dancing with three 20ft long pythons wriggling around her body and arms.

Offstage they were housed in a large metal container and fed on live animals, particularly rabbits. Public Health Inspectors visited the theatre on Tuesday 11 December 1951 seeing the three large pythons in the container.

With them was a live rabbit, which was in a state of abject terror. The snakes were pointing their heads, open mouthed, hissing and about to strike at the defenceless, trembling animal until it was rescued by the inspectors. The caretaker of the snakes, Mr Alexander Talmon Gross, admitted feeding the rabbit to the snakes, but said he had been told to do so by their owner, Miss Neumaier.

The case was held at the Acton Middlesex Magistrates Court on Wednesday 5 March 1952 and the evidence was heard. The Court were informed that Miss Neumaier had returned home to Germany, although Gross was present. After a lengthy hearing, Gross was fined £5 with the alternative of one month's imprisonment, the case against Miss Neumaier was adjourned.

## 1954 – MR TONY FAYNE

Commencing Monday 20 September 1954, Tony Fayne, one half of the Fayne & Evans comedy act were engaged at the Empire. At the end of their first performance on the Monday evening, Fayne was informed that his wife, Mrs Norma Fayne, had given birth to identical triplets at a Croydon Hospital. The babies, all girls, were born at twenty minute intervals and weighed in at six pounds six ounces, six pounds and ten ounces and five pounds and ten ounces. Mr & Mrs Fayne, who lived in Thornton Heath already had two daughters, Jacqueline and Pamela.

Fayne & Evans parted in 1959, probably caused by Evans' alcoholism. Fayne continued in show business becoming famous as the straight man for Norman Wisdom in the 1960s. They received national press coverage when, Wisdom, as part of their comedy routine, was prevented from singing with the band by Fayne. At this point a burly man from the audience entered the stage and commenced punching him. He was shouting 'I paid to see Norman

Wisdom, if he wants to sing, let him'. The offender was removed and the act continued with Fayne covered in blood. Fayne eventually retired from show business, and died in New Milton, Hampshire on Monday 30 November 2009 aged 85, Evans died in Bristol on Thursday 14 February 1980, aged 57, after years of alcoholism.

## 1959 – MISS HYLDA BAKER

For the January 1959 pantomime, 'Cinderella', at the Empire, Hylda Baker was offered her lifelong ambition of starring in a London Pantomime playing the part of an 'Ugly Sister' with her famous companion 'Cynthia'. She was cast alongside singer Joan Regan and television personality MacDonald Hobley playing Cinderella and Buttons respectively.

Unfortunately, six weeks prior to rehearsals, Hylda Baker collapsed on the stage at the Sheffield Empire, and was diagnosed with bronchial pneumonia. Her doctor insisted that she cancel her contract at the Chiswick Empire and rest at home in Blackpool for an indefinite period. She followed doctors orders and was replaced by The Burt Twins.

Hylda Baker had a history of ignoring doctors orders though, having two years earlier in 1957, whilst appearing at Blackpool Palace and suffering from shingles, had continued to perform against 'Doctors orders' at Blackpool, following that with a performance at Sheffield, where she collapsed.

Hylda Baker was born on Saturday 4 February 1905 into an entertainment family, and a talented performer commencing her stage career at the age of ten.

By the age of fourteen she was able to write, produce and perform her own shows against many challenges from the male dominated industry. She created an unforgettable stage act with her companion 'Cynthia', dressing her companion (but who was always a man) in weird women's clothes and giving her a sullen, gormless and uncommunicative manner. Hylda Baker always selected extremely handsome young men for this part, usually well over 6ft tall, which, alongside her height of 4ft 11in immediately created a comical effect.

One of the latter 'Cynthias' was Matthew Kelly who became one of the UK's most sought after leading television presenters of light entertainment shows, before returning to his acting career in theatre and television roles.

In later years Hylda Baker starred as Nellie Pledge in ITV's 'Nearest and Dearest', and in the 1960 film 'Saturday Night and Sunday Morning'. Hylda died in Epsom, Surrey aged 81, on Thursday 1 May 1986 after a long illness.

## 1959 – MR CLIFF RICHARD

*Cliff Richard*

Cliff Richard appeared at the Empire for the week commencing Monday 27 April 1959 which attracted hundreds of screaming teenagers. However, many traditional audience members were critical of such behaviour. Their fears were confirmed on Friday 1 May 1959, when certain members of the rowdy audience started to throw electric light bulbs, eggs and tomatoes at Cliff as he opened the second house of the show. This show of great enthusiasm for him, was followed by a fire extinguisher thrown from the circle into the stalls, injuring a young lady. Fire extinguisher foam was also sprayed on the audience, and chaos resulted. The manager had no alternative but to call the police, cancel the remainder of the show to ensure audience safety and had to refund money to the many disappointed customers.

## 1959 – MISS JEAN BARBOUR & PETER

Jean Barbour and her partner, Peter, both puppeteers, stilt walkers and acrobats, were appearing on the same bill as Cliff Richard and they witnessed the chaos of that Friday evening's performance only to experience problems of their own two days later.

On Sunday 3 May 1959, they visited the theatre to collect their props and transfer them to the Finsbury Park Empire where they were performing the following week. On visiting their dressing room they found that a number of items had been stolen, including Jean Barbour's fur coat, all of their performing clothes, including a pair of 6ft long trousers used in their stilt walking performance. The police found the trousers outside the theatre. Obviously the wrong size for the burglar! Nothing else was recovered, and the burglars were never apprehended.

# CLEETHORPES PIER PAVILION

*The Cleethorpes Pier Pavillion Theatre*

## 1866 – CLEETHORPES PIER

The fishing port of Cleethorpes developed as a seaside holiday destination in the early/mid 1800s especially when the Town Councillors decided that a railway station should be opened in 1863. This decision proved very successful and many thousands of visitors from the industrial heartlands of the Midlands and Yorkshire greatly added to the port's economy. The next stage in the tourist development of Cleethorpes was to introduce additional visitor attractions, therefore plans were submitted in November 1866, for a Pier.

The project, designed by the engineers Messrs J. E. & A. Dowson, of London, cost £8,000 and was built by Messrs Head, Wrightson & Co of Stockton on Tees. Due to the important influence of the railways at that time, the project was financed by the Manchester, Sheffield and Lincolnshire Railway Company.

The Pier was 1200ft long, 20ft wide and, at the very end, there was an additional platform 120ft long and 84ft wide which had steps descending to sea level for visitors to enjoy boating trips.

The Pier was finally opened to the general public many years later, at 2.00pm on Saturday, 30 August 1873 by Mr Grant Thorold and Mr E. Bannister, Directors of the Railway Company. They thanked the numerous contractors for building such an added attraction to Cleethorpes. On the first day, almost 3,000 visitors paid 2p to walk the length of the new Pier and an additional 37,000 paid 1p each to stroll its length over the next five weeks.

## 1885 – CLEETHORPES PIER PAVILION

By 1885, the owners had made significant, expensive improvements to the Pier attracting thousands of people each summer to enjoy the facilities. On Friday 11 September 1885, the Directors of the Railway Company announced that they were planning to erect a large concert hall at the end of the Pier where dancing and entertainment would be allowed. Whilst undergoing construction, on Saturday, 24 April 1886, a fire was discovered under the deck planking, apparently from some hot ashes left by the workmen. These were quickly extinguished with no damage caused. This would not be the only decking fire.

The concert hall was opened in June 1886 providing excellent dancing, entertainment and meeting facilities which were extremely popular. Especially popular was Little Jim, the boy frog, entertaining the crowd in an enormous water tank for a sixteen week season during the summer of 1887. In May 1888, due to the popularity of entertainment, the owners decided that the Pavilion would become a permanent theatre, so plans were made and implemented.

On Tuesday 17 July 1888, the owners of the pier submitted an application for an alcohol licence for a proposed new building on the pier. This was surprisingly denied, as the building at the front of the Pier was allowed a licence. The new Grand Concert Pavilion, located at the very end of the 1200ft long pier, included a large stage, dressing rooms, refreshment rooms, shops, outdoor seating facilities etc. It opened for business in September 1888, the Pavilion proving to be a success as a number of famous acts appeared, all attracting large audiences, especially during the peak summer months.

## 1903 – FIRE

On Monday 29 June 1903, the popular morning musical concert held in the Pavilion, concluded around 12.30pm, and the audience made their way along the Pier to the promenade. Following a suspicion of smoke, it was discovered that there was an outbreak of fire between the wooden beams and iron girders supporting the floor at the end of the pier. The theatre, erected mainly of glass and wood, built around an iron framework, was in danger, as the fire was now spreading under the wooden beams, and approaching the floor situated under the theatre.

A number of potentially catastrophic situations met together as the Pier floor had been coated in a highly flammable, weather protective, tar type substance and this, coupled with the very hot weather, made the wood in various parts of the theatre very dry. In addition, the actual floor of the Pavilion, as it was used for dancing, had been heavily waxed which helped the flames quickly spread to the whole of the theatre floor. This, in turn, spread to the other areas of the theatre and the situation was becoming extremely serious as the whole building was becoming a mass of flames.

The Great Central Railway Company's fire engine was summoned, along with the Cleethorpes and Grimsby engines, but the fire was spreading rapidly. The smoke was thick, black and blinding due to the various chemicals coated on the wood. Many firemen were overcome by fumes and they also had a major problem of an acute shortage of water as the tide was receding. The flames were now engulfing the stage, dressing and store rooms of the Pavilion where the wardrobe and musical instruments belonging to the performers were kept. There were many costumes belonging to Miss Ada Phillips, and also a cinematograph projector and films, plus many musical instruments, belonging to the orchestra. In particular, there was a 100 guinea piano, located on the stage. All of these were completely destroyed.

Only twenty minutes after the discovery of the fire, the Pavilion was virtually destroyed and, by now, the whole of the Pier was in serious danger as the fire was spreading rapidly along the wooden floor heading towards the promenade and destroying everything in its path Desperate measures were needed.

An instruction was given by Police Inspector Bowles for the firemen to cut off the fire from the rest of the pier by creating a six foot wide gap in the wooden decking approximately half way along the pier in order to create a fire break.

At around 1pm an additional fire brigade arrived from Grimsby, it was immediately directed to fight the fire from underneath the burning Pier but the receding tide meant the heavy fire engines drawn by horses were bogged down in the soft sand. The horses were unable to move the brigade's equipment to nearer the seat of the fire, therefore visitors, firemen and police manhandled it as far as possible. Due to the receding tide, sea water could not be used and street hydrants were too far away for their use, an impossible situation.

The fire was finally extinguished around 2.30pm as it had effectively burnt itself out and all that was left of the end of the pier and the Pavilion was a mass of charred wood, twisted girders, iron railings and a large heap of smouldering debris on the beach below. The fire break was a successful operation, the fire was halted from spreading and the fire brigades were stood down at 4pm.

The cost of rebuilding would be in the region of £3,000, it was fully insured, but the loss of summer income to the proprietors, Great Central Railway Company could not be accurately estimated but would certainly run into many thousands of pounds. It was agreed that a marquee would be constructed in the nearby promenade gardens to ensure summer entertainment could, at least, continue in the absence of the Pavilion.

## 1904 – REBUILD

In June 1904, a concert hall was designed by Mr S. George-Moore, contractor and Mr A Thorne, both of London, working under the supervision of Mr P. H. Thorne, Clerk of Works, with an expected build time of one year.

The completed building exceeded all expectations but, surprisingly, the new location was to be in a completely different part of the pier. It would be situated a mere 175ft from the Pier entrance, rather than the 1200ft walk to the end of the pier It would be built as an extension on one side of the pier, offering numerous additional benefits, principally eliminating a half mile walk, in inclement weather, or having to run the length of the pier to catch the last train!

The Pavilion, costing £21,500, measured 110ft by 60ft and was fitted with a high degree of glass to maximise the beautiful sea and promenade views. The architect also designed eighteen large opening windows, each one measuring 9ft wide by 6ft high, whilst the top rows were divided into twenty-four small windows of leaded Cathedral glass. There were also fourteen 5ft wide double emergency exit doors leading to the pier walk-ways. The whole interior was painted white, the roof was supported by twelve steel arched ribs of a 40ft span carried on twelve ornamental cast-iron columns, imprinted with the contractor's name, Alfred Thorne of Westminster which is still visible today.

The centre portion of the auditorium floor measured 20ft square and had a high quality pitch pine sprung floor installed for the delight of dancers. Using removable seating to allow for these regular dances, the multi-use Pavilion could seat 1200 people in the auditorium for variety shows. The stage measured 25ft deep and 30ft wide, and would accommodate the majority of touring shows without much difficulty. The auditorium was illuminated by four, 450 candle powered chandeliers. High quality dressing rooms, green room, workshops and offices were provided behind the stage, for the comfort and enjoyment of performers, staff and management.

## 1905 – THE NEW PAVILION

The new Pavilion opened on Saturday 10 June 1905 with a grand concert, starring Miss Ada Crossley, contralto; Miss Violet Ludlow, soprano; Mr Joseph Hanson, tenor; Mr Foden-Williams, comedian and Mr E. Von Gelder, violinist. For the benefit of people who could not gain entrance on the Saturday night, the show was repeated the following afternoon.

The Pavilion had a successful time during the early/mid 1900s and included a wide range of entertainment, including celebrity concerts starring Henry Gill, baritone; numerous music hall artists such as Major & Minor, comedians; The Tudor Sisters, vocalists and Jack Crosby, comedy cartoonist & magician.

*Ada Crossley*

## 1936

The owners sold the Pier to the Cleethorpes Council in 1936 coincidentally the same year as the resort gained borough status.

## 1940

In early 1940, the Pier, along with the majority of others around the UK, were breached for defence purposes. As a result, the pier was reduced in length by almost two-thirds, from 1200ft down to 335ft.

Scrap metal from the demolition was transported to Leicester City's football ground in Filbert Street to assist in the building of their new stand following its bombing and fire damage during the war.

Ballroom dancing was a major attraction and many professionals such as Mr Cyril Bourne & Miss Margaret Burgess gave regular exhibition performances. A great deal of radio programmes featuring local dance bands were broadcast during the intervening war years and were extremely popular at the time.

## 1960s

The 1960s were becoming a difficult time for the Pavilion Theatre as it struggled to attract the leading stars of the day, therefore steps had to be taken to improve the situation. The summer seasons at the Pavilion were a financial disaster. For example, in 1962 the council lost over £2,000 and they decided to hire a complete show for the following summer of 1963. They selected the 'Tony Melody Show,' a very talented singer and impressionist supported by Mr Tony Valdi, singer; Mary Chappell, singer; Eric Martin, singer; the Meltones, Harry Rowley and Margarette Little.

During the winter of 1965/6, the council closed the pavilion and carried out a major refurbishment including a new bar and restaurant. In the summer of 1966, the financially draining, traditional summer seasons variety shows were abandoned in favour of weekly variety with popular stars such as Vince Hill, Dave Allen, Clinton Ford, the Raindrops etc. Sunday night would be dedicated to wresting bouts or for top pop groups. Afternoon Bingo was also introduced as an added attraction for the many visitors.

*Cannon & Ball*

## 1970s

The Council decided to revert back to presenting summer shows in the mid/late 1970s, the quality of the summer shows significantly improved, therefore attracting much larger audiences. Performers in the mid/late 1970s were;

- 1975   The Rockin' Berries and Ray Allan (With Lord Charles)
- 1976   Norman Collier and The Brother Lees
- 1977   Cannon & Ball and Tony Christie
- 1978   Charlie Williams and Terry Webster
- 1979   The Nolan Sisters
- 1980   Lonnie Donegan and Clodagh Rodgers

The threat of fire was never far away. On Saturday 27 September 1975, a fire broke out at the rear of the theatre, caused by high winds blowing sparks from a tool being used during a £6,000 ongoing roof repair. These sparks set fire to the rest of the roof, which spread to the stage and its surrounding areas. The workmen quickly extinguished the flames but had to urgently carry out temporary repairs to ensure the planned wresting event was able to take place on the following evening.

## 1985 – CHANGE OF OWNERSHIP

The Council were experiencing significant losses during the summer shows of the 1960s and 1970s and they sold the Pier to Funworld of Skegness, who quickly offered the Pier for sale, initially offering it back to the Council who refused to consider their offer.

Nightclub owner, Mr Mark Mayer bought the pier, including the Pavilion, for £10,000 on Wednesday 24 July 1985 and spent a quarter of a million pounds transforming The Pavilion into the 'Pier 39' (named after an old Steamer Pier in San Francisco). This refurbished, modern night club, opened on Wednesday, 4 September 1985 and that was the end of live, traditional variety entertainment as far as the Pavilion Theatre was concerned.

## 2011

Over the next few years the Pavilion had many night club owners and it was quite an interesting period as numerous businessmen tried hard to make a success of it, but without success. Unfortunately, none of these activities included the use of the theatre facilities and on Friday 2 September 2011, the then owners surrendered their licence pending an investigation into a series of violent incidents and serious disorder. It was re-opened on Thursday, 1 December 2011 under new management, and renamed Tides Bar and Restaurant.

## 2013

The owner eventually put it up for auction on Saturday 2 February 2013. Swindells Auctioneers offered it at a guide price of £400,000, but they subsequently announced it had been sold to a mystery buyer for a figure in excess of the guide price. The contents listed in the Auction Catalogue included, two restaurants; a fully equipped stage; fitted kitchens; 12 original cast iron pillars; pitch-pine wooden floor; 4 dressing rooms plus many other items such as sound systems, LED lighting, etc.

Three months later, in May 2013, Swindells Auctioneers announced that the sale had collapsed as the potential buyers had failed to meet their contractual obligations. However, shortly afterwards, in July 2013, the Pavilion re-opened after Mr Bryan Huxford purchased it, commencing a total refurbishment. In November 2013 Huxford's multi million pound vision for the future of the Pavilion was unveiled, including the creation of a high quality restaurant named 1873 (the name reflected the year in which the Pier had first opened), a new bar and tea-rooms.

The Pavilion had closed to undergo this major refurbishment in late 2014, reopening in August 2015, to rave reviews and thousands of people flocked to see the multi-million pound transformation. Their efforts to create a success were rewarded in March 2016 when it won the prestigious 'Pier of the Year Award', a truly wonderful achievement for a small seaside town. However, in September 2016, just over one year after this expensive transformation, the Huxford family announced that the Pavilion was, once again, available to purchase at an undisclosed amount. The agents instructed to handle the sale of the Pier and theatre premises were Andrew Watt of CBRE and Carl Bradley of Clark Weightman.

## 2016 – CHANGE OF USE

In November 2016 it was announced that a very successful family restaurant business would become the new owners of the Cleethorpes Pier including the Pavilion. They were 'Papas Fish and Chips' and would create the 'World's Biggest Fish and Chip Restaurant' and take-away, based entirely in the Pavilion Theatre premises.

*Papa's Fish & Chip Restaurant*

*Papa's Fish & Chip Restaurant Dining Area*

Able to accommodate 500 diners, the theatre and side rooms underwent an expensive, but tasteful refurbishment, finally opening for business in March 2017 and attracting thousands of diners.

The old front bar was transformed into the fish & chip out-sales area. The tea-room, colonnade and the theatre auditorium were sympathetically restored without altering the main theatre features in any way, in fact, the stage was upgraded with a view to holding live entertainment at some time in the future.

The highly rated, original pitch-pine floor was also refurbished, cleaned and polished. The original iron supporting columns are now a feature of the dining area, the decor style and colour is the same as those present in the original theatre days. The stage, complete with maroon theatre curtains, sound and lighting units, now sits, together with the dance floor, in all its former glory, anxiously awaiting entertainment. Theatre evenings have been planned where entertainment/dining evenings are being seriously considered.

Let us sincerely hope that Cleethorpes Pier and Pavilion, through 'Papas' proven business acumen and professionalism, will have many years of stability and be the same highly valued attraction to visitors as was the original Pier built 144 years earlier.

# DID YOU KNOW...?

## 1888 – MR ROBERT BASKER

The Pier was undergoing major refurbishment in the 1880s but one unfortunate person was found drowned under the Pavilion on Wednesday 4 July 1888. He was named as Mr Robert Basker, aged 40, working as a bailiff for the landlord of the White Swan, Grimsby. A letter, addressed to his wife, pleading poverty was found in his pocket, it was believed he had committed suicide.

## 1955 – MISS SANDRA ALLDRYCHE

Juvenile Dance Festivals, held on an annual basis at the Pavilion, attracted hundreds of young girls who regarded it as a perfect venue to display their dancing talents. Sixteen child dancers, between the ages of four and five years old entered the East Coast Children's Dance Festival on Thursday 1 September 1955. Amongst them was five year old, Miss Sandra Alldryche. She had started dancing only four months previously, after spending most of her life in hospital, suffering many serious illnesses requiring numerous operations.

Miss Alldryche had only recently left hospital, entered her first ever competition and was awarded a third place against strong relatively, experienced, competition. A credit to her and her endurance.

## 1976 – 'CINDERELLA'

Pantomime was a regular feature for many years, and an incident occurred on Friday 9 February 1976 when the cast of 'Cinderella' had to be rescued from the theatre when they were cut off from reaching the promenade due to high seas which caused flooding on the promenade to a depth of four feet.

The full cast were marooned for many hours. However, they were entertained by the fun and music of the principal comedians, Nicholas and Nickelby, plus other entertainment from Tony Mandell who played Buttons, Monty Simpson and Jimmy Slater who were the Ugly Sisters, Janet West as Dandini and Victoria Williams as the Fairy Godmother.

They were all rescued, along with two real life ponies, without injury, in the early hours of the morning and relived their experiences for many months.

## 1979 – NOLAN SISTERS

Miss Anne Nolan a member of the singing Nolan Sisters, married Blackpool Football Club player, Mr Brian Wilson, at the Church of the Sacred Heart, Blackpool, on Saturday 23 June 1979. Her sisters, Denise, Maureen, Linda, Bernadette and Colleen acted as bridesmaids and were dressed in apricot and white which almost matched the Blackpool Football Club's playing colours of tangerine and white.

The happy pair left for a brief honeymoon but had to return quite soon as the Nolan Sisters were heading the summer season show at the Pier Pavilion commencing on Wednesday 12 July 1979, continuing until Saturday 1 September 1979.

# ECCLES CROWN

*The Eccles Crown Theatre*

## 1899 – THE LYCEUM THEATRE

Mr Richard Flanagan, owner of the Queen's and St James's Theatres in Manchester, decided to build a theatre on the corner of Church Street and Mather Road in Eccles, five miles from Manchester City centre. It was designed by local theatre architects, Campbell and Horsley, and able to seat 2,500 people with everyone having a perfect view of the stage.

The Lyceum Theatre comprised of the orchestra stalls, dress circle, balcony and upper balcony (known locally as the 'Gods') all supported on four columns at each level. The decorative plaster fronts of the tiers were in an Adam style. The stage was 67ft wide, 38ft from the proscenium to the back wall and 26ft across the proscenium opening. The act drop had a facsimile of the opening of the Theatre Royal in Manchester in 1845. The fire curtain was embossed with the heraldic insignia of the Borough of Eccles and the ornamentation of the proscenium was composed of the representation of Shakespeare's 'The Seven Ages of Man', painted by Hugh Freemantle. In addition there were stained glass windows of poets and playwrights installed around the theatre in an attempt (they said) 'to educate the poor and uneducated'!

There were seventeen dressing rooms situated across four floors on one side of the theatre with superior quality fittings. They even included a small cooking range and an electric calling bell. The theatre fittings throughout were in the English Renaissance style and the upholstery was in blue and there were gold velvet plush curtains to match the decorations. Every consideration was given to safety. The windows of the foyer opened onto a verandah running the full length of the front of the building, which could be utilised should the theatre need to be evacuated.

## OPENING

On Thursday 23 February 1899, Flanagan invited a number of principal guests to a private opening ceremony of the Lyceum, including His Worship the Mayor of Eccles, Dr Hamilton, the Mayoress, the Mayor of Salford, Sir W. H. Bailey, Sir Richard Mottram and Mr R. A. Armitage. Dr Hamilton performed the opening ceremony and he gave a lengthy, impassioned speech, emphasising the need for suitable drama to be presented and he stressed that the Lyceum should have a moral influence upon life in Eccles. It was expected that the theatre would be a home for Shakespeare performances but this policy was quickly forgotten. The invited guests witnessed a concert programme involving Miss Lizzie Skeet, Miss Jessie Young, Mr Thurgate Simpson, Mr J. G. Hewson and Mr J. H. Greenwood.

The following Monday 27 February 1899, the Lyceum was formally opened to the public, with the National Anthem sung by Miss Lizzie Skeet, one of the performers and an enthusiastic audience. This singing was followed by the concert programme, 'The Gay Grisette' presented by the Associated Manager's Company and starred Mr Colin Mackay as Captain Jack Canary, Mr G. Bastow as Amos Basingstoke, Mr Geo. L. Montague as Blossom and Mr Maitland Dicker as the Sultan of Sahara.

In March 1899, the Lyceum had the audacity to present a ten minute Bioscope, a new silent cinema system, entitled 'The Spanish Bullfight' and this was clear evidence that the management were moving away from the original policy as outlined by Dr Hamilton in his opening speech.

## 1903

From the very early 1900s, it was obvious that the residents of Eccles were not enamoured with Shakespeare. Audiences were disappointing, therefore, in order to continue in business, Flanagan had no alternative but to present weekly variety and modern drama from 1903. The initial costs of funding the Lyceum had to be met, increased admission charges also proved unpopular as they were 1p more than other local theatres. As part of the move to variety, he closed the Lyceum in early 1903 and carried out a full re-decoration and modernisation programme.

## RE-OPENING

The re-opening took place on Monday 3 August 1903 when the bill included Miss Ada Fawn, burlesque actress; Mr Bert Woodward, trick cyclist; Mr Joe Graham, ventriloquist; Les Belles Americaines, acrobatic dancers plus numerous additional variety acts.

## 1907

Business did not improve for Flanagan. The Lyceum closed for business on Saturday 23 March 1907 with almost £12,000 owed in mortgage arrears. Local theatre owners, Messrs W. H. Broadhead & Sons, immediately commenced negotiations with the owners to acquire The Lyceum. It was their intention to purchase a high quality theatre of outstanding design, less than eight years old, built of the finest materials available at the time.

## 1907 – THE CROWN THEATRE

On Monday 30 September 1907 Flanagan announced that he had finally sold the Lyceum to the expanding amusement group of companies, Messrs W. H. Broadhead & Sons of Manchester, who announced that the theatre would, in future, be known as 'The Crown Theatre'.

Due to the excellent condition of the theatre, little improvement work was required. Therefore one week following the purchase, on Monday 8 October 1907, the Crown opened for business with a variety bill including David Pool, ventriloquist; Correze & Keith, jugglers; Little Tim, comedian and a sketch from the pantomime, 'Cinderella'.

Mr William Henry Broadhead, together with his two sons, William Birch and Percy, had acquired a large number of Lancashire entertainment centres in the early 1900s, including theatres, cinemas and dance halls in Manchester, Bury, Liverpool, Salford, Preston and Morecambe.

Unfortunately, during the negotiations for the Lyceum, Mr William Birch Broadhead died on Sunday 3 March 1907 at the young age of thirty-four, following a bout of pneumonia causing a heart attack.

## 1919

Mr Percy Broadhead, Williams Henry's remaining son, became President of the Provincial Entertainment Proprietors and Managers Association. He was a firm believer in treating employees fairly and in November 1919 he concluded an agreement with the Manchester and Salford Branch of the Theatre Trade Union. This agreement awarded significant basic wage increases to all staff, overtime in excess of normal hours and all rehearsals would now be paid. Additionally, working Bank Holidays would attract a double time payment. This agreement was regarded as being extremely far sighted as far as employee relations were concerned.

## 1930

Rumours were circulating in 1930 that Mr Percy Broadhead planned to convert The Crown into a cinema and although he committed to continue it as a variety theatre, his plans were soon to change. Mr William Henry Broadhead, who had been suffering ill-health, died at his home in Blackpool on Sunday 12 April 1931 aged 82. That was effectively the end of the Broadhead empire.

## 1932

The Broadhead Trustees ordered that the Crown Theatre must be offered for sale on Thursday 11 February 1932. The advertisement stated that the items included in the sale were all the theatre contents plus three refreshment bars together with the relevant licences, and twelve dressing rooms. It also included property, electrical and carpenter's offices. The total area of the site was 1,322 sq yds, the building covered 1,016 sq yds with a payable rent of £68.75p per annum. It was announced that the buyers of the Crown were the H. D. Moorhouse Circuit who controlled around 60 cinemas, most of them in Lancashire. The new owners closed the Crown for a number of weeks for alteration, refurbishment, including a new cream and gold colour scheme and installation of new rear projection equipment.

Their other theatres in the Broadhead group, such as the Hippodrome, and Junction Theatres in Hulme, the Royal Theatre in Salford and The Metropole in Openshaw, Manchester were eventually offered for auction on Wednesday 26 April 1933 by local auctioneers, W. H. Robinson & Co.

Since its opening in 1899, originally as a dedicated Shakespeare theatre, it had moved quickly to variety entertainment and attracted many famous stars to its stage over the years. A very young Charlie Chaplin appeared in 1910, George Formby, both Senior and Junior were regulars.

Frank Randle appeared in the 'Bounding Randles' before he became a headline act, even Max Miller travelled from the south coast!

*George Formby*

## 1955

In 1955, ownership of The Crown was obtained by the Snape Group and they continued the tradition of showing films with some variety performances but, similar to the majority of other theatres in the country, they found the economic situation to be very challenging indeed.

## 1963

In 1963, the entertainment changed to Bingo when some major structural alterations took place as the stage house was demolished leaving only the auditorium and front of house areas intact. However, many thousands of people continued to attend the Crown Bingo until it closed in December 1990.

## 2003 – 2019 – THE END

On Wednesday 16 April 2003, English Heritage awarded the Crown Theatre/Cinema, Grade 2 Listed Building Status, which would ensure the future for the building. However, since its closure, the condition of the building was seriously deteriorating due, principally, to the leaking roof causing some of the ceiling decorative plasterwork and tiles to collapse into the circle and auditorium.

In 2005, the Crown was purchased by Mr Geoffrey Klein, a property developer. Three years later in 2008, it was sold again to Westgate Developments who planned to build accommodation on the site, but the Crown continued to rot and decay.

The Crown was placed on the 'Theatres At Risk' list in 2012. By then, the building had deteriorated even further as the third and fourth floors were now unstable and water penetration was now damaging the second floor. In addition, the structure of the building was felt to be unsafe as the front elevation wall on the fourth floor was now insecure and in danger of collapsing into Mather Road.

Upon further inspection it was found that there was extensive corrosion to the internal steelwork making the building unsafe to enter. Lamination to the steelwork was affecting the main staircase from ground to second floor level, possibly resulting in the total collapse of the stairway in a similar manner as had happened to the one from the auditorium into the cellar. The local council boarded-up the building and bricked up the rear section in order to make it secure to ensure no-one could enter it due to its dangerous condition. This was not particularly successful as local residents often saw people within the premises.

## FIRE

The situation was to become much worse as at 04.45am on the morning of Sunday 1 December 2019, Manchester Fire Brigade were called to the Crown but they were unable to enter the building due to its perilous state and had to fight the fire from the local streets. The 35 firefighters managed to bring the fire under control by 1.30pm but the Crown had burnt itself out and the interior was now almost totally destroyed.

The Manchester Fire Brigade said that the only aspect remaining was the brick outer shell and some internal brick walls but, the flooring, staircases, balconies, stage and even the roof, had collapsed. They commented that the fire was particularly challenging as they only allowed two firefighters at a time into the concrete entrance hall at the foot of the main staircase, in order to fight the fire, but this had little effect. They had to be mindful of the amount of insecure flooring and falling debris from the balconies and roof. The cause of the fire was unknown but assumed to be accidental arson. The disastrous fire would have no effect on the planning permission as the outer walls were still standing and the proposed apartment housing plans could still be completed.

## FUTURE

The current position is that the building cannot be salvaged in view of its present state, and local residents are hopeful that the recent plans to demolish most of it and convert the site into 82 flats and retain the facade will be successful. If built, music and laughter may be heard once again within the retained facade, and new residents may be welcomed into the Crown at some time in the future.

## DID YOU KNOW...?

### 1899 – FATALITY No 1

Within days of the official opening of the Lyceum in February 1899, Mr Fred Mason, working as a painter and decorator for Messrs A. & R. Dean, Birmingham, was fatally injured when one of the planks gave way and he fell 45ft into the auditorium from scaffolding. His wife brought an action for compensation on Friday 28 April 1899 for £300, this was refused as the contractors argued that the building was incomplete, therefore the claim was refused by the County Court Judge.

Mrs Mason appealed against this judgement in the Court of Appeal on Friday 23 February 1900 under the Workman's Compensation Act (1897) and their Lordships decided that the County Court Judge was wrong and the claim should be allowed within the meaning of the Act. The appeal was allowed and Mrs Mason was awarded £300 in compensation and the costs of the appeal.

It was rumoured that the ghost of Mr Fred Mason haunts the theatre to this day!

## 1899 – FATALITY No 2

On Friday 16 June 1899, Mr Samuel Hitching, aged 19, an assistant gas-man at the Lyceum fell through a trap door, fracturing his skull. He was rushed to hospital but tragically died fifteen minutes after admission.

## 1900 – MR SAMUEL FRANKLIN CODY

*Samuel Franklin Cody*

In June 1900, a revue called 'The Klondike Nugget' was performed by, what was billed as (in those days) real-life 'Cowboys and Indians' including traditional western music, galloping horses, gunfights, lassoing skills etc featuring Samuel F. Cody, the brilliant American showman. He was born in Iowa, USA on Wednesday 6 March 1867 and toured with his famous revues but his main interest was flying aeroplanes and developing large kites.

In 1912 he became one of the first men to build and fly an aeroplane, and his kites attracted the interest of the Government for future development within the armed forces. He died near Farnborough on Thursday 7 August 1913, test flying one of his designs, which collapsed in mid air. He is buried at the Aldershot Military Cemetery.

## 1905 – MR JOHN MURPHY

On Monday 22 May 1905, Mr John Murphy, an employee at The Crown, appeared before the Mayor in the Manchester Magistrates Court. He was charged with being drunk on Saturday 20 May 1905. Allegedly, Murphy had attended the Mayor's place of work demanding a meeting, only to be told he wasn't available, to which he replied "it's a good job, it has saved his life as I intended doing for him".

When Murphy was told he would be sent to an 'Inebriates Home' he said he would prefer Strangeways Prison instead. He was fined £1 plus costs, or one month's imprisonment.

## 1905 – FATALITY No 3

On Wednesday 22 November 1905, the County Coroner, Mr J. F. Price, held an inquest at Patricroft, a suburb of Eccles. It concerned the death of Mrs Charlotte Burroughs, who was found in a kneeling position at the bottom of the toilet steps in the Lyceum. The inquest heard that she had been suffering from 'fainting fits'. The toilet and steps had more than adequate lighting and no blame could be attached to the owners of the theatre.

A verdict of death from natural causes was returned, and it was noted that Mrs Burrough's broken arm had not contributed to her death.

## 1908 – MR ARTHUR BEALE

Mr Arthur Beale, the famous Lancashire comedian, was booked to appear at the Crown during week commencing Monday 21 December 1908. He was taken ill whilst performing at the Liverpool Empire the previous week. Unfortunately he passed away in a Liverpool Hospital a few days later. His death was due to double pneumonia.

## 1909 – THE MARS TRIO

The Mars Trio of Gymnasts were performing at the Crown on Wednesday 6 October 1909 when an accident occurred which created great concern. One of the troupe was making his third revolution on the horizontal bar, head downwards, when the bar broke and the gymnast fell 20ft, head first, onto the wooden stage. He escaped with slight injuries.

## 1931 – MR WILLIAM HENRY BROADHEAD

This once very successful entertainment business, Messrs W. H. Broadhead & Sons founded in 1896 by Mr William Henry Broadhead, consisted of numerous of theatres, dance halls, cinemas, etc in the North West. He added The Crown to his portfolio in September 1907 along with the enormous Morecambe Winter Gardens complex.

Born on a farm in Mansfield in 1848, William started work as a builder in Liverpool, married at the age of 23, opening a building and decorating business in Manchester before moving to Blackpool in 1883 due to health problems. His first venture into entertainment was buying Blackpool Baths, which proved successful, therefore he quickly expanded his operation into many forms of entertainment for the 'working man'. Appointed an Alderman, he became Mayor of Blackpool on two occasions, 1905/6 and 1910/1911. He also served as a magistrate making him regarded as one of the pillars of society.

On Sunday 12 April 1931, Alderman William Henry Broadhead, aged 82, passed away at his home in his beloved Blackpool. His funeral on Wednesday, 15 April 1931 at the Blackpool Cemetery, was one of the largest ever held in Blackpool. In addition to his family, mourners included representatives from Blackpool, Lytham St Annes and Morecambe Councils, every theatre, dance hall and cinema he had ever owned, local police and fire service personnel plus thousands of people lining the streets who had been entertained by him over the years.

William's remaining son, Percy, born in 1878, had gradually taken full control of the Broadhead Group in the 1920s due to his father's deteriorating health. All the various theatres, cinemas's etc were auctioned and the business effectively disappeared. Percy died in 1955 at the age of 76.

## 1971 – CEILING COLLAPSE

On Friday 13 August 1971, 250 people were in the Crown enjoying a game of Bingo when the ceiling collapsed causing plaster and wooden slats to rain down upon them. At first it was feared that some people may be seriously injured but the vast majority suffered from cuts, bruises and shock. Twenty people were transported to hospital, three women required X-rays and one lady had seven stitches inserted in a deep cut on her head.

The Bingo manager, Mr Gerald Love, said that only two numbers had been called when the ceiling fell. The condition of the building was obviously deteriorating as it closed permanently a few years later, never to re-open.

# EDINBURGH EMPIRE

*Edinburgh Festival Theatre*

## 1864 – THE SOUTHMINSTER

There have been numerous theatres in Nicolson Street since the early 1830s with varied names such as Ducrow's Circus, Pablo Fanque's Ampitheatre, Dunedin Hall, and the Southminster Theatre.

## 1875 – FIRE No 1

The Southminster was built entirely of wood in 1864, capable of holding an audience of 2,000, but unfortunately it was destroyed by fire on Sunday 14 March 1875 along with the Old York Hotel where the dressing rooms were situated. Re-building commenced on Monday 19 April 1875 and it was expected to reopen by Christmas 1875.

## 1875 – THE QUEEN'S THEATRE

The new theatre replacing the Southminster, was re-named the Queen's Theatre, and would be one of the finest built in Edinburgh to date. It was capable of accommodating 3,000 in that splendid building. The internal colours were white, grey, pink and gold. There were two palatial stage boxes. The ceiling was perfectly flat with illustrated panels enclosed within a circle and with a huge 'sun-burner' light in the centre.

The striking proscenium had a 30 feet wide opening, was 38 feet high with lavish ornamentation. The stage had a width of 80 feet, a depth of 43 feet with a height of 60 feet and was capable of handling the most difficult and cumbersome scenery.

It opened on Monday 13 December 1875, with numerous dignitaries present and an audience of 3,000 people who appreciated the full opulence of the building. They were initially entertained by the full assembly singing the National Anthem. Mr Henry Levy, the owner, thanked everyone for their attendance and particularly, Mr Sey, the architect for his wonderful design. This was followed by the Royal Opera Company, Covent Garden, London, performing the opera 'La Sommanbula' starring Mr Naudin as Elvino and Miss Vines as Lisa.

## 1876 – BANKRUPTCY

Unfortunately the Queen's Theatre would appear not to have a future as it closed for business due to Levy's bankruptcy, on Saturday 29 January 1876, only six weeks after opening.

At the official hearing on Friday 3 March 1876, Levy's financial state of affairs showed a deficiency of £2,243. This was due mainly to exceeding the building estimates and trading at a loss since its opening. In his defence, Levy said that he had initially agreed a fixed budget with the architect Sey, of £4,000. However, these plans were changed considerably, thus increasing the final cost to £7,000. Levy accepted he had virtually lost control of the costs, allowed modifications to the plans without costings, and worse still, making no profits during the short trading period.

On Saturday 25 March 1876, Messrs Lyon & Turnbull offered The Queen's Theatre for auction at a reserve of £8,000. The bids did not reach that figure therefore it was withdrawn. On Friday 5 April 1876 the theatre was offered for auction again, but the £7,000 reserve, although now reduced, still failed to attract a purchaser. On Saturday 23 June 1876 it was finally sold for £6,000 to Mr Thomas Baird, a builder from Edinburgh.

Baird did not own the theatre for long as he quickly sold it to a local syndicate, the Queen's Theatre Company (Edinburgh) for £6,250 within a few weeks. The new owners leased it to Howard & Logan, who were the lessees of the Edinburgh Theatre Royal, for two years at a rent of £3,000 per annum, and the building was insured for £8,000.

Problems arose when Mr James B. Howard applied for a licence for the Queen's to the Edinburgh Justices of the Peace on Thursday 14 September 1876. One of the Justices, Mr Josiah Livingston, stated that live entertainment had already commenced the previous week, and clearly the theatre did not have a licence. Howard said he had believed that a licence was already in existence as it had been a theatre for some time and apologised for the oversight. The Justices unanimously granted the licence.

Relations between the owners and the lessees rapidly deteriorated. On Friday 26 January 1877 in the Court of Sessions, the Queen's Theatre Company (Edinburgh) sued Howard & Logan for unpaid rent for the period between Friday 11 August 1876, the actual purchase date, and Friday 1 September 1876, the first performance date. Judge Lord Craighill heard the full evidence, recommending a compromise between the parties regarding the outstanding rent, both of them sharing the costs of the hearing. This was accepted.

## 1877 – FIRE No 2

The theatre had gone through a difficult start to its life and matters would deteriorate further in the spring of 1877. On Wednesday 4 April 1877 at 11.50pm that evening, local neighbours saw flames in the first floor windows beginning to burst through the stage roof, the fire being clearly out of control.

The heavily populated surrounding area saw residents panicking, as only a couple of years earlier the Southminster Theatre had been destroyed by fire and they had begun to fear the worst. The fire brigade was quickly summoned, only to find the interior a burning furnace with almost everything on fire, the roof collapsing into the auditorium amid a shower of sparks and flames illuminating the night sky. This collapse caused more concern as the walls began to buckle, weakened by the absence of a roof to support them.

The east wall fell on one local man who was assisting the firemen. He had a lucky escape and had to be carried home by his friends. Unfortunately two firemen were not so lucky. Mr Adam Lowe suffered a broken arm and Mr David Martin a badly bruised leg. At 1am the internal proscenium wall collapsed into the auditorium bringing with it a number of metal roof beams and so destroying the stage. That was the end of the Queen's Theatre.

The cause was never established, although it was reported to police by neighbours that, during the two week closure prior to the fire, three men were seen moving scenery out of the stage door.

Quite surprisingly, the directors of the company accepted a sum of £6,000 from the Northern Insurance Company deciding not to rebuild the theatre and dispose of the structure as it stood. John Turnbull Smith, Auctioneers offered the site for sale on Tuesday 24 July 1877 at 2pm.

## 1877 – WELDONS CIRCUS

It was announced on Friday 28 September 1877 that Mr Weldon, a circus proprietor from Hull, had purchased the site and walls for £3,000 planning to open a circus which would also act as a multi-purpose concert hall. Weldon erected a 3,000 seater building on the site using the footprint of the old Queen's Theatre, opening to a capacity audience on Saturday 20 October 1877. The numerous acts ranged from equestrian displays and contortionists to jugglers and the traditional clowns.

## 1879

At the Edinburgh Bankruptcy Court before Sheriff Hallard, on Friday 4 April 1879, Weldon was accused of being bankrupt. He had purchased the old Queen's site for £3,000 and erected a circus costing £1,500. He regularly sub-let the building to other circus owners and received a weekly rent and was operating at a profit, in fact his assets were £1,345 and his liabilities £1,150 leaving a surplus of £162.

## 1879 – NEWSOME'S CIRCUS

Mr Newsome, an experienced circus owner, leased the Weldons Circus premises, and immediately carried out a major refurbishment of the building, including installing new seating, drapes and carpets.

On the opening night, Monday 6 September 1879, Mr and Mrs Newsome entered the ring to rapturous applause whilst the orchestra was playing 'Auld Lang Syne'. Numerous traditional circus acts appeared in addition to the amusing clowns. Mr Alfred Brown and Mr A. C. Boswell turned somersaults whilst riding a horse at full gallop. Misses Charini and Amalia presented two highly trained horses marching to music. The star attraction was Sarina, appropriately called 'the boneless wonder' who put his body in a series of shapes and positions which were thought impossible.

Six weeks later, on Wednesday 22 October 1879, Newsome purchased the old Weldon circus for £2,200, experiencing many successful years of presenting circus acts but deciding to change direction.

Newsome leased his building to Mr Sam Hague's Minstrels of Liverpool, for week commencing Monday 12 September 1887. Hague locked and secured the premises at 10pm the following evening after a successful presentation.

## 1887 – FIRE No 3

The following day, on Tuesday 13 September 1887, Hague's Minstrel Show completed at 10pm, and the audience departed. Hague carried out a full inspection of the building, and finding everything in order, locked all the doors at 10.50pm. At 11.15pm, smoke was seen by neighbours coming from the windows of the theatre, and they immediately notified the fire brigade who rushed to the scene. Arriving within minutes, they found the circus blazing from end to end especially as the interior was built with a tremendous amount of wood and the roof was covered in a highly flammable felt material.

Situated on the rear external wall of the circus were the wooden stables containing the horses. With the aid of neighbours, the firemen rescued all of them, leading them to safety. Unfortunately, a cat and its two kittens perished in the blaze. The firemen faced a hopeless situation as there was insufficient water available for the hoses to effectively fight the fire. They were helpless and just had to watch the building being reduced to ashes for almost an hour before sufficient pressure was available. No reason could be found for the cause of the fire. Hague believed he saw someone hurriedly leaving the circus as he arrived shortly after the fire was discovered, but as he was unsure, the matter was not pursued by the police.

A few days earlier Hague had agreed to lease the circus to Mr Horace Edward Moss for three years, being Moss's first venture into the theatre world, planning to convert the building eventually into a theatre. In not too many years, Moss became the biggest Theatre Impresario owning over fifty venues throughout the UK.

On Thursday 15 September 1887, an urgent meeting was held by the Edinburgh & District Water Trustees Committee at the request of the Lord Provost into the scarcity of water for the fire. It appeared that the supply of water had been reduced by adjusting the supply valves for use at night as an additional three million gallons had been used during the day time!

It was agreed that there should be better communications between the fire service and the water management team in cases of emergency, to ensure the valves were immediately adjusted.

## NEW BUILD

Mr & Mrs Newsome immediately planned, through their architect, Mr J. Murray Robertson, to rebuild the circus and/or a theatre on a more permanent and palatial basis than previously. A number of safety recommendations were insisted upon by the local council. These stipulated that all the walls, stores, dressing rooms etc must be built of brick and cement, and the roof must be constructed from iron. The decorations were magnificent, the walls and ceilings of the boxes and corridors were covered in Japanese paper. All curtains were in an olive colour, and pine framed fold up seating in maroon was provided. A new ventilation system was installed, the building was illuminated with forty-eight gas burners and numerous fire hydrants were installed in all areas.

The cost of the build would be between £4,000 and £5,000. It was said that the safety precautions insisted on by the magistrates had increased the cost by a third. Particular attention was paid to the amount of fireproofing and means of escape in the event of a fire or other emergency. In addition, two large water tanks, holding 7,000 gallons, were installed in the eaves of the roof for release in the event of a fire. The 3,000 seater building, measuring 154 feet by 94 feet, was one of the finest in Scotland. The fixtures & fittings were of the highest quality and design, modern ventilation was provided to all areas and only the finest carpets were fitted.

## OPENING

Working day and night, the building took only six weeks to complete, opening on Saturday 31 December 1887. Several city dignitaries were present, including the Lord Provost Clark and Lady Clark, who heard an amusing address by Mr Louis Egerton, the Ringmaster. The entertainment commenced with a children's presentation of 'The Gathering of the Clans', followed by a humorous interlude from Mr Newsome; Vokes the clown and a pony. These acts were followed by Miss Margarita, a slack wire specialist, a troupe of performing dogs, pigeons, and, to everyone's surprise, pigs. The headline act was the Newsome family who performed their specialist equestrian act, 'with confidence and grace' was how it was described at the time.

## 1890 – NEW OWNER

Newsome continued to lease his circus/theatre to various people. Moss had taken up his option to lease the building from 1887, however, on Saturday 10 May 1890 it was announced that Moss had purchased the property. Moss eventually became the owner of the large chain of Empire Theatres, all starting with the acquisition of Newsome's Circus.

## 1891 – THE EMPIRE

On Thursday 11 June 1891, Moss submitted planning permission to the Edinburgh Dean of Guild Court to demolish Newsome's circus along with some adjoining property, and erect a new, purpose built theatre, designed by Mr Frank Matcham. Permission was approved, and building work commenced a few months later. The end result was a theatre of magnificent proportions, perfectly designed, elegant and full of decorative beauty which would, without doubt, completely satisfy the high standards demanded by the residents of Edinburgh. The theatre could accommodate 3,000 people with the cost of building and decorations calculated at £25,000.

The remains of the old circus were removed. In order to increase the size of the new build, several adjacent properties were purchased which would significantly improve the external image of the building. Internally, the prime objective was one of fire safety. All passages and staircases were wide, built of brick or stone, little wood was used. Numerous exits were provided, fire appliances and hydrants were situated at every level including behind the stage.

Audiences were impressed with the sheer elegance of the building. Many rooms were decorated in gold and silver with an Indian theme throughout and stately marble staircases led to the circle. Its entrance was aesthetically pleasing, full of Indian palms, a waterfall with its water falling into marble shell basins all lit by stylish electric lighting. The elegant theme continued throughout the theatre, focusing all eyes on the beautiful proscenium arch decorated with the finest designs.

The auditorium consisted of stalls and pit, a grand circle with private boxes, an upper circle and a gallery. No columns were erected, therefore every seat had an uninterrupted view of the stage which was 75 feet wide and 40 feet deep and could be converted into a circus ring if needed. Performers would appreciate the quality of the dressing rooms, a significant improvement over the old standards.

## 1892 – OPENING

On Monday 7 November 1892, at 7:15 pm, the Empire opened again. A tremendous cheer greeted the appearance of the Combined Regimental Bands of the Carabiniers (6th Dragoon Guards) and the Argyle and Sutherland Highlanders playing the National Anthem accompanied by Miss Giulia Warwick. In addition to Miss Warwick, the performers included Miss Cora Stuart, musical sketch; Mr Ben Natham, comedian; Mr Albert Christian, vocalist; Miss Katie Cohen, vocalist; Professor Marville and his troupe of Canine Wonders; Mr Harry Atkinson, vocalist; The Brothers Poluske, comedians; The Craggs, acrobats and Evans & Luxmore, musical eccentrics. All the acts were accompanied by the Grand Orchestra of thirty musicians conducted by Mr Edmond Bosanquet.

## 1896

The success of the opening night continued for many years and the Empire attracted the most popular acts which performed in front of many thousands of people. This included, in 1896, the presentation of the first motion pictures ever seen in Scotland. George V became King in May 1910 and he and Queen

Mary visited Edinburgh. During their visit, they commanded that a Royal Variety Performance should be held at the Empire in the near future, but events were to overtake them.

## 1911 – FIRE No 4

On Monday 8 May 1911 the American impresario, magician and illusionist, The Great Lafayette, commenced a two week engagement at the Empire at a salary of £350 per week. That was a tremendous amount of money in those days and the equivalent of just under £40,000 per week at today's value. The supporting acts were Peter Bermingham, comedian; Warsaw Brothers, masters of mimicry; Rhoda Paul, soubrette; Mile Elldu, soprano and The Bensons, comedians.

The history of The Great Lafayette is intriguing. He was born Sigmund Ignatius Neuburger in Germany, and moved to America in his late teens accompanied by his beloved pet dog who died shortly afterwards.

This move to the USA was the start of his show business career. He had struggled in the early years to make a name for himself, however, his luck changed when his close friend, Harry Houdini, gave him a replacement dog in 1895, called 'Beauty'.

Lafayette's career escalated from that point to international fame. He regarded his dog Beauty as his lucky charm and she accompanied him on his world travels becoming a very pampered and much loved pet.

Although Lafayette was a hard task-master, who demanded perfection, his staff regarded him as one of the kindest people they could ever work for. He encouraged them to save money for 'a rainy day' often adding 10% to their wages. This could only be accessed when they were not working due to Lafayette's holidays or other commitments. On Tuesday 9 May 1911, Lafayette had almost concluded his performance of 'The Lion's Bride' with the stage set in jewelled splendour as a harem, including luxurious cushions, draperies and fittings. Suddenly one of the overhead electric Chinese lanterns began to smoulder. It then burst into flames and dropped onto the stage, igniting those furnishings.

The flames quickly spread to the remainder of the set, the audience slowly realising that there could be a serious incident developing that was not part of the act. This became obvious when the orchestra, upon instructions from the manager, began to play 'God Save the Queen' as smoke was beginning to engulf the Theatre. Over two thousand people in the audience escaped within a few minutes, and without injury, through the many fire exits situated around the Theatre.

Upon sight of the flames, the stage crew instantly lowered the fire proof safety curtain but it did not reach floor level as stage hands were fighting the fire in the vicinity immediately below it. As a result, a gap existed between the floor and the bottom of the curtain, allowing a strong draught to blow under it which fanned the flames making the problem worse. The theatre lost all of its electrical power and, as a result, the whole building was plunged into darkness causing more panic amongst the backstage staff.

The horror was rapidly escalating, many of the performers, stage hands, scene shifters etc were caught unawares, some perishing in the inferno. The Edinburgh firemen fought the fierce blaze bravely and managed to contain the flames, preventing them from spreading to the neighbouring buildings and the main body of the Empire.

Lafayette, his lion and his favourite horse, all died in the flames. His body being discovered later, in the stables situated underneath the stage. It was believed that he had desperately tried to save his horse, but all escape routes were blocked due to locked doors. The decision of locking these doors had been made on the personal instructions of Lafayette in order to ensure no one discovered his well kept magic secrets.

The following morning the stage, as viewed from the auditorium, was unrecognisable, everything around it had been destroyed, the fixtures and fittings and three blackened brick walls stood in the roofless area. Piles of smouldering debris were scattered around the stage which had presented thousands of acts over the years.

Underneath it was a burned mass of pipes, wires, cables and stage remnants. The rest of the theatre was largely undamaged as the fire curtain had successfully prevented the flames from spreading to the auditorium and beyond.

What was believed to be the body of The Great Lafayette was recovered at 5am on the Wednesday morning and this body was displayed in an open coffin at the top of the grand staircase. The massive coffin, was made of panelled oak, with bronze mountings, enclosing another of oak, and lined with lead. In the corners of the staircase lay the remains of his lion and his horse which had been recovered adjacent to his body.

There was a great deal of confusion, when, on clearing the wreckage of the Empire two days later, in a room under the stage, the workmen found another body. It was wearing a set of clothing and matching diamond rings identical to those that Lafayette had worn on the evening of the fire. They then realised the secret of one of his tricks was having 'a body double'. Clearly, both men, in identical clothing and wearing identical jewellery, had died in the fire.

The question of which was the actual body of Lafayette and which was the body of his double, continues to the present day. Which body was buried as Lafayette? Did a switch take place after discovering the second body?

At 12 noon on Friday 12 May a body, (but which one?), was removed from the mortuary of W. T. Dunbar & Sons, Undertakers, Edinburgh and transported to Glasgow for cremation. Only two people accompanied the unmarked coffin, Mr Will Collins, Lafayette's business manager and Mr Dunbar the undertaker. After the cremation, the ashes were placed in an urn and brought back to Edinburgh for the official funeral the following Sunday.

Whatever the outcome of this puzzle, on Sunday 14 May 1911, a carriage with an urn containing a set of ashes, and pulled by horses wearing black plumes, went to Piershill Cemetery, Portobello Road, Edinburgh. Over 200,000 people lined the streets paying their respects. At the cemetery, Lafayette's urn of ashes was laid between the legs of his beloved dog Beauty who had died days earlier. The vault is marked as a monument to remember the career and catastrophic end of 'The Man of Mystery'. However, the mystery remains, which Mystery Man lies in the vault? The Great Lafayette or his body double?

Mr Will Collins believed that Lafayette may have anticipated his own death when his beloved dog Beauty, had died only a few days before the fire. Lafayette had given Collins precise instructions as to how his own funeral should be arranged and conducted. He felt that his 'luck had gone' when Beauty died and his career was finished.

Lafayette had already arranged for a vault for Beauty at Piershill Cemetery earlier in the week, little did he know he would shortly be joining his beloved dog, or did he? As required under the Fatal Accidents Inquiry Act, a public enquiry was held in the Sheriff's Court, Edinburgh, on Thursday 15 June 1911 to establish the reasons for the death of ten people at the Empire on Tuesday 9 May 1911.

*The Great Lafayette Grave*

The victims of the fire were named as Ignatius Neuberger, known as 'The Great Lafayette', the following members of his company; James Edwin Baines, musician; Walter Edward Scott, musician; John Whelan, musician; Alice Dale, performer; Joseph Coates, performer; Charles E. Richards, (who acted as Lafayette's stage double); Alexander Rae Joss, labourer; James Watt, labourer and James Neilson, stage hand. Witnesses gave detailed evidence and many commented that the people on the stage or relaxing in the first and second floor dressing rooms could have escaped immediately through the exit doors had they not chosen to take time to collect their personal effects.

The jury returned a formal verdict of death due to suffocation. They added a rider recommending that, in future, City Authorities exercise more care both with regard to the safe construction of theatres and more frequent inspection of electric lighting and water hydrants.

Work commenced immediately to repair the damage to the stage and dressing rooms. Matcham was appointed to produce a rebuild design with structural alterations ensuring that the most modern fire-proof building materials were used at every opportunity. Wood was almost totally dispensed with, all supports were built of steel, concrete, brick and iron. There were three clear exits from the stage area leading into the street, all fitted with fire resistant doors with instant opening 'panic bolts'.

Elsewhere, London County Council had demanded that the fire curtain specification for their theatres should be significantly improved due to the number of fires. Matcham and Moss insisted that the upgraded London standard should be introduced elsewhere which consisted of two sheets of asbestos cloth, between which a sheet of asbestos was fitted and stretched over a steel frame. Fourteen new dressing rooms were built, four on the stage level, and ten at the rear of the stage, separated by fire resistant, close fitting doors which would prevent smoke and flames entering those areas.

A smoke extraction unit was installed over the stage which would be automatically activated should there be a fire. Whilst the auditorium escaped damage by fire, all the seating was replaced by more comfortable ones and the original circle and balcony seats re-upholstered. Due to the smoke and water damage, the theatre had a total redecoration by the London based company, F. De Jong & Co, in an Oriental design, coloured in pale blue, yellow, white and gold.

During the reconstruction of the Empire, Moss made arrangements with Howard and Wyndham Ltd for the business of the Empire to be transferred to the nearby Theatre Royal during the temporary closure. This ensured that all permanent staff and entertainers could continue to be paid their full earnings during this temporary arrangement.

## RE-OPENING

On Monday 7 August 1911 music and laughter was heard from the Empire for the first time in three months as it reopened to a sell-out audience. Appearing on the bill were Le Roy, Talma & Bosco, magicians; The Dayton Family, acrobats; Keens & Adams, song & dance; The Findens, comedy playlet; Katie Moss, violinist; Rochez's Monkeys; The Manchester Mites, juvenile singers and Marjorie Lawrence, comedienne.

## 1927

The Management of the Empire decided to temporarily close the theatre for a year in September 1927 in order to carry out a major re-furbishment based on designs submitted by Messrs William and T. R. Milburn of Sunderland. Their original thoughts were to only rebuild the stage area and make some other minor alterations. They were successful in purchasing additional adjoining property and were able to make significant improvements and extensions.

To all intents and purposes, the Empire was totally re-built, the three tier gallery, grand and upper circles disappeared and were replaced with a two tier grand circle and a spacious balcony. The width of the stage was increased from 75 feet to 88 feet therefore enabling the larger touring productions to be accommodated. Seventeen dressing rooms were built on the north side of the stage and each 'star artistes' accommodation would have bathing and toilet facilities.

A passenger lift and a laundry room were built in close proximity for the additional comfort of visiting entertainers. The decorations were in the style of Venetian Renaissance, with blue and silver relief. The seats were upholstered in Rose du Barry velvet with matching draperies in all other areas and a new system of ventilation was installed. Five hundred additional seats were fitted and the whole theatre freshly decorated in an amber and gold colour scheme.

## 1928 – RE-OPENING

For the re-opening on Monday 1 October 1928, the successful Drury Lane, London musical 'Show Boat' was presented, starring Mona Magnet and J. Blake Adams as the principals and Ena Hudson, Trissie Sturley, Adah Dick, Gilbert Holland, Beryl Walkley and Alex Lennox as supporting artistes. At the conclusion of the show, Mr R. H. Gillespie, managing director, made his welcoming speech and wished the theatre every success in the future.

This show was staged for three weeks before being replaced with the musical comedy 'Mr Cinders', which appeared at the Empire as part of its UK tour. It had commenced in Blackpool on Tuesday 25 September 1928 and finished at the Adelphi Theatre in London on Monday 11 February 1929. Actor/comedian, Bobby Howes and vocalist, Binnie Hale performed the leading roles assisted by David Hutchinson, Eileen Redcott, Basil Howes and Jack Hellor.

## 1933

Refurbishment seemed to be the order of the day as in June 1933, the Empire was closed yet again for several weeks for further remedial work. A new colour scheme of rose, amber and silver was introduced which gave the Theatre a brighter atmosphere, dispelling what was now considered to be its previous bleak scheme. The barrier separating the stalls from the pit was removed and a centre gangway was provided to reduce the inconvenience and discomfort of patrons reaching their seats.

Following a number of complaints, steps were taken to improve the acoustics by installing high quality sound equipment, manufactured by British Acoustic Films Ltd. including five additional stage microphones. To improve stage lighting, eight 1,000 watt lamps and one single centre stage unit of 3,000 watts were installed and significant improvements in the power of the limelights were made.

Re-introducing twice nightly performances, the Empire opened on Monday 7 August 1933 with Nervo & Knox, Naughton & Gold and 'Monsewer' Eddie Gray who brought continuous laughter to the opening proceedings. There was no particular pattern to the show and their unique brand of humour entertained the maximum capacity audience for at least two hours. The Empire attracted many famous and well respected names over the next thirty years or so with stars such as Harry Lauder, Joe Loss, Morecambe & Wise, Harry Worth etc.

*Laurel & Hardy playbill*

Probably the most famous people to appear at the Empire were Laurel and Hardy who appeared three times, to sell out audiences, during weeks commencing Monday, 30 June 1947, Monday, 28 April 1952 and Monday, 12 April 1954.

## 1950s – 1960s

In the early and mid fifties, the Empire maintained its audience numbers, presenting shows with stars such as Joan Regan and Tommy Cooper during week commencing Monday 25 October 1954.

Dark clouds began to gather over the Empire in the late 1950s and early 1960s due to other forms of entertainment being more popular such as

Here is our Route list - so you will know where we are.

APRIL. 28TH. EMPIRE. EDINBURGH.
MAY. 5TH. HIPPODROME. BIRMINGHAM.
"   12TH. GAUMONT. SOUTHAMPTON.
"   19 "  EMPIRE. LIVERPOOL.
"   26TH. OLYMPIA. DUBLIN
JUNE 2ND    "        "
"   9TH. OPERA HOUSE. BELFAST.
"   16TH.    "        "
"   23RD. REST.
"   30TH. EMPIRE SHEFFIELD.
JULY 7TH. HIPPO. BRIGHTON.
"    14TH. PALACE. MANCHESTER

JULY 21ST. QUEENS RHYL.
"   28TH. ALHAMBRA BRADFORD.
AUG. 4TH. GAUMONT SOUTHEND.
"   11TH. HIPPO. COVENTRY.
"   18TH. GARRICK. SOUTHPORT.
"   25TH. WINTER GDNS. MORECAMBE.
SEPT. 1ST. HIPPO. BRISTOL.
"   8TH. VACANT AS YET.
"   15TH. HIPPO DUDLEY.
"   22ND. NOT FIXED YET.
"   29TH. NEW THEATRE. CARDIFF.

Morecambe date may be changed but will let you know - anyway will sure be seeing you - all news till then. Eda sends love & we are all well & happy with you both. as Ever -

Fond Thoughts.

Stan.
xx

*Stan Laurel's handwritten appearance list for 1952*

television, night clubs etc. Theatres were beginning to lose their popularity, resulting in many closing down.

In November 1961, Leslie A. Macdonnell, Managing Director of Moss Empires announced that the Empire would close the following January due to heavy financial losses which could no longer be sustained. He agreed to suspend the planning application for change of use, pending consideration of proposals submitted by the representatives of the Federation of Theatre Unions in Scotland.

The final show, commencing Monday 1 January 1962, was the old favourite, 'Oklahoma' starring Don McManus as Jud; Kevin Scott as Curley; Paula Hendrix as Laurey; Susan Irwin as Ado Annie; Jerry Dene as Ali Hakim; Charles Yates as Will Parker and Nita Croft as Aunt Eller. The Empire closed after the performance on Saturday 20 January 1962 and its future was in serious doubt.

## 1962 – NEW EMPIRE CASINO – BINGO

In May, 1962 it was announced that the Empire had been sold to Mecca Ltd for £160,000 in shares, rather than money. Mr Eric Morley, Mecca's Assistant Managing Director said he would turn it into a centre for Bingo and conference facilities but continue to make it available for live entertainment, such as ballet, pantomime and other theatrical events. They agreed to spend £50,000 on redecorations and modernisation prior to its reopening, giving the Empire the improvements it needed as the decorations were showing their age.

The renamed New Empire Casino was unable to gain an alcoholic drinks licence therefore the original stalls bar was refitted with new red plush seating and the circle bar was converted into an area for snacks and refreshments. The old dressing rooms were converted into a suite of offices including the manager's office. The New Empire Casino opened on Thursday 14 March 1963 becoming one of Edinburgh's top Bingo centres with a membership exceeding 25,000.

## 1991

On Thursday 14 March 1991, Edinburgh's District Council's ruling Labour Group, voted to buy the Empire from Mecca Ltd, who were now owned by the Rank Group PLC. Purchase of the Empire would cost around £2.6m but a far greater amount of money would be required to significantly upgrade the facilities in order to meet the Council's plans for its future. It would be funded by a combination of local authority contributions and sponsorship from the private sector.

Work immediately commenced with the refurbishment and the total cost of the work was estimated at £20m. Upon completion, Edinburgh would possess the biggest and best equipped entertainment stage in Britain, larger than the Royal Opera House, Covent Garden, London and complete with 'state of the art' backstage and technical features. It would also be able to accommodate 120 musicians and seat 1900 patrons. The new Theatre would also be the new home for Scottish Opera and the Scottish Ballet offering a year round festival of music, dance, opera, ice shows, concerts, drama, musicals, variety etc.

## 1994 – THE EDINBURGH FESTIVAL THEATRE

Now called the Edinburgh Festival Theatre it opened for business on Saturday 18 June 1994 and the most impressive feature was, and still is, the new entrance, a modern glass fronted structure designed by architect Colin Ross. It provided a perfect contrast between this new style and the splendour of the auditorium of the original Theatre.

Comfortingly, the old Empire's future was assured.

## DID YOU KNOW…?

## 1876 – MR CHARLES LENNOX

On Tuesday 4 January 1876 at the Edinburgh City Police Court, Mr Charles Lennox was charged with mischievously disturbing the gas supply to the theatre thus potentially endangering lives. On Saturday 1 January 1876, Lennox had been dismissed from his job as 'gas man' by the owner Mr Henry Levy, for being drunk whilst on duty at the theatre.

Lennox became abusive, used obscene language, and threatened to affect the gas supply in some way which could 'blow the house to atoms'. When the stage floodlights were lit, they ignited flammable material which was quickly extinguished by the stage staff or the theatre could have been destroyed but for their quick action. Lennox, in his defence, said that the allegation was untrue, witnesses said that his actions could have created a panic amongst the audience potentially causing loss of life. Sheriff Hamilton imposed a fine of £2 with the alternative of twenty days imprisonment.

## 1904 – MESSRS LAWSON, MILLER AND STEVENS

On Monday 14 November 1904 Mr George Lawson, Mr John Miller and Mr Robert Brown Stevens pleaded guilty in Edinburgh Police Court to stealing £2.70p from the Empire on 3 November and a further £3.25p two days later.

Their plan was quite clever. Stevens, a cashier at the pit entrance, sold tickets to customers and Lawson, a ticket checker, kept the tickets instead of placing them in a box. Lawson then passed the tickets to Miller who handed them back to Stevens to re-sell them. The police witnessed them in action, calculating that, between 7pm and 7.45pm on both nights, there were a total of 35 tickets unaccounted for. The judge found all three guilty especially as Lawson and Stevens had conspired together to commit the offence with Miller acting as a go-between.

He sentenced Lawson and Stevens to 21 days imprisonment, Miller received 7 days.

## 1905/07 – MR JAMES ADAM McKEE

On Saturday 5 March 1905, one of the cashiers left the Theatre with £35 of takings and disappeared. On Friday 26 July 1907, over two years later, at the Edinburgh Sheriff Court, Mr James Adam McKee pleaded guilty to actually stealing the larger amount of £36.45p from the Theatre in March 1905. Employed as a cashier, he had stolen the takings, had immediately left the country as he was in great financial difficulty and said he had no alternative. He had not committed any previous offences but Sheriff Gardiner Miller could not excuse McKee's actions and sentenced him to prison for 60 days.

## 1907 – MR JAMES BEATTIE

The second house performance was approaching completion around 11pm on Monday 15 April 1907, when Mr James Beattie, a cattleman, attempted to enter the theatre through the stage door, only to be refused entrance by Mr Alexander Forsyth, the stage door-keeper. A struggle ensued where Beattie struck Forsyth.

At that moment, Mr John Stirling, aged 57, a cashier at the theatre, attempted to control the situation as peacemaker, but received a blow to his face from Beattie. He fell onto the pavement striking his head on the pavement which knocked him unconscious. He was rushed to the Edinburgh Royal Infirmary where he died less than an hour later due to a fracture of the skull. Beattie was initially charged with murder.

The hearing was held in Edinburgh Court on Friday 31 May 1907 where Beattie pleaded not guilty to murder. He said he was enjoying a half-day holiday in Edinburgh and admitted he was drunk and was unaware of the incident. The jury returned a verdict of guilty of assault, but asked the judge to consider leniency. In view of Beattie's previous convictions for assaulting three women and two men, not previously notified to the jury, the judge sentenced Beattie to four months imprisonment.

## 1909 – SIR HARRY LAUDER

*Sir Harry Lauder*

Sir Harry Lauder, the highest paid performer in the world in the early 1900s, was the first British artiste to sell a million records with his song 'I Love a Lassie'. He achieved world wide success attracting sell-out audiences wherever and whenever he performed.

There had been a strange incident involving Sir Harry the week before he appeared at the Empire, during week commencing Monday 21 June 1909. It involved a large bull dog he purchased in Blackburn, on Friday 18 June 1909.

Immediately after his purchase, he despatched the dog in a cage, by rail, to his wife who lived in Tooting, London. His wife eagerly anticipated its arrival. She travelled to the Euston station with her brother, Mr Harry Valance, to collect the dog.

Somehow the dog escaped from its cage at Willesden station, on the outskirts of London, and in attempting to re-capture it, two railway porters were severely bitten. Mrs Lauder and her brother rushed to Willesden station.

Upon arrival, she tried to control the dog but was also savagely bitten by it on both her legs, causing severe wounds. Valance, her brother, was bitten around his throat causing some damage. Mrs Lauder fainted at the sight of their injuries, both were subsequently taken to St Thomas's Hospital in London, where their wounds were treated. The dog was destroyed.

Sir Harry arrived at his home from Manchester on Sunday morning 20 June prior to leaving for Edinburgh, to greet his badly shaken and bandaged wife. They both agreed to purchase another bulldog in the near future because, as he phrased it 'if burglars visit my house in the future they will get a warm welcome'.

Sir Harry was born in his grandfather's house in Edinburgh on Thursday 4 August 1870. His first occupation was as a coal miner paid 50p per week which he endured for ten years before becoming a full time performer. During his successful career he toured the USA, New Zealand, Australia and South Africa until semi-retiring in the mid 1930s. He died in his Strathaven home on Tuesday 28 February 1950.

## 1911 – THE GREAT LAFAYETTE

On Tuesday 9 May 1911 The Great Lafayette and his body double Charles Richards, died in a fire at the Edinburgh Empire. It is rumoured that the theatre is haunted by the ghost of a tall, dark stranger. Could this be The Great Lafayette or is it perhaps his body double?

## 1911 – MR ALBERT KENDALL

On Wednesday 25 May 1911, Mr Albert Kendall was charged at the Edinburgh Police Court with stealing a gold watch, a gold Albert chain, a gold seal plus the sum of two shillings from a dressing room at the Empire on or around Wednesday 10 May 1911. This was most distressing for many people as the alleged theft was carried out at the time of the Lafayette fire tragedy where people had died in the massive blaze.

Kendall was employed as a fireman at the Empire for two years. On the day of the fire, a musician had hung his coat in one of the dressing rooms under the stage as he changed into his formal dress. The musician escaped from the fire but could not reach his dressing room at that time, and returned the following day to search his dressing room when it was safe to do so, finding his coat but with his possessions missing. About ten days later, Kendall offered the watch to a pawnbroker in Leith, giving a false name.

Mr Norman M. McPherson, legal representative for Kendall, said that his client had 'given his full endeavours at the time of the fire' and had actually saved a man's life through his bravery. McPherson admitted that Kendall's crime was in the worst possible taste and agreed that some punishment must be given, but hoped leniency could be considered. Bailie Geddes, passed a sentence of a £2 fine and 20 days imprisonment or 30 days if the fine was unpaid.

## 1930 – MR BERNARD MYER WEINER

A case in the Old Bailey, London on Thursday 13 February 1930 involved the play 'Open Your Eyes', which was due to be presented at the Empire. Mr Bernard Myer Weiner was accused of obtaining money by false pretences from Mrs Frances Mary Hales. He persuaded her to invest money in the production in which Mrs Hales' son and Mr Weir's daughter would appear. Mrs Hales advanced £2,800 but only £1,650 was invested in the production.

This amount of money had been handed to the author of the play, Mr Frederick Jackson, but as he had not received the full payment, he closed the play down.

Weiner had told Mrs Hayes his name was Mr Patrick Weir from Dublin, (not Bernard Myer Weiner from Russia), with an impressive investment record, otherwise she would not have invested in the play, irrespective of the potential of earning 60% from box office takings.

Weiner was found guilty and Detective Sergeant Greenacre proved to the court that Weiner had numerous previous convictions for similar offences as he was a very plausible and cunning rogue. He was jailed for three years.

## 1936 – MISS RENEE HOUSTON

Miss Renee Houston, a famous Scottish comedy actress who appeared in a number of television shows and starred in many films, was seated in her dressing room at the Empire on Tuesday 28 April 1936. Two university students, Mr John Roderick Mackay Johnston and Mr Kenneth Brauer, entered her room as part of their 'Rag Week' fund raising plan, intending to 'kidnap' Miss Houston, but they caused serious injuries in the process. She was forcibly struck on her face, dragged from her dressing room, escorted through the back stage area, pushed into a car and taken to another area of Edinburgh fearing for her life. She was to be held in captivity until the £25 ransom was paid by the theatre management.

Following the payment of the £25 ransom, a medical examination was carried out on Miss Houston establishing that she was suffering from a cracked rib, severe shock as well as numerous other injuries. The two Edinburgh University students appeared in the Edinburgh Sheriff Court on Thursday 16 July 1936, charged with 'illegally securing the custody of Catherine Houston, professionally known as Renee Houston'. Miss Houston was not aware of any kidnap attempt and she was genuinely frightened at the events of the evening.

Summing up, Sheriff Robertson said that there was no excuse for their conduct whether it be for charity or otherwise. He fined both students, Johnston £5 or 30 days in jail and Brauer £3 or 20 days in jail.

## 1939 – MR JOSEF GOTZ

The audience were unaware of a serious incident which took place back stage on Friday 17 March 1939 during the revue 'Doorlays Wonder Rocket' when they were applauding 16 year old Miss Trudi Bora for her dance performance between four leopards as well as her fondling them during the course of her act. As they were being securely fastened to the stage by their trainer, Mr Josef Gotz, one of them clawed his arms and legs needing him to be rescued by the stage hands.

Gotz was taken to the Edinburgh Royal Hospital where numerous stitches were inserted in his wounds necessitating an overnight stay. The attack was apparently a regular feature as Miss Bora had already been mauled three times in the previous few weeks. Mr William E. Barratt, manager of the revue company, said there was no danger to the public as the leopards were securely fastened at all times.

## 1948 – MRS JESSIE THORNTON

The Empire often featured International Ballet Festivals. A serious incident took place on Wednesday 8 September 1948 when Mrs Jessie Thornton, aged 80, was queuing in the street to attend a performance by the Sadler's Wells Ballet. Whilst in the queue, she was pressed forward into a door which opened suddenly causing her to overbalance and fall quite heavily. Mrs Thornton was taken to the Edinburgh Royal Hospital with a fractured femur, but unfortunately she died on Friday 1 October 1948.

## 1954 – MR ROY ROGERS

Mr Roy Rogers, an internationally famous 'singing cowboy', appeared in almost one hundred films as well as countless TV and radio shows during his career with his popularity continuing well into the 1950s. He had chosen to undertake a UK variety show with his wife, Dale Evans and his Golden Palomino horse, Trigger. They were appearing at the Empire during week commencing Monday 22 February 1954.

On their closing performance on Saturday 27 February, Roy Rogers fired his revolver, shooting at plates thrown into the air whilst sitting on Trigger and enthralling the audience with his shooting skills. Unfortunately some of the shots ricocheted from part of the stage fittings, resulting in two shots hitting Trigger on his flank and one hitting Roy Rogers on his nose.

*Roy Rogers & Trigger*

# EXETER THEATRE ROYAL

*Exeter Theatre Royal*

## 1734 – THE OLD EXETER THEATRE

The Old Exeter Theatre opened to the public on Waterbeer Street, (later called Theatre Lane), on Monday 30 December 1734 and continued to entertain the residents of Exeter for many years.

## 1820 – FIRE No 1

On Tuesday 7 March 1820 between 2am and 3am a fire was discovered. Several fire engines were summoned but, on arrival, the flames had burst through the roof leaving the interior one mass of flames and out of control. The imminent danger was to the neighbouring properties as burning embers, pieces of scenery, drapes etc were raining down onto them. The firemen concentrated on saving five houses in St Southernhay Place, and a building directly in front of the theatre which, after a long and difficult battle, they managed to do.

The theatre was totally destroyed. The owners admitted that they were under-insured by around half of the building's replacement value, but planned to re-build it as soon as possible. Less fortunate were the performers who lost all their personal effects, valuables, clothing etc in the fire and the theatre management organised a benefit fund. The fire was thought to have been caused by the wadding of some muskets igniting scenery, as the melodrama 'The Falls of Clyde' was being performed. This wadding must have smouldered for a while before bursting into flames.

## 1821 – THE NEW THEATRE

The New Theatre, designed by Mr Lethbridge, and built by Mr Lake, was situated in Bedford Street, and exceeded all expectations with its beauty and opulence with many people thinking it to be the finest in England at that time. The most outstanding feature being the decorations. The fronts of the boxes were ornamented in gold and silver, the lower circle had a large laurel leaf in the centre, the second circle bore the National Emblems of Oak, Rose, Thistle and Shamrock, whist the third circle had a Grecian Foliage Scroll.

The ceiling was dome shaped with four decorated panels. A circular dome was situated in the centre which also regulated the temperature and ventilation of the theatre. The proscenium was framed by four square marble columns with gold caps and bases supporting an elegant arch, which displayed the National Union Arms in gold. The auditorium was lit by a Grecian Style chandelier with twenty-four lights, fitted with painted glass shades. The drop curtain, painted by Mr Andrews, represented Shakespeare's figures of Tragedy and Comedy.

The New Theatre was scheduled to open on Thursday 11 January 1821, however the opening act booked for that week, the Exeter Company of Comedians, failed to arrive from a booking in Guernsey, where they had been performing the previous week. This caused much concern to the management who did not receive any explanation for the absence of these performers. They had no alternative but to postpone the opening show. The theatre eventually opened one week later than planned on Thursday 18 January 1821 with a presentation of Shakespeare's Macbeth, starring Mr Frimbley and Mr Fisher.

## 1872 – THE THEATRE ROYAL

In 1824, the New Theatre had been re-named the Theatre Royal continuing to attract large audiences for almost the next fifty years. However, Mr F. W. H. Neebe, the lessee, closed the theatre in July 1872 to undertake a major refurbishment which included considerable work to all areas of the theatre. He appointed Mr C. E. Ware, the City Surveyor, as supervisor of the work and one of his first tasks was to improve the facilities for the ladies. The crush room outside the dress circle was removed, replaced by a private, fully carpeted cloak room with all the modern facilities.

New comfortable seating was fitted in all areas, decorated with maroon fabric which contrasted beautifully with the newly painted, sea green tinted walls. Special attention was paid to improving the sight lines, the circle floor was lowered, the rear stalls flooring was raised ensuring that, in future, all patrons would have a perfect view of the stage. In addition, the floodlights were concealed below the stage floor, giving an uninterrupted view of the scenery and performers. The old, green stage curtain was retired after many years service and replaced by one in red, provided by Mr Mark Rowe of nearby High Street.

An impressive new feature was the improvement in decorations, the fronts of the gallery, circle and boxes were outlined in grey, maroon and gold. A new act drop scene of the 'View of the Teign above Dunsford Bridge' was painted by Mr Widgery and Mr W. H. Cracknell. The theatre decorations were completed by Mr Hutchinson. Mr Cummings carried out the building alterations and Messrs Willey & Ford provided the new gas facilities.

The re-opening took place on Monday 30 September 1872. The invited guests were the Mayor of Exeter, Mr J. Harding, the High Sheriff of Exeter, Mr H. C. Lloyd and many members of the Town Council. The evening commenced with the Irish drama by Dion Boucicault entitled 'Arrah-Na-Pogue' and concluded with the whole company and audience singing the National Anthem.

## 1880

The theatre was closed again for another significant refurbishment in mid July 1880 by Neebe, who was celebrating twelve years as manager. No expense was spared.

The major improvement identified by Mr H. Wills, the architect, was re-styling the approaches to the theatre by creating more entrance/exit doors, also purchasing the milliner's shop and the residence at the front of the theatre to enlarge the entrances. Internally, he extended the width of the corridors leading to the circles and gallery, re-decorated all the walls and replaced the flat fronts of the dress and upper circles with cream and gold colour mouldings enhanced by a gold coloured gilding comprising of 20,000 leaves.

Improvements were also made to the ventilation system for the comfort of patrons, but specific attention was taken to upgrade to the stage facilities. The stage area was increased by reducing the area of the green room. A further improvement resulted in the 'wings' being able to be suspended and no longer man-handled, saving time, damage and improving space and efficiency.

The well attended opening on Monday 30 August 1880, included the Mayor of Exeter and the Sheriff. The opening performance was Mr Charles Wyndham's Company in 'Mary's Secret' and his new comedy 'Betsy'. Upon conclusion of the performances, Neebe made his welcoming speech and personally thanked everyone, especially Wills, for the wonderful transformation of his beloved theatre and wished it many years of success. From a personal point of view he was to suffer a disappointment.

## 1884

On Wednesday 15 October 1884, Mr Frederick Edwin Harrison Neebe, lessee of the Theatre Royal, Exeter, was declared bankrupt of the sum of £3,003 to unsecured creditors. He was a man of honour with many years standing in the entertainment industry. His experience of theatre management included being the lessee of theatres in Devonport, Bath and Weymouth. He blamed his losses on poor attendances, legal costs, heavy travelling expenses and depreciation of assets such as scenery. Neebe offered 25p in the pound. Half was paid in February 1885 and the other half in February 1886, and he would continue as manager of the Theatre Royal, reporting to a trustee committee. After a brief discussion the matter was resolved to everyone's satisfaction.

However, the situation was to become much worse four months later.

## 1885 – FIRE No 2

On the morning of Saturday 7 February 1885, a fire raged through the Theatre Royal which was to cause considerable damage to the building and surrounding property.

On the previous evening, Friday 6 February, Mr Frank Emery's Pantomime Company had been performing 'Beauty and the Beast' to a full audience. The theatre emptied around 10.30pm when the manager, Neebe, locked all the doors and ensured the theatre was safe and secure, leaving at 11.15pm.

Shortly before 6am on Saturday morning Police Sergeant Mock was patrolling the town centre when he saw flames breaking through the roof at the rear of the building. He immediately gave the alarm and the fire engines raced quickly to the scene. By the time they arrived, the theatre was blazing fiercely from end to end and the firemen naturally concentrated on ensuring the flames did not spread to the adjoining properties. The strong wind was blowing flames, burning pieces of canvas and embers towards them. The flames illuminated the whole city and a large crowd, including the Lord Mayor, attended the scene to witness one of the fiercest blazes ever seen in Exeter. There was only one fatality, a pig belonging to a clown.

Many of the performers, tradesmen, staff and musicians lost their possessions but the most unfortunate of them all was Mr Frank Emery and his company of twenty-six who suffered total losses. The owners of the Theatre Royal organised a fund raising event the following Wednesday evening for Emery at the local Victoria Hall, under the patronage of the Lord Mayor, which would include many local artistes giving their time, free of charge, including, of course, Emery.

This was the second time Emery had suffered a severe loss, as, only a few months previously, a fire in the luggage van of their train had destroyed all of his property. On Friday 27 February 1885, a benefit evening was held in the Royal Public Rooms for Neebe to partly compensate him for his recent losses caused by the fire at the theatre. It was supported by voluntary effort from the performers as most of them had been involved with Neebe, during his sixteen years as lessee and manager, especially appearing in his famous pantomimes.

The appreciative audience thoroughly enjoyed the evening and saw numerous individual performances concluding in a farce entitled 'Neebe in a Pigskin' which must have had some relevance! In his speech Neebe thanked everyone and said he hoped that the theatre would be re-built as the people of Exeter deserved high quality live entertainment.

On Monday 20 April 1885, it was announced that Mr C. J. Phipps, architect, had submitted plans for the erection of a new theatre on the old site of the Theatre Royal, plus an adjacent site previously occupied by the stables of the New London Hotel. The theatre's frontage would face Eastgate and would have side entrances in New North Road and Longbrook Street, costing £5,500 to build plus a further £4,500 for fixtures and fittings, all raised by forming a new company with a value of £10,000. In order to create additional income, six shops would be incorporated into the new theatre and, in view of previous incidents, emphasised that safety would be paramount in his final design.

Work commenced as soon as planning permission was obtained and the finance now in place with an opening date planned for October 1886.

## 1886

The new theatre was very impressive indeed. The auditorium consisted of four private boxes, a dress circle, five rows of pit stalls, upper circle, pit and gallery. It was designed by Mr C. J. Phipps, built by Mr Bevan of Plymouth with Mr Browne as the Clerk of Works. It had a capacity of approximately 1300, seating 650 in the pit, 170 in the dress circle and 500 in the upper circle and gallery.

Phipps planned numerous means of evacuating the theatre in the event of an emergency, but either these exits were inadequately designed or not installed at the gallery level which would have very serious consequences within a few months. The stage measured 55 feet by 49 feet and the proscenium measured 25 feet across the top and was designed and fitted by Mr Robinson, late of the Savoy Theatre, London.

On Wednesday 3 February 1886, it was announced that Mr S. Herberte Basing had taken a three year lease on the new Exeter Theatre at £500 per annum. On Thursday 27 June 1886, unfortunately two workmen erecting the theatre, Mr Greenham and Mr Elliott, were seriously injured when they fell from scaffolding.

The opening ceremony took place on Wednesday 13 October 1886 with the Mayor, Mr R. R. M. Daw, as guest of honour. He was presented with a special token which allowed him, and all future Mayors, free admission to the theatre. At 7.30pm the Mayor officially opened the theatre and speeches were made by various guests, and the curtain was raised at 8.00pm to the playing of the National Anthem under the musical direction of Mr Sidney Ward. This elaborate opening was followed by the presentation of Robinson's comedy, 'Breach of Promise' which featured Mrs Edward Saker, Miss Clare Harrington, Mr F. M. Paget, Mr Lytton Grey and Mr T. W. Hanson. During the interval, the orchestra played a selection from 'The Merry Wives of Windsor' and 'The Mikado'.

Less than twelve months later, the Theatre Royal would suffer a major disaster which is remembered in Exeter to this very day.

## 1887 – FIRE No 3

On the night of Monday 5 September 1887, the fourth act of the first performance of the touring production of Mr Wilson Barratt's popular drama 'Romany Rye' was about to start when the disaster unfolded. There were about 700 to 800 in the audience when one of the stage hands, lowering a gauze curtain, saw it make contact with a gas jet designed to illuminate the stage. This curtain caught fire, the blaze spread rapidly onto the scenery at the back of the stage. Immediately the theatre fireman began fighting the fire using the nearby fire hose.

Disaster loomed. An external stage door was opened as a means of escape for the performers, but, unfortunately it was left open, allowing the incoming draught to fan the flames causing the fire to spread even more rapidly. The smoke and flames spilled through the proscenium opening into the audience who started to panic as they realised the extent of the fire. They all made a rush to the fire exits, the stalls and circle had clearly defined exits, therefore people made their way onto the street with relative ease.

*Theatre fire in 1887*

However, in one instance, a fire door leading from the stalls to the street was locked and only brute force from people pushing against it, managed to force it open or many more could have perished by that oversight. Whilst the people in the stalls and circle were able to make their escape, those in the gallery, leading to New North Road, were less fortunate and, as a result, suffered the biggest loss of life.

In the original plans it was stated that there would be two exits from every part of the house but, apparently for cost saving purposes, there was only one from the gallery. The flames were now spreading through the theatre, the gallery audience were attempting to make their way down the single exit staircase but the acrid smoke and the sheer volume of people made their escape almost impossible. In addition, the fire escape route from the gallery was poorly designed as there was only one narrow single stone stairway which had four turns creating a 'log jam' effect as people, in their panic, became entangled at each turn.

There was also an additional cruel twist of fate caused by a temporary pay-box, which had been located at the top of the gallery's stone exit staircase. Due to people rushing past this temporary structure, it was pushed, accidentally, down the first flight of stairs. Because of its size and bulk, it wedged itself tightly across the bend of the second turn of the stairway, effectively blocking the only means of escape for the unfortunate people trapped behind it.

Dozens of people who died were eventually located in this stairwell. Fortunately some people were able to make their way through an upstairs external window onto the roof, but many were imprisoned in the gallery and met their death in horrendous conditions.

Many others chose to jump from the roof onto the street, hundreds of feet below, rather than face a horrible death in the fire. Ladders were brought from a nearby builder's yard to assist the local firemen who bravely climbed up to pull women and children out of the upper windows. Many of those waiting to escape died in the process. A wheeled ladder was placed in the auditorium and it was able to reach the front of the circle. Very few gallery people were rescued by this method as they did not have the presence of mind to descend one flight of stairs to the circle level.

Whilst the shell of the theatre was built of stone and red brick, the interior was made of primarily flammable products, especially wood, which had provided a ready fuel for the fire to spread so rapidly.

The most serious omissions by the builders were the lack of the installation of an iron fire curtain and water hydrants near the stage, although included in the plans, they were never fitted.

The installation of fire curtains in theatres was only legally mandated after this disastrous fire which had resulted in the tragic loss of so many lives.

Hours later, when the fire had been extinguished, a large number of volunteers began searching the debris with the horrendous job of locating family and friends who had not returned from the theatre.

Many of the victims were unrecognisable and the majority died from asphyxiation either from smoke or from the effects of being crushed. Some could only be recognised by their jewellery, or what remained of their clothing/personal effects. Identification was often impossible, leaving many relatives uncertain of where in the theatre their loved ones had died.

There were many stories emanating from the fire. A Great Western train driver lost his wife and eldest daughter in the gallery, leaving him with his remaining eleven children, the youngest being only a few months old.

A happier story concerned PC Ching who rushed into the auditorium many times to rescue people, with only a handkerchief over his mouth and nose. He grabbed a lady in distress who, when they reached safety outside, he was surprised to find was his wife, and he had not even been aware she was attending the theatre that evening.

In total, it is thought that possibly 186 people died in the UK's worst ever theatre fire disaster and a National Appeal for the victim's families raised almost £21,000.

## 1887 – THE AFTERMATH

On Wednesday 21 September 1887, the Coroner's inquest into the deaths concluded a verdict of accidental death for all of the victims, however the Coroner was severely critical of the licensing magistrates, the builder and the architect. He found the magistrates inspection of the theatre to be sadly lacking as they had been misled as to the existence of a second exit from the gallery and 'jumping' from the gallery to the circle levels did not constitute an 'acceptable' method of exit.

A further inquiry was launched into the disaster by Captain Eyre Shaw, Commander in Chief of the Metropolitan Fire Brigade, who criticised Phipps, the designer. He defended himself by stating that many elements of his original design had not been carried out by the builder. The positive outcome from the disaster was that it gave Captain Shaw much more ammunition to introduce stricter regulations for safety precautions in public buildings, especially theatres.

The fire had affected the residents of Exeter and a 'Theatre Fire Relief Committee' was formed. On Monday 9 April 1888 a window was dedicated in the parish church of Newport, Essex to the son of the Vicar, Mr Robert Morgan Tamplin, who perished in the fire with his friend Mr Gossett. They were only identified by pieces of their jewellery.

*The Theatre Royal Memorial*

The Committee also agreed to spend £100 upon a permanent memorial in Exeter cemetery with the words 'In memory of more than 160 persons who perished in the fire at the Exeter Theatre, Monday 5 September 1887'. There was indecision for some time as to the exact number of deaths.

A decision was made at the time to delay any announcements concerning the future of the Theatre Royal due to the public feeling surrounding the tragedy. Various opinions were considered such as firstly, starting afresh at a different site in Exeter. Secondly, totally re-building it on the existing site. Then thirdly, rebuilding on the existing site but incorporating some of the original and remaining walls.

The final decision was very difficult to make as the Directors continually changed their minds which resulted in stalemate and, due to this deadlock, the Chairman resigned his position. It was resolved when Dr Domville, the new Chairman organised a vote of the shareholders who decided in favour of option three, adapting the original walls into the new design and rebuilding the theatre within the existing footprint.

## 1888

Bankruptcy raised its head again on Wednesday 16 May 1888. Mr Sidney Herberte Basing was declared bankrupt, predominately, as a result of the disastrous fire the previous September. He had taken a lease on the theatre in February 1886, had incurred unexpected expenditure on travelling, lighting equipment, scenery, printing etc which had eaten into his finances prior to the opening. Once the theatre was open in October 1886 he was making an average profit of £50 per week which was helping to reduce his debt and the future looked secure. The fire was a complete disaster for him and had left him in this impossible position.

In June 1888, the directors placed the new design and build in the hands of Mr Alfred Darbyshire who was assisted by actor Mr Henry Irving. The finished building was indeed an excellent structure, with a beautiful central staircase leading to the grand circle. At each end of this circle, on the same level, were four private boxes, two on each side. In view of the recent history, every part of the theatre had its own separate emergency exit leading directly to the street through forward opening 'crash' doors. The Theatre could seat around 1,000 people and the total build and fitting out budget was £15,000.

The stage was completely isolated from all other parts of the theatre and there was no opening in the proscenium wall other than the actual stage. A fire proof Titancrete safety curtain was fitted which could be lowered in ten-seconds, and capable of being locked into solid masonry situated beneath the stage. For the benefit of everyone, it had the words 'Safety Curtain' printed across it in bold letters.

The floors were manufactured of Titancrete and every staircase was completely fireproof, built of brick and stone with no dangerous corners. Another great improvement was the installation of 510 electric lights, thus eliminating the need for gas, which was the prime cause of the earlier fires. All other fire and safety precautions were well in excess of the new legal requirements of the time.

## 1889 – RE-OPENING

The re-opening was held on Monday 7 October 1889 and, as the safety curtain rose, the audience witnessed a painting of 'Dartmoor' by Mr William Widgery, which became a regular 'act drop' hiding the scene changes for many years to come. Selected for the opening performance was Gilbert and Sullivan's 'Yeoman of the Guard' presented by the D'Oyly Carte Company. The cast was headed by Mr Cairns James as Jack Point, Mr Charles Rose as Fairfax, Miss Jessie Moore as Elsie Maynard and Miss Kate Forster played Dame Carruthers.

During the interval, a telegram was read from Mr Henry Irving, wishing the new Theatre Royal every success and happiness in the future. At that juncture, Mr Alfred Darbyshire, architect; Mr Dart, builder; Dr Domville; chairman of the board and Mr S. L. Giffard, theatre manager were given a standing ovation for their wonderful efforts in the rebuilding of the Theatre Royal to such an excellent standard.

## FUTURE YEARS

Following this successful opening night, the Theatre continued to attract many thousands of people from Exeter and surrounding areas to witness the high quality entertainment provided. Artistes treading the boards were wide and varied from Sir Henry Irving, Violet and Irene Vanburgh, Fred Karno, Noel Coward, George Formby Snr, etc. The Theatre Royal introduced 'animated photographs' on Monday 2 November 1896 with 'Rescue Up the River' and 'The Czar's Visit to Paris', followed in 1901 by a film of Queen Victoria's funeral. As required by a new law, in May 1909, the management had to build separate, enclosed boxes for the projection equipment and they commandeered two of the private boxes located in the circle.

At the same time the Theatre Royal was given a total make-over, the orchestra pit was extended to accommodate an increase of musicians, from nine to fourteen and the whole theatre was re-painted and re-decorated. In place of the hard, uncomfortable seats, luxurious tip-up velvet ones had been provided and all carpets were replaced by bright, high quality and hard wearing Axminster. Lighting was fully upgraded and an added attraction was a handsome new chandelier, overhanging the circle, illuminating the theatre in a warm and welcoming glow. Even the spartan pit bar was re-decorated and refurbished with new lighting, new fittings, seating and decorations. There was a new door, leading directly into the auditorium. Amongst the many alterations, the most spectacular one was a new act drop based on a painting by Mr John Shapland depicting the 'Estuary of the Teign'.

The re-opening of the Theatre Royal took place on Monday 2 August 1909 with the Percy William's company in 'The Fatal Wedding', an American drama by Theo Kremer which starred Miss Lulu Wohlmann in the role of Jessie.

## 1939

A further closure took place in the spring of 1939 where the architect, Mr Fred Jerman, redesigned the interior by rebuilding the grand circle and removing some ground floor pillars ensuring that all seats would now have an uninterrupted view of the stage. It re-opened on Monday 7 August 1939 with the comedian, Norman Long topping the bill, ably supported by Leslie Rome & Connie Leonard, comedians; Harry Jerome, comedian; Sylvia, musician; Gladys Church, vocalist; Gintaro, Juggler; Will Power, gymnast and Dave & Maureen, dancers. The following week, Carroll Levis was presenting his famous 'Discoveries' show.

## 1954

In August 1954, the owners of the Theatre Royal, the Exeter Theatre Company, agreed a contract with the Rank Organisation and Twentieth Century Fox for the installation of the wide screen CinemaScope system with Stereophonic Sound. The first film to be shown was the biblical epic, 'The Robe'.

Many stars of the period performed on the stage including Harry Secombe, Arthur Askey, Morecambe & Wise, Ted Heath & his Music and Dickie Valentine.

The initial indication that the Theatre Royal was having financial difficulties came in 1954 when the management reported a loss of £4,000 as they tried to 'balance' the mix of live variety and films. Neither were particularly successful other than the annual pantomime. In an attempt to halt the decline, the Directors ploughed money into the theatre. For example, in 1960 and 1961 they installed over 600 new seats and re-decorated the stalls in pastel shades of pink and red in an attempt to increase audiences. Unfortunately this action had little, or no effect on audiences. Due principally to the expansion of television, the economic and financial situation was deteriorating quite rapidly in the early 1960s putting the Theatre Royal's future in serious doubt.

## 1960

After much consideration and debate, the 1960/61 Christmas pantomime of 'Babes in the Wood' went ahead to limited success but the 73rd consecutive one in 1961/62 of 'Ali Baba', running from Tuesday 26 December 1961 to Saturday 13 January 1962, was less successful. In the cast were Donald B. Stuart, Tony Scott, Grace Rich, Johnny Dallas, Ralph Broadbent, Gail Leslie, Eleanor Beam's Young Ladies and the Bill Dane dancers. This would be the last ever.

In desperation, the manager Mr Cliff Gwilliam, immediately following the pantomime, advertised for sale, four complete Theatre Royal pantomime productions, in order to raise some much needed funds. The sale included scenery, wardrobes, sets, scripts etc, for 'Ali Baba', 'Cinderella', 'Babes in the Wood' and 'Dick Whittington'. His advertisement stated 'No Reasonable Offer Refused'.

## 1962

The Directors issued a warning in April 1962 that they would be seeking a buyer for the theatre, 'as soon as possible and at the best price'. This followed years of financial losses and they admitted the theatre had not made a profit since 1953. The published losses in 1959 were over £1,000; 1960 showed losses of £6,500; 1961 was £1,400, in fact, it cost over £400 per week to just to open the theatre.

One of the most popular summer shows over the previous years had been the Clarkson-Rose production of 'Twinkle'. Therefore, it was booked for the summer season commencing Monday 9 July 1962 for an eleven week summer run, in the hope of attracting sufficient audiences to ensure the theatre's future. Unfortunately it was a failure and attendances were very low, in fact, some matinees had more in the cast than in the audience. It struggled along before closing on Saturday 22 September 1962. That was the end of Exeter's Theatre Royal.

On Thursday 8 November 1962, the complete contents of the Theatre Royal were offered for auction by Saunders, Redfern & Co and included 900 tip-up seats, the screen, flood and spot lights, a 'Bechstein' baby grand piano, stage props, lighting, fittings etc. Some of the projection equipment, however, was rescued from the scrap merchants and ended its days in the Cinema and Theatre Museum in Covent Garden.

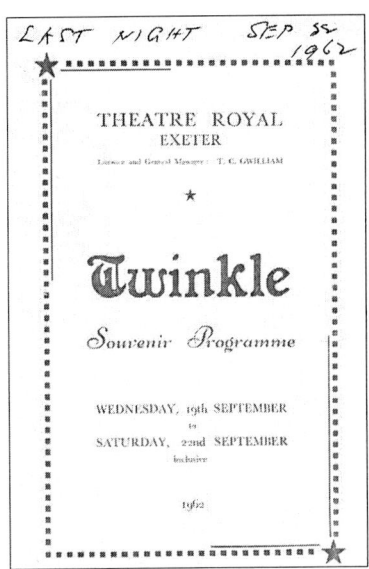

The Last Ever programme    The Theatre Royal Survival Request

The most sensible offer for the Theatre Royal was received from Mr George Northcott but his final offer of a cash injection of £100,000, half for the building and the other half for renovation costs to turn it into a Community Theatre/Arts venue was rejected.

Instead of accepting Northcott's offer, the Directors took an alternative offer of £85,000 from the Prudential Assurance Company to buy the theatre outright, which gave a larger distribution sum to shareholders rather than keep live theatre in Exeter. Many thought this was a very short-sighted decision.

On Thursday 28 February 1963, the shareholders in Exeter Theatre Co Ltd, attended a meeting to wind up the affairs of the theatre. A resolution that the company should be wound up voluntarily was agreed and that Mr W. Brand of Messrs Godfrey & Brand of Exeter be appointed as liquidator. The annual report of the directors for the year ended 30 June 1962 showed a trading loss of £11,658.

Northcott ultimately decided to invest his £100,000 in another Exeter venture and the Northcott Theatre opened in 1967, so community theatre in Exeter wasn't lost after all. It is still successfully entertaining the people of Exeter today.

The local council did not interfere or make any movement towards helping the Theatre Royal, the new owners immediately demolished it in June, 1963, replacing it with a modern, bland office block and shops, named Portland House. It was reported that, during demolition, a spiral staircase was stolen and a £25 reward was offered for its recovery.

## 2015

In 2015, planning permission was agreed to demolish Portland House and build 150 student apartments plus ground floor retail units, opening within a couple of years. However, elements of the Theatre Royal do still exist somewhere in Exeter as its demolished remains of rubble were used as hardcore for local roads and streets.

The Theatre Royal certainly had a chequered history during its lifetime, it had many happy and joyful times but one can never forget the tragic loss of life in the fire of Monday 5 September 1887.

## DID YOU KNOW...?

## 1867 – MR WALTER GRAHAM

Exeter was to hit the headlines on Thursday 11 July 1867, when Mr Walter Graham was charged with intent to cause an explosion and destruction of the Theatre Royal. Graham, was the son-in-law of the lessee Mr Belton, and had been in the employment of the theatre as stage manager until a few months previously. He was seen acting suspiciously during the evening.

At 10.30pm a light was seen by the stage door, and upon investigation by Mr Norman, a manager, he found that every gas tap had been turned on in all parts of the house and only two of them had been lit. Luckily, the previous night had been warm and there had been a capacity audience. Therefore the ventilators and sky-lights were opened, including a new ventilation system located in the roof. This allowed the gas to escape and reduced the danger of explosion.

Without this gas escape route it was highly likely that the theatre would have exploded within a few hours and serious damage caused to the theatre, the adjacent dwellings and many surrounding buildings. Graham was heard boasting in a local public house that he had been the culprit. He was duly arrested and charged, but later stated that he had entered the theatre, intending to sleep and left. Graham had a history of mental illness and had threatened Belton with violence on more than one occasion.

The case was held at Exeter Assizes on Wednesday 7 August 1867 and, after a long hearing, Graham was found not guilty, admitted he had been unwise in entering the theatre but had no malice intended and was released from custody.

## 1868 – MISS KATE REIGNOLDS

A serious incident occurred on Saturday 31 October 1868. Miss Kate Reignolds, a young American actress, was playing the lead part in the drama 'Stolen, or the 'Street Ballard Singers' when she was required to cross a 'bridge' about six feet above the stage. In the first half of the drama, she did this without problem but when she repeated it in the second half, the 'bridge', a wooden plank, gave way causing her to fall heavily onto the stage. The theatre joiner was blamed for failing to install adequate fastenings at the ends of the plank which caused it to collapse.

Immediately, the act drop was lowered, other performers and staff ran to her aid but she was clearly badly shaken and, possibly seriously injured. A doctor was called who could not detect any broken bones but diagnosed serious bruising to her liver and severe shock. As she was being taken to her lodgings in a cab, the manager Mr Belton, explained the position to the audience and stated that the drama could not continue without the leading lady. The show continued with Mr & Mrs Finlayson and Neebe, the lessee, leading the singing, unfortunately other performers retired early for the evening due to shock.

## 1953 – STRIKING MUSICIANS

The theatre had quite an interesting time over the next two years. The members of the orchestra went on strike at the end of the pantomime on Saturday 28 March 1953 demanding that the four recently declared redundant musicians should be reinstated. This dispute continued throughout the summer months which eventually resulted in all of the musicians being dismissed.

The Theatre Royal, during 1954, decided to present a ten week season of repertory with the occasional variety show with the accompaniment of a single organist. However in April 1954, the musical show 'Lilac Time' was presented using non-union musicians assembled from various parts of the country and conducted by the General Manager, Mr Cliff Gwilliam. The end was not in sight and a question was raised in the Commons on Wednesday 14 July 1954 by Colonel G. Wigg, who accused the War Office of allowing Army bandsmen to work in a strike-breaking action at the Theatre Royal.

After two years of dispute and ill-feeling, it was reported on Thursday 12 July 1956 to the Association of Touring and Producing Managers, chaired by Mr Tom Allen, that the dispute between the Musician's Union and the Theatre Royal, Exeter had been settled.

# GLASGOW COLISEUM

*Glasgow Coliseum*

## 1903 GLASGOW COLISEUM

Moss Empires Ltd, founded by Sir Horace Edward Moss, already had thirty-eight theatres throughout the UK, but decided to build Glasgow's third one. The Moss Empire Group already owned the Palace Theatre on Sauchiehall Street, had a large interest in the Hippodrome Theatre in New City Road and now this new one was to be situated in Eglinton Street.

Building began in 1903, the design, by Mr Frank Matcham, would be modelled on his other theatres, particularly the Ardwick Empire in Manchester, although on a much larger scale, and be constructed by Morrison & Mason Ltd. The planned seating capacity was 4,000, therefore at two houses per night, it meant 8,000 people could be entertained nightly. Including matinees, that would exceed over 60,000 per week, bordering on 3 million people per year!

It was advertised as the largest theatre in the world. Built in a Flemish design, the corner of the theatre had an octagon ashlar tower built of dark red brick. The theatre was easily identified by a large revolving illuminated sign with the word 'Coliseum' in bright electric lighting. In order to maximise income, the building frontage included a number of single storey shops including, of course, the mandatory sweet shop.

The vestibule was of an Italian design with imitation stone attached to the walls and divided by white marble columns. The floors were covered with rich Turkish rugs and carpets. The auditorium was beautifully decorated in an Italian Renaissance style with impressive paintings depicted on the ceiling and box facades. Luxurious tip-up seating was provided by Messrs R. Lazarus for the boxes, stalls and grand circle. The pit and gallery were not neglected as they were fitted with high quality seating, covered in Rose Du Barry upholstery. The proscenium opening was 36ft wide, flanked by marble pillars, with rose coloured velvet stage curtains costing £500, in an embroidered design, and complemented by a rich silk fringe and matching trimmings.

Due to the history of fires in theatres, specific attention was paid to fire safety. A hydraulic fireproof curtain of solid steel, weighing 82 tons, was installed to separate the stage from the auditorium. In addition Matcham installed thirty-six emergency exits, all six feet wide, complete with crash doors, each one fitted with an automatic alarm. Every area of the theatre was fitted with fully equipped fire hydrants and extensive training on their use was given to all staff. The dressing rooms were of superior quality and built as a separate block at the rear of the stage. They included such benefits as fitted carpets, dressing tables, toilets, heating (provided via hot water pipes) and electric lighting. Very different from the old type of basic, cold and unfriendly ones.

## 1905 – THE OPENING

On Friday 15 December 1905, Sir Edward and Lady Moss, Mr Oswald Stoll and Mr Richard Thornton (his business partners) with their wives, hosted a reception for the dignitaries of Glasgow. Also in attendance were Matcham, Lord Provost Bilsland, Mr W. McKillop the local MP, Councillors and representatives of the majority of the contractors who built this beautiful theatre. Mr Wm. Moore, the leader of the orchestra provided a musical interlude.

The public opening, at 7.30pm on Monday 18 December 1905, had a capacity audience, including many other local dignitaries from Glasgow Corporation. They witnessed an excellent variety show starring Charles Coborn, singer; Hurley & Cole, comic actors; Tom Edwards and his dummy 'Curly', ventriloquist; Sinclair & Whiteford, comedians; The Mayvilles, comedians; Rose Archer, impressionist and Prince Kokin, juggler.

## 1924/25 – PANTOMIME

Over the years, the Coliseum presented a wide range of popular twice nightly shows including revues, variety, pantomime, musical plays and the ever-popular Carl Rosa Opera Company. This was a very successful period, the Coliseum attracted the top acts of the day to be seen by many thousands of people over the next twenty years. The last ever pantomime during the winter of 1924/25 was 'The Forty Thieves' starring G. H. Elliott, Emilie Hayes, Kitty Evelyn, Geoff Hirst and McGregor & Hood.

G. H. Elliot, born Friday 3 November 1882 in Rochdale, a singer who performed with a painted brown face and dressed all in white, was extremely popular, so much so the pantomime had to close a week early on Saturday 31 January 1925 as he was summoned to appear in the Royal Command Performance before the King and Queen the following week at the Alhambra Theatre in London.

He also appeared in the 1948 and 1949 Royal Command Performances. Working until 1960 when he suffered a stroke, retiring to Brighton where he died on Monday 19 November 1962, aged 80.

Following the pantomime, the management presented an increased number of films to assess the demand as live entertainment was suffering falling audiences.

## 1924/25 – CINEMA

On Thursday 6 November 1924, it was announced that the Scottish Cinema and Variety Theatres Ltd (later the ABC Group) would take over the lease of the Coliseum in February 1925. It planned to concentrate on films. On

Monday 2 March 1925, the Coliseum re-opened under their management with the promise that occasional live entertainment performances would be presented, but, in fact, they were few and far between.

Mr W. Holding, Chairman of the Moss Empire Group, said that the sale had been completed as they were concentrating on their other theatres in Glasgow and the Coliseum had been difficult to manage. He pointed out that the entertainment tax was especially onerous as they had paid £157,000 in 1924 and almost £2m during the previous ten years. He wished the cinema group every success in their new moving picture venture at the Coliseum.

## 1927

The cinema had a major overhaul in April 1927 when the 'Optha-Stereo' metallic type of screen was fitted which gave clearer definition, irrespective of the angle viewed. The first film to be shown using this new screen was 'The Big Parade' starring John Gilbert, Renee Adoree and Tom O'Brien.

The Coliseum was the first cinema in Scotland to screen 'talkies' when in 1929 the 'Jazz Singer', starring Al Jolson, featured to sell out audiences. On Friday 6 June 1930, as a pioneer of 'talkies' in Scotland, the Coliseum installed apparatus on a number of seats to help people with hearing problems. Headphones were attached to seats, and connected to microphones located on the stage in front of the screen.

## 1931

On Monday 4 May 1931, the Coliseum was closed for at least six months for a major refurbishment, making it one of the largest and most artistically decorated in Scotland. The major work involved lowering the floor at the rear of the auditorium by three feet, as the line of the circle interfered with the sight of the screen by the audience in those seats. As an additional benefit, two of the columns supporting the circle floor were removed, the side boxes were dispensed with, allowing many more seats to be added on the ground floor. All the old seating was replaced with new, more comfortable modern ones, the gallery seating was re-furbished and re-upholstered.

The most striking features were the decorations. The entrance lobby was painted in gold, red and orange, the staircases in red and orange and all the other internal walls in an ivory colour. The new lighting was magnificent especially the proscenium, where the stage curtains were floodlit from the side with an alternating colour changing scheme going from red to blue, then green to yellow and back to red.

*Richard Dix*

Cinema technology was not ignored, the old projection box at the back of the circle was removed and a new, more spacious one built at the rear of the upper circle. It contained two Rose projectors, a spotlight, a Western Electric 1932 sound system working in conjunction with a Westone screen which could be varied from 23ft to 38ft.

Another feature was that the current capacity was increased from 2,000 to 3,500, the prices were 6p in the circle, 5p in the front stalls and 2p in the rear stalls with reductions for the afternoon performances. It re-opened on Monday 7 September 1931 with the western 'Cimarron' starring Richard Dix and Irene Dunn. The Coliseum was now regarded as one of the most artistically decorated cinemas, as well as the largest in Scotland.

## 1937 – FIRE No 1

Whilst fire would eventually destroy the theatre in later years, a smaller one occurred on the evening of Friday 22 October 1937 when 2000 people were enjoying the film 'Shall We Dance' starring Ginger Rogers and Fred Astaire.

The manager suddenly entered the stage, paused the film and asked the audience to leave in an orderly fashion. They were taken by complete surprise as they had no knowledge of any potential danger.

*Ginger Rogers*

Apparently, the revolving turret electric sign, 100ft above the street, had ignited and smoke was billowing over the nearby streets but did not affect the cinema interior. The fire brigade attended, the blaze was quickly brought under control, and fifteen minutes later, the audience were allowed back into the cinema to watch the remainder of the film.

## 1963

In May 1963, the Coliseum closed again for the installation of the new widescreen projection process of 'Cinerama' which required major alterations to accommodate the new bulky equipment and the massive 60ft concave screen.

The system demanded a new large projection box, therefore one was erected at the rear of the balcony. A mechanical hoist was needed to lift the enormous reels of film to and from the ground level. In addition, the front of the balcony was removed, a new internal sound surround was installed, a false ceiling fitted to hide the old balcony, leaving only a single circle. Full length curtains covered all the walls, adding to the sound quality. Major alterations to the ceiling included a checkerboard pattern, a new proscenium was installed and the exterior had corrugated iron cladding to modernise its appearance. The total cost of this refurbishment was in the region of £100,000 which eliminated any possibility of the Coliseum presenting live entertainment in the future.

In future the Coliseum would be called 'Cinerama'

## CINERAMA

On Thursday 26 September 1963, the Coliseum Theatre re-opened as Cinerama, in a blaze of publicity, featuring 'How the West Was Won' starring John Wayne, Henry Fonda, Gregory Peck, James Stewart and Debbie Reynolds.

Due to the complexity of the system, the shortage of films, the distorted angles of actors on the screen and the problems with repairing film breakages, the popularity of 'Cinerama' was short lived and it reverted back to featuring traditional films.

## 1980

After much discussion and deliberation at Council level in early 1980, involving the development of Glasgow, the Planning Department issued a Compulsory Purchase Order Scheme for the theatre and, as a result, the Coliseum/Cinerama closed its doors on Saturday 11 October 1980 with Jack Nicholson starring in 'The Shining'.

## 1986

This scheme was never implemented and the theatre stood empty for seven years looking sad, unwanted, decaying and neglected. On Tuesday 17 June 1986, Historic Scotland designated the Coliseum/Cinerama as a Grade B listed building and, at the same time, included it on the 'Buildings At Risk' register.

## 1987 – 2006

After being empty for seven years, County Bingo acquired the Coliseum/Cinerama in 1987 but found the interior to be in a poor decorative condition therefore major improvements had to be made before it could be utilised. They removed any remains of the old Cinerama equipment, created an 'inner' shell for the auditorium, replaced the floor and installed yet another suspended ceiling. In effect, it was a building within a building. Some repairing and re-rendering work was required on the exterior of the building to make it fully waterproof. In 1993, two of the old Cinerama projectors were transferred to the National Science and Media Museum in Bradford where they are retained for future generations to see.

Bingo continued until January 2003 when County Bingo decided to close the Coliseum. The building, once again, sat empty, neglected and decaying until it was sold in 2006. It remained unused and the Council had to draw up an Urgent Repairs Notice to ensure it remained weather tight on an ongoing basis, until a final decision was made regarding its future. The decision would be taken out of their hands.

## 2009 – FIRE No 2

At 1.30am on Monday 25 May 2009, a fierce fire engulfed the Coliseum, believed to be caused by arson. 60 firefighters from the local Calton and

Polmadie stations fought the blaze with five pumps and three aerial rescue platforms but their efforts were in vain. The building was well alight, the fire was obviously out of control. When they arrived, neighbouring houses, roads and streets were in danger of catching fire or being seriously damaged if the theatre walls collapsed.

Flames shot out of the building's distinctive campanile tower, smoke billowed over the city sky as dawn broke and the roof collapsed in a mass of flames into the auditorium. Unfortunately the fish & chip shop and the newsagent's shop within the Coliseum complex were unable to be saved. Scores of firemen battled the blaze for over five hours but it was obvious that the end result would have to be demolition.

*After the Fire at The Glasgow Coliseum*

The building was in a very dangerous condition, the roads and streets around it were immediately closed for three weeks. Instructions were given by the Council for its immediate demolition. A proposal was made that the frontage of the building should be supported by scaffolding and retained for inclusion in any future development but this suggestion was not found to be feasible. Three weeks later, in mid June 2009, this beautiful building was totally demolished, the site was cleared in the vague hope that another theatre or entertainment complex would be built on the site.

No such proposal was forthcoming and this patch of scorched earth lay empty for almost ten years until the New Gorbals Housing Association, in partnership with Urban Union, acquired it to accommodate their next phase of housing development. This will be a truly fitting tribute to a wonderful building as in its place will be family accommodation bringing fun, happiness and laughter back to the site of the much loved, but long departed, Coliseum.

## DID YOU KNOW…?

### 1905 – MR JAMES HUDSON & MR JOHN TIMMINS

The building of the Coliseum was also a tragic time as, at 8pm on Thursday 10 August 1905, three employees were placing a 16 ton girder into position, some 70ft high in the roof area, when the holding chain on the crane snapped, taking the girder and three men crashing onto the theatre floor.

Two men, Mr James Hudson, foreman engineer, and an unidentified labourer were killed instantly, the third casualty, Mr John Timmins, a labourer, was taken to the Glasgow Royal Infirmary with both legs fractured and injuries to his skull and ribs.

### 1907 – MR ALEXANDER RUSSELL

An incident occurred on Saturday evening 1 March 1907. A drama concerning football was being played with three English International players taking part, Messrs Crabtree and Athersmith of Aston Villa and Mr Spikesley of Sheffield Wednesday.

An occupant of a private box, Mr Alexander Russell became so excited that he fell fifteen feet into the stalls and landed on Mr William Forsyth, a clerk, who suffered a broken neck.

### 1909 – Dr. WALFORD BODIE

The world famous performer, 'Dr.' Walford Bodie, appeared at the Coliseum during week commencing Monday 8 November 1909 with his unique mystical act which had made him one of the world's most famous and mysterious performers. He claimed that he could cure invalids by hypnosis and the use of electricity, therefore audiences attended in their thousands to witness

*Dr Walford Bodie*

such claims. He used his extensive knowledge of electricity by changing the electric charge from amps to volts and gave patients a 'mock electrocution', accompanied by sparks and lightning effects, which, allegedly, could return them to full health.

This method was extremely dangerous and could cause patients to collapse into unconsciousness, and, to make matters worse, he falsely added Dr and MD to his name and implied he could cure any ailments. These claims, his false medical qualifications and his act were heavily criticised by many thousands of people, particularly medical students, who saw him as a 'quack' and many objected in the strongest terms, believing he should be banned or jailed.

On the opening night, Monday 8 November 1909, Bodie was pelted with eggs by students of Glasgow University but completed his performance. The theatre management and the police felt this demonstration could develop into something more serious before the end of the week.

Their fears were realised on Thursday 11 November 1909, when Bodie entered the stage with his female assistant, many hundreds of these medical students threw a large quantities of eggs, rotten fruit, vegetables, smelly fish scales and flour towards him. Bodie and his assistant quickly left the stage, the safety curtain was immediately lowered but a dozen or more students clambered over the heads of the orchestra's musicians, attacked the safety curtain and assaulted the attendants who were tying to restore order.

Non-student members of the audience began arguing and fighting with the students, causing mayhem in the auditorium. At that stage over 100 waiting police emerged from both sides of the orchestra stalls and eventually removed the offending students from the theatre. In the meantime, Bodie re-entered the stage, tried to negotiate with the students, apologised to the audience for the disturbance but was shouted down with chants of 'quack' from the students and he again retreated to the safety of his dressing room. Once in the streets, the demonstrators continued demonstrating until the police presence restored order.

Bodie was extremely concerned at the events of that evening, the remainder of that week's performances were cancelled in fear of further disturbances and the incident was classified as a major riot. A dozen or so students were arrested and charged with affray and assaulting the police. The court case against the students was held at Glasgow Police Court on Saturday, 20 November 1909 to justify their actions at the Coliseum on Thursday 11 November,

There was a certain amount of damage in the theatre, Mr Andrew Jarvie denied tearing the asbestos curtain, he agreed a hole had been made but said it was caused by the stage staff to allow the police to crawl through it to apprehend the students. Jarvie was discharged, however, Mr Thomas Fraser Noble was fined £1.05p, or seven days in jail for stealing the knobs off the orchestra rail and Mr John Norman Sutherland fined a similar amount for throwing tomatoes and potatoes, one of which hit a police inspector.

Bodie took time away from the stage to assess the situation. Following tremendous demand from his followers, he re-commenced his shows in 1911,

Bodie continued performing his act for many years, however, at the Pleasure Beach, Blackpool in early October 1939 he collapsed on stage and was rushed to Blackpool Hospital.

Mr Walford Bodie, real name, Mr Samuel Murphy Bodie, born in Aberdeen on Friday 11 June 1869, died on Thursday 19 October 1939. He had been performing for over 50 years, claiming to have cured 'thousands' of people. He is buried in his home town of Macduff in Aberdeenshire.

## 1918 – MR MARK SHERIDAN

A sad event was to affect the Coliseum in mid January 1918, The famous comedian, Mark Sheridan, real name Mr Fred Shaw, was taking the principal role in his own company show entitled 'Gay Paree' which included among its performers, his wife, son, daughter and nieces amongst its cast of 40.

He was very famous at that time for writing, recording and performing the famous songs, 'I Do Like To Be Beside The Seaside' and 'Who Were You With Last Night'.

Mark Sheridan, personally financed the revue, 'Gay Paree' at a cost of £2,000. He employed a cast of over 40, opening the show at the Coliseum on Monday 14 January 1918 when he played the part of Napoleon Bonaparte rather than his comical self. The presentation left the audience critical of the content and its lack of comedy material. Mark and the cast received a hostile reception from them before departing for his room at the nearby Bath Hotel. He was clearly dispirited at this outcome as he held the audience at Coliseum in the highest esteem. He often said it was his favourite theatre hence his decision to open 'Gay Paree' at that theatre.

*Mark Sheridan*  *'I Do Like to be Beside the Seaside' sung by Mark Sheridan*

At 11am the following morning, Mark Sheridan vacated his hotel room, stated he was going for a calming walk prior to attending the theatre for rehearsals at 1pm, but he failed to arrive, which was very unusual for such a professional and dedicated performer.

Later that day, at 2.30pm, two members of the public found the dead body of a man in nearby Kelvinside Park, with a pistol lying by his feet. Upon investigation by the police, the body was identified as Mark Sheridan. There was a bullet hole in the middle of his forehead.

On that evening, the audience had assembled for the first house when Mr Baxter, the theatre manager, appeared in front of the curtain to announce that the show was cancelled as Mark Sheridan had died suddenly that afternoon. The audience were completely shocked, many left the theatre in tears at this very sad announcement of such a popular comedian who had topped the bill on many occasions at the Coliseum.

The funeral took place on Friday 18 January 1918 at Cathcart Cemetery on the outskirts of Glasgow attended by his family and numerous music hall friends. There were dozens of wreaths sent by fellow entertainers who were unable to attend his funeral.

Mrs Maude Ethel Shaw, his widow, continued with the contractual obligations of 'Gay Paree' until October when she sold the performing rights to another impresario.

That was not the end of the matter. The executors of Sheridan's will, his wife Mrs Maude Ethel Shaw, Mr Thomas Shaw and Mr Thomas Frederick Dunn appeared in front of the King's Bench on Wednesday 20 November 1918 suing Equitable Life Assurance Society for £5,000.

*Mark Sheridan's Grave*

This was for non-payment of two life assurance polices taken out by Mark Sheridan in October 1917. The executors argued that the shooting was a pure accident whist he was rehearsing the part of Napoleon Bonaparte, and that somehow the trick must have 'gone wrong'. He had no reason to take his own life as he was earning upwards of £10,000 per annum, had a full diary for 1920 and had a happy and settled family life.

After hearing many witnesses, including George Robey, the jury found in favour of the Assurance Society.

## 1921 – MR GEORGE HENDRY

Mr George Hendry had enjoyed an evening at the Coliseum on Saturday 5 March 1921 and was leaving the theatre at around 10.30pm. Attempting to cross the road, he was knocked down by a taxi, witnessed by hundreds of people also departing the theatre. He suffered serious injuries, was taken to Glasgow Royal Infirmary where he died shortly afterwards.

## 1924 – MR JOHN ACEY

The famous singer, G. H. Elliott was appearing in the annual pantomime, 'Dick Whittington' with Miss Emilie Hayes (his wife) and Miss Violet Carmen, at the Coliseum on Monday 31 January 1924. G. H. Elliott's driver of three years, Mr John Acey, received some exciting news. A distant cousin, who Acey, aged 41, could not remember ever communicating with, had died recently leaving him a small estate of over one hundred acres situated thirty miles from Cardiff, plus a substantial house and £20,000 in cash.

Acey quickly gave his notice to G. H. Elliott telling him he was planning to retire to Wales. Elliott offered him congratulations on his windfall, wishing him good luck and happiness in Wales.

## 1928 – THE SULTAN OF MUSCAT AND OMAN

The Sultan of Muscat and Oman was touring Scotland and made a request to the manager of the Coliseum asking if he could be given a private film showing on Thursday 4 October 1928. Mr David A Stewart, the manager, instantly agreed to this request and featured the screening of the news film made by Pathe Gazette of the Sultan visiting places in Scotland. He also included excerpts of the comedy film 'The Circus' to complete the evening.

'The Circus', was written, produced, directed and starred in, by Charlie Chaplin with Harry Crocker, Merna Kennedy and George Davis in supporting roles. Whilst audiences were falling about laughing, Charlie Chaplin had undergone a desperately sad time making the film. His beloved mother died, he was experiencing a bitter divorce from his second wife, Lisa Grey and the film studio caught fire, To make matters even worse, the Inland Revenue were seeking significant back taxes from him.

On a positive note, it was the seventh highest grossing silent film in cinema history, taking more than £3 million pounds in 1928.

## MR WILLIAM SCOTT WILSON

Mr William Scott Wilson who was an intriguing giant of a man, served in many wars, was taken a prisoner of war by the Boers suffering horrendous conditions and was one of the few survivors of the Battle of Magersfontein in South Africa in 1899.

Wilson settled in Glasgow and became famous following an incident at the Coliseum when Yuko Tani, the famous Japanese wrestler was taking on all comers, easily beating the first opponent in one minute, resulting in the audience demanding their money back. Wilson volunteered, wrestled Yuko Tani furiously for ten rounds, slamming him onto the floor on occasions, but was eventually beaten, but received a standing ovation for his efforts,

Wilson died in the Southlands Hospital, Shoreham, Kent on Monday 21 October 1936, aged 55 after a very exciting life.

# HUDDERSFIELD PALACE

*The Palace Studios*

## 1908

As in many other towns and cities, the residents in the late 1800s were seeking additional forms of entertainment. The most popular type of the day was live theatre. The people of Huddersfield wanted a second theatre to complement the Theatre Royal, which had opened in 1880. The site of the former Rose and Crown Hotel, on the corner of Venn Street and Kirkgate, became available following the hotel's demolition. In December 1908, Mr Frank MacNaghten of the MacNaghten Vaudeville Circuit, owners of a number of Northern based theatres, successfully submitted a plan for the building of a luxury theatre on that site.

## 1909

Once planning permission was granted, building work commenced on Tuesday 2 March 1909 and Messrs Richard Horsfall & Son of Halifax were appointed architects. The Palace Theatre, estimated to cost around £11,600, would be in a similar style to the Palace and Hippodrome Theatres in the nearby town of Halifax. The building work was awarded to Messrs Smith Bros of Burnley and Messrs Jonas Binns & Sons of Halifax were to be responsible for the painting and decorating.

The facade had three bays of three storeys, the narrower two outer bays had towers rising above the centre, the left hand tower having a steep slated roof, the right hand one, a copper drum and dome. The facings were brick with stone dressings and the exterior was completed by a street level, iron covered canopy, across the full width of the frontage.

The exterior was described at the time as an 'imposing structure' and the interior was equally impressive with its elaborate furnishings and decorations supplied by Messrs H. Lazarus & Son of Great Eastern Street, London. The seating and upholstery of ruby plush velvet, with the curtains and draperies in the same colour plus gold appliqué relief work. The latest tip-up seats were fitted to the stalls and dress circle with comfortable balcony seating, having the capacity for 1,600 people. The stage measured 60ft wide and 30 ft deep enabling the majority of the touring shows to be accommodated.

The Palace was opened on Monday 2 August 1909 by Frank MacNaghton introducing to the audience the Mayor, Alderman John Holroyd and the Mayoress of Huddersfield. The Mayoress was presented with a bouquet of red and white carnations by Mr Reginald Foster, the theatre manager. In addition to the Mayor were Councillors and Officials of Huddersfield Corporation plus a number of JP's, all of whom were seated in the six luxurious side boxes.

The programme opened with the singing of the National Anthem by The Garricks Four and the audience. This was followed by a stream of talented and popular entertainers. Top of the bill was 'The Man of Many Parts', Charles T. Aldrich who was described as the most versatile performer on the music hall circuit. The performers that evening were the Arthur Gallimore Trio, comedians; Arthur Woodville, comedian; Bernard and Weston, comedians & dancers; Four Sidney Girls, vocalists and The Garricks Four, vocalists & dancers.

The bill also included 'Bioscope', a very early cinema projection system, which fascinated the audience as they could see moving pictures displayed on a screen, but films were never a regular feature at the Palace.

The Palace enjoyed many years of success and thousands of people visited the theatre to see the stars of the day and more often than not 'House Full' notices were displayed at the front of the theatre, but a disaster in 1936 would change the theatre for ever.

## 1936 – FIRE

During week commencing Monday 20 January 1936, the comedian, Sandy Daw, was heading a revue, 'The Means Test', with a cast of 25, billed as a non-stop laughter and musical show in seven scenes. He was supported by Bert Randall & Eddie Bee, the principal comedians, Geoffrey Denton, Marian Francis, Dolly Lewis, Vera Grafton, Gordon Norville and Dick Wilson all playing significant parts. That Monday's first night was a huge success but King George V died five minutes before midnight, therefore, out of respect, the following Tuesday and Wednesday performances were cancelled.

On Thursday 23 January 1936, at 6.20pm, twenty minutes before the show was planned to start, the staff were setting the stage. The cast were preparing in their dressing rooms, the musicians seated in their band room, relaxing and talking to each other prior to the commencement of the show. What should have been a 'normal' evening suddenly changed with lasting consequences for the Palace.

Approximately 200 people were already seated in the theatre when there was vivid flash from the main control box, situated at the side of the stage, followed immediately by two further huge flashes which could be seen in the auditorium through the closed stage curtains.

The stage hands immediately operated the fireproof safety curtain which closed off the stage, and they commenced spraying the control box with water. There was insufficient water pressure from the theatre hoses to have much effect. The main control box burst into flames which quickly spread to the scenery causing panic amongst the performers who realised the imminent danger.

The back stage staff fighting the rapidly spreading fire, were ably assisted by Sandy Daw, one of the show comedians, who had just arrived at the theatre a few minutes earlier for the twice nightly show. He took control of one of the hoses.

He immediately instructed another performer, Mr Gordon Norville, who was playing 'the villain', to demand that the others immediately evacuate the theatre. Norville, whilst the fire began to rage, bravely carried out a detailed search of every dressing room, band room etc to ensure that everyone was safely evacuated.

Once outside, the performers, who were dressed in their 'first scene' costumes and heavily made-up, were given blankets supplied by a local hotel to protect them from the bitterly cold January night. History was repeating itself, as five years earlier on Wednesday 13 May 1931, the same cast, performing 'Laughter Parade', had suffered a similar fire disaster when they had to evacuate the Theatre Royal, Loughborough, losing all of their personal belongings.

The audience were still oblivious of the events back stage until the lights failed, and at that point, the manager, Mr Frederick Pitt, in complete darkness, asked them follow the emergency exit signs and leave the theatre. While the audience were filing out, artistes, stage hands and office staff were battling to control the flames to stop them spreading to other parts of the theatre.

This was not possible once the flames burst through the safety curtain into the auditorium. Firemen and staff entered Pitt's office and carried the safe and company files into the street but his personal effects would be lost in the fire. Upon reaching the street, Pitt realised that his pet bird, Koko, was still in his office. He re-entered the blazing building and successfully rescued the bird.

The fire spread very rapidly and within a quarter of an hour, flames were shooting 20 feet through the stage roof and they could be seen for miles around. It was reported that 20,000 people congregated in Kirkgate, Market Street and Venn Street to witness this tremendous fire in anticipation that the entire theatre would be destroyed. Spectators were also in danger as the tower copper dome, situated on top of the building, collapsed sending showers of heavy roof slates and flames into the adjoining streets, As a sad reminder of the King's death, a few days earlier, the flag pole on the front of the theatre, complete with its flag at half mast, collapsed onto the fire fighters in a mass of flames.

All the stage effects, costumes, musical instruments, scenery etc were destroyed in the fire and it would be very doubtful if the cast would be able to perform at the Theatre Royal, Barnsley the following week. Sandy Daw said that if anyone could provide a venue in Huddersfield, he would gladly organise a fund raising event to raise money for these losses. Sandy Daw alone suffered personal losses of £700 and unfortunately, 40 people would lose their jobs.

The local hotels, shops and houses were deprived of their electricity for many hours and they remained in darkness until the early hours of next morning when the engineers were able to re-connect the supply. The fire brigade experienced considerable difficulty in fighting the fire due to insufficient water pressure from the hydrants. By 10.30am, the fire was under control but clouds of smoke and steam were pouring from the theatre and the firemen were still extinguishing the few remaining flames. The interior of the theatre was totally destroyed, the cellar dressing rooms were flooded with water to a depth of three feet and the offices were badly smoke damaged. Luckily the three external walls and the beautiful frontage, minus the roof, were still standing and could be included in any refurbishment.

Work commenced immediately by Roland Satchwell and Ernst Roberts to re-build the Palace at a cost of £45,000. The facade had a similar design to the old one but overall, the exterior remained unchanged from the original structure except filling in the tall windows on the frontage.

A new larger stage was built. All the ancillary stage equipment was replaced including the fly tower and nine new, modern dressing rooms were built for the benefit of performers. To minimise the danger of fire, hardly any wood was used in the re-construction and automatic sprinklers were installed. A new fresh air ventilation system was fitted and the heating system extended into the corridors. A unique type of concealed lighting located in the ceiling was created. The new seating was recorded in the local press as 'wide and comfortable', certainly a vast improvement on the original, uncomfortable, seating.

## 1937 – RE-OPENING

The building did not proceed in accordance with the refurbishment time plans. It was due to open in December for the 1936 Christmas pantomime. Because of the acute shortage of steel, plus other structural and logistical problems, the opening was delayed by two months.

It was finally re-opened on Monday 1 March 1937 starring the Blackpool Arcadian Follies and Harry Korris the radio comedian. It was a sell out and the audience were delighted to see the re-furbished and improved Palace in full operation again. Korris, born in Onchan on the Isle of Man on Thursday 8 October 1891 was a popular comedian in the majority of northern theatres but never neglected appearing in the Isle of Man. He was regularly on radio, made three films with Frank Randle and toured with ENSA throughout the second world war. He eventually retired to Blackpool where he occasionally performed, raising significant money for local charities. He died in his adopted town of Blackpool on Thursday 3 June 1971 aged 79.

Throughout the remainder of the 1930s and 1940s, the Palace had a very successful period and many thousands of patrons attended to enjoy the famous performers of the day,

## 1953 – 1954

During 1953 and until mid 1954, the Palace entertainment policy changed from traditional variety to musical comedy, but this was not successful and audiences continued to dwindle. Mr Harry Cunningham, the theatre manager, felt that the decline was primarily caused by the number of people buying or renting television sets therefore they did not have the money to spend on live theatre.

*Gracie Fields*

The problems came to a head on Monday 14 June 1954 when the owners, MacNaghton Vaudeville Circuit, announced its closure. Redundancy notices were served to the fifty employees, including the orchestra of nine. Cunningham, the manager, gave the reason as 'declining patronage during the past two years'. The Palace had been the home of variety and revue in Huddersfield for nearly half a century where Charlie Chaplin, Gracie Fields, George Formby, Old Mother Riley, George Elrick. Norman Evans, Tessie O'Shea, Izzy Bonn, Peter Cavanagh, Max & Harry Nesbitt etc had been 'treading the boards'.

This was terrible news as far as theatre in Huddersfield was concerned as the owners of the only other live theatre, the Theatre Royal, had announced its pending closure a few weeks previously. The last performance at the Theatre Royal was on Saturday 21 August 1954 with the play 'The Light of Heart'. This closure was in spite of the Huddersfield Corporation agreeing a subsidy of £40 per week. However, the Theatre Royal management declined this offer due to its restrictive conditions.

## 1955 – 1957

That was not quite the end of live theatre in Huddersfield, as the Palace reopened on Easter Monday 7 March 1955 starring Lee Lawrence, the popular singer. He died five years later in 1960, of a heart attack at the young age of 40 whilst touring the West Indies.

During the period of closure the theatre had undergone extensive renovations and modernisation including new and improved seating, total redecoration and the installation of a new lounge bar. The management also booked the top stars of the day to appear during the following weeks including Albert Modley, Al Read etc, hoping to attract huge audiences.

The first few months were successful from an audience capacity point of view but the numbers began to fall alarmingly in early 1957 and the financial difficulties became more severe, putting its future in doubt again. Just over eighteen months after re-opening, the Palace closed its doors again on Saturday 17 August 1957 and it appeared that the public of Huddersfield had fallen out with live variety and wanted other forms of entertainment. The threat of demolition was looming for this beautiful theatre, unless it could be re-opened as a theatre or have a change of use.

## 1959

However, the Palace was not dead yet! In April 1959, the Huddersfield Town Council Watch Committee granted permission for internal structural alterations to be made to the Palace to create a 'Continental Music Hall' similar to the ones in Hull and Middlesborough. The new owners were, Messrs Ultrans Ltd, a London firm of cinema and theatre owners. Opening on Thursday 28 May 1959, this new style of entertainment at the Palace would have variety and cabaret acts with dancing to a live band when the acts were not performing.

Another significant change from traditional theatre was customers sitting at tables, rather than in rows of seats, where they were served with food and drink whilst the entertainment was in progress. The cost of admission for a stalls table was 25p and 12p for a seat in the original circle. This new concept, of presenting entertainment along with dining, initially attracted large audiences but it was not to last.

## 1962 – 2010

The venture lasted until Saturday 27 October 1962 when it closed due to lack of customers principally during the early part of the week although there were sufficient numbers present at weekends but the total project was not financially viable. The staff of 60 were made redundant.

In early 1963, the theatre transformed into the Palace Casino, a similar type of venture, which continued for a some years and a further change in the use occurred in 1978 when it became the Palace Bingo Hall. Bingo continued until 1988 when it moved to a more modern building in Huddersfield therefore the theatre was disused once again and the building structure began to deteriorate. Would it be demolished now?

In 1989, the theatre was converted into the Chicago Rock Cafe, constructed largely using the auditorium. The stage was removed, the orchestra pit boarded over and the seven dressing rooms bricked up. It was subsequently acquired by the Society Night Club but closed in late 2010 due to the anti-social behaviour of some of its patrons. That was the end of entertainment as far as the Palace was concerned and everyone expected that it would finally be demolished.

## 2010

The Palace had been threatened by demolition many times over the previous fifty years but had always avoided the embarrassment of disappearing from Huddersfield's skyline, although the site was very valuable in view of it being situated in the centre of the town. The Town Council, in 2008, had planned a £40m extension of the nearby Kingsgate Shopping Centre and the Palace was included in these plans therefore implying that it could be subject to compulsory purchase. The Council eventually changed their plans in 2010 and the Palace was placed on the open market for offers around £350,000.

The same year, the Palace Theatre Restoration Trust was formed with the object of achieving grade two listing for the building and, eventually, reopening it as a Community Theatre.

## 2011 – STUDENT ACCOMMODATION

It was purchased in 2011 by a Leeds property developer, Mr Sammy Sekhon who, in July 2012, applied for planning permission to convert it into student apartments which did not involve any external alteration, just major internal alterations.

This application was granted and major work commenced in 2014 taking a year to complete. The interior was completely gutted which was particularly disappointing as the previous owners had not removed much of the original fixtures and fittings such as the safety curtain and its moving gear. Most of the other areas had been boarded up, boxes, circle, upper circle, dressing rooms and orchestra pit and, fortunately, they remained in a reasonable condition but now would be lost forever. The stage had been removed some years earlier to create a dance floor but many of the Palace's beautiful decorations and architecture could still be seen and admired.

Sekhon planned to build 15 studio apartments on the ground floor, install a bar and build a further 19 studios on each of the remaining five floors. The overwhelming good news was that the Art Deco facade frontage on Kirkgate and the lantern roof would be fully preserved as were the four outer walls.

It stands today as a proud monument to its famous history and is living proof that old theatres can be converted to modern day requirements. It is such a shame that so many theatres were demolished and are gone forever.

The Palace lives on, despite the many attempts to demolish it, the attractive exterior remains as a permanent reminder of the entertainment and laughter it gave the people of Huddersfield for over one hundred years. It truly deserved to have a totally new life.

# DID YOU KNOW…?

## 1909 – SERGEANT T. M. PHILLIPS

On Saturday evening 27 November 1909, at the Huddersfield Palace, Sergeant T. M. Phillips formally of the Liverpool Regiment, broke his own amateur world record of continuous Indian Club swinging by completing a forty hour spell using a pair of clubs weighing 2lbs. He commenced 'swinging' at 7am on Friday 26 November and finally completed his task at 11pm on the following Saturday evening.

Phillips said he could have continued for a longer period but once he had achieved the record he placed his clubs on the floor, a doctor examined him and found him to be in perfect health. His next plan was to make an attempt on the world professional record of sixty hours held by Mr Tom Burrows, an Australian.

## 1913 – MR JOE WHITLEY

On Saturday 4 October 1913, the first house of the show 'Mr Harry Burns Holiday Revue' was coming to an end when, Mr Joe Whitley, one of the limelight operators shouted, very loudly, 'turn if off' and was obviously in some distress. The limelight, the first spotlight used in theatres, was produced by heating quicklime to a high temperature, which, when mixed with hydrogen and oxygen, created a very bright light.

Whitley was apparently attempting to delicately renew a carbon burner when he received an electric shock, causing him to panic. In doing so, the two comedians on the stage quickly left for their dressing rooms. Someone in the audience shouted 'fire'. Many of them began to panic until, Mr Henry Curwin, manager of the Company, also playing the Dame, appeared on stage and urged the audience to remain in their seats as it was a minor problem,

The conductor had the presence of mind to instruct the orchestra to play, 'The Wedding Glide' for the next turn, six girls entered the stage dancing as the audience settled once again into their seats. This was not before a number of ladies in the audience had fainted.

Whitley was taken to hospital, treated for shock and burns, but he was allowed home after treatment.

## 1914 – MR TOM FOY

Tom Foy, born in Manchester in 1879, was a well known Northern comedian. He topped the bill at a number of theatres in the early 1900s. His most popular sketch was 'Tom Foy and his Donkey' which amused thousands of people over the years. He was topping the bill at the Palace from Monday 23 November 1914 when a rumour was circulating that his famous donkey had died and Tom Foy was presenting a new sketch entitled 'In Trouble Again'. Tom Foy denied this rumour, stating that his donkey was 'resting' in his stable until their pantomime season started in Belfast in a months time.

Almost three years later, Tom Foy died. He collapsed on stage at the Argyle Theatre in Birkenhead, was taken to hospital, where he passed away two weeks later on Tuesday 7 August 1917.

## 1926 – MR HARRY HUDDLESTON

At Huddersfield Court on Thursday 14 January 1926, Mr Harry Huddleston of 'His Majesty's Prison, Manchester' was accused of breaking and entering the Palace the previous day and stealing £35 in cash, a gold fob chain and a pair of boots.

Huddleston had entered the theatre through a window at the rear of the building, drilled holes into the door of the manager's office, removed a panel to gain entry and opened the safe with a drill to steal the items. He was arrested in Manchester and even though he was wearing the stolen boots, he pleaded 'Not Guilty'.

## 1935 – MRS DORIS JONES

Mrs Doris Jones brought an action in the Civil Court, on Friday 3 May 1935 against Mr Frederick Pitt, general manager of the Palace for causing the death of her husband on Saturday 16 June 1934 by dangerous driving. Her husband, Mr John Henry Jones, aged 23, a colliery mechanic, was riding his motor cycle in Shepley, near Huddersfield, with Mrs Jones as a pillion rider, when he collided with Pitt's motor car. Jones died from his injuries at Huddersfield Hospital eight days later.

Mrs Jones alleged that Pitt was driving on the wrong side of the road, but this was strenuously denied. Pitt said the motor cycle appeared to wobble and skid into his car. The Coroner said that was the likely cause of the accident and that Jones was probably riding too fast for the conditions therefore Mrs Jones lost her case for damages. Pitt was told he was not to blame and should not hold himself responsible.

Pitt did not ask for costs against Mrs Jones.

## 1936 – HUDDERSFIELD WATER PRESSURE

An urgent meeting of the members of the Huddersfield Borough Waterworks Committee was held on Wednesday 12 February 1936 to consider the problem with water pressure in the town, following the criticism after the Palace fire. The fire brigade management said that there was insufficient pressure from the hydrants and they had to run lengths of hoses from the canal in Quay Street, half a mile away, causing a significant delay. The weakness in the pressure created concern amongst other businesses and home owners in the town centre and they demanded that the Waterworks Committee take immediate remedial action.

## 1938 – KORINGA

Koringa, who was booked to appear at the Palace week commencing, Monday 18 July 1938 had a unique act. She called herself 'the only female Fakir in the world'. The act consisted of Koringa handling snakes and crocodiles, rolling bareback among broken glass and climbing a ladder of knife blades.

On Thursday 21 July, Koringa performed her act without any problems. The seven crocodiles were placed in two separate tanks, regularly inspected during the evening until the theatre was secured for the night. The following morning Koringa called in at the theatre, to feed them and found three of the crocodiles, named Hitler, Goering and Goebbels, dead in one of the tanks.

A crocodile expert was called to establish the reason for their deaths but he was unable to offer the correct cause of their death. He felt they could have been electrocuted by the water heating system or the water had been contaminated in some way.

## 1949 – TROUPE TOKAYERS

Commencing Monday 15 August 1949, The Troupe Tokayers performed an acrobatic act where one of the members jumped onto a spring board, somersaulted 14ft into the air and landed in a sitting position in an armchair fastened to a tubular pole held by another member. The following evening, Tuesday 16 August, the 'jumper' carried out the normal procedure except that he totally missed the armchair and crashed down 14ft onto the stage, badly injuring himself. He tried to regain his feet but staggered around, the audience then realised it was not part of the act as the safety curtain was lowered.

A request asking 'is there a doctor in the house' was unsuccessful. An ambulance was called for the injured gymnast, unfortunately none of the Troupe could speak English which complicated matters. The injured man was allowed back to his accommodation after x-rays and treatment, the Troupe Tokayers were unable to complete their week's contract whilst he fully recovered. A substitute act, the Seanore Trio, were rushed from a sister theatre in Halifax for the remainder of the week.

# KINGSTON EMPIRE

*Kingston Empire Theatre 2011*

## 1909

In early 1909, new theatre plans, designed by the famous theatre architect, Mr Bertie Crowe, were submitted to the local council by the proposed proprietor, Mr Clarence J. Sounes, who had spent the majority of his working life in the theatre. He was successful in his planning application and building work commenced almost immediately. It was decided to call his theatre 'The Kingston Empire Music Hall' but it became locally known as simply, 'The Empire'.

The external elevation was of Modern Renaissance style, constructed in terracotta imitation Portland stone. An interesting addition was a fully illuminated ornamental wrought iron and glass veranda, protecting the patrons from bad weather. Another special feature was a 60ft tower built at the south-east corner, which was illuminated at night and could be seen for miles around.

The main entrance in Richmond Road led to the box office and a grand staircase to the circle. The circle featured a spacious promenade, 61ft long, plus a beautiful, fully carpeted ladies tea-room with many spacious settees and armchairs. At the rear of the circle was a fireproofed box for projecting the new Bioscope cinema system onto a screen mounted on the stage for showing films between the variety acts.

The decorations were in the Grecian Renaissance style complemented by white with gold edges. The impressive stage curtain and all internal curtains were in shades of blue and gold, as were the seating and carpets, The whole building was lit by electricity, which also powered the enormous fans situated in the roof, ensuring fresh ventilation at all times. All levels of the building had a minimum of two permanently illuminated emergency exits, with an additional third one in the pit area, allowing the maximum audience of 2,000 being able to evacuate the theatre within a few minutes.

An enormous amount of consideration was given to fire safety, the stage was completely isolated from the auditorium by a steel framed and double covered asbestos curtain which could be operated from either the side of the stage or from the stage manager's office. In addition there were four fire hydrants adjacent to the stage and two additional ones in each of the pit, circle and gallery making a total of ten. The stage roof was constructed in such a manner that the large skylight could be opened in the case of fire to extract smoke and fumes. As a final commitment to fire safety, all stage doors and the ones leading to the auditorium were self-closing. The Empire's main structures were erected in fire proof materials including the staircases leading from the circle and gallery.

It was a well known fact that many theatre dressing rooms were dark, dingy, cold, had inadequate toilets, terribly cramped conditions and only had cold water available. The ten new ones at the Empire, were exactly the opposite, they were light, airy, heated and provided with hot and cold running water as well as 'decent' toilets.

## 1910 – OPENING

The opening date was Monday 24 October 1910 when Sounes invited the Deputy Mayor, Alderman Dr. W. E. St Lawrence Finney JP, officially opened the Empire. In his introductory speech, Dr. Finney particularly thanked Sounes for his unstinting efforts in bringing such a marvellous building to Kingston and said that the finished article was an absolute credit to him and Crowe. He emphasised that the policy of the theatre would be to provide inoffensive entertainment so that families could attend without embarrassment. He wished the Empire every success and the audience appreciated this speech and also gave Sounes three rousing cheers.

Sounes had provided a quality entertainment programme for this special event which included many stars of the day. Top of the bill was the 'Great Raymond', a magician of extreme skill and he was supported by Little Sunbeam, a junior Marie Lloyd; Ryde & Beeman, acrobats; Tom Clare, singer; The Comedy Meisters, comedians; Dorothy Ward, musical comedy; Arthur Gill, impressionist; Luella Cross, singer and Joan Deering, singer. The prices on that opening night ranged from 1p in the gallery to 75p for the finest box.

## 1914 – FIRE No 1

In spite of the attention to detail concerning the installation of fire safety equipment, a disaster occurred on the morning of Friday 17 April 1914, causing damage of £10,000. At 2.30am, a police sergeant was cycling past the building when he saw flames breaking through the stage roof of the Empire. He raised the alarm, the fire brigade was on the scene within a few minutes finding the rear of the building well alight, and the roof over the stage ready to collapse, which it did within a few minutes. In doing so, it brought down the safety curtain but it had contained the fire within the stage area for a while until the firemen arrived, otherwise the Empire may have been totally destroyed.

Additional fire engines arrived to assist, but they could not prevent tremendous damage to the scenery, stage curtain, stage fixtures and fittings. Due to the fire prevention systems installed at the build stage, the flames did not damage the dressing rooms as they were protected by a brick wall two feet thick. Unfortunately the majority of the musicians lost all their instruments as they were rendered useless by either fire and/or water, one tearful musician lost several of his instruments, including a violin which he had purchased for 50 guineas a few weeks previously.

The stage was now open to the sky with the remaining steel roof girders hanging perilously overhead which could have collapsed on the remains of the stage at any time. A number of the front seats in the auditorium were severely damaged by the heat from the fire. All other seating, carpets etc were either scorched, smoke damaged or drenched with water.

One animal had a lucky escape, the stage manager's fox terrier, living in a kennel on the roof, was heard barking. PC 1020 Jones, climbed a vertical iron ladder, situated within the raging fire at the back of the stage, to rescue the dog.

The leading presentation that week was 'Humanity' performed by Mr John Lawson and his Company. Weirdly, the various scenes led to the climax of the burning down of a house which was set on fire by the villain of the piece! Supporting this drama were High Davis Co., acrobatics; Tom Leamore, comedian; Miss Ethel Newman, comedy sketch; Tom Brierley, shadowgraphs; The Zanoni's, jugglers and Elsie Malpass, dancer.

After the fire Lawson stated that he had lost stage scenery to the value of £175 in respect of 'Humanity'. The cast's wardrobe stood him at a further loss of £60. The majority of the other acts lost their 'props' including 'The Zanonis's' eighteen 'Indian' juggling clubs, almost impossible to replace at short notice, therefore they had to cancel their future theatre bookings for a number of weeks.

Sounes immediately recalled to the Empire the original architect Crowe, who instantly agreed to oversee the necessary repairs to ensure its early re-opening, hopefully within three to four months.

## RE-OPENING

The re-opening took place on Monday 20 July 1914. The Empire presented to the audience a bright and cheerful appearance which was a credit to the architect and all other contractors who completed the repairs within such a short time-scale. A number of improvements had been introduced, major upgrading of the house and, especially, improvement to the poor stage lighting which had received criticism in the past. Also provided were new stage curtains, seating, carpets and upholstery and, in addition, the audience would benefit from the most modern type of heating and ventilation. It could provide cool air in the summer months and heating during the winter.

The Mayor of Kingston, Councillor C. F. Burge, opened the proceedings by thanking Sounes for re-building the theatre in such a short time and wished it every success in the future. Sounes took to the stage and thanked everyone for attending the improved Empire and said that all steps had been taken to ensure it was one of the safest theatres in the country. These words were to come back and haunt him within a few years.

The opening night's performers were headed by Charles Austin, 'Napoleon of Mirth' in a sketch entitled 'Parker on the Panel'.

Austin was born Thursday 4 April 1878. He developed an act as an incompetent policeman. He was 'King Rat' of the 'Grand Order of Water Rats', an entertainment charitable organisation, for an unprecedented six years which occurred in various years between 1912 and 1932. He died in London on Friday 14 January 1944, aged 65.

The supporting acts on opening night were Miss May Knight, comedienne; Scotta Trio, instrumentalists; Chas J. Lavley, impersonator; Les Neslos, aerial act; Eight Stella Girls, singers and dancers and May Knight, comedienne.

Over the years people flocked to the Empire and enjoyed the shows presented to them. However, another, more serious fire, would put an immediate halt to their enjoyment placing the future of the theatre in doubt once again.

## 1919 – FIRE No 2

On the night of Tuesday 10 June 1919, history repeated itself. On this occasion, at midnight, a passing postman on his way to Kingston Railway Station to collect mail, saw smoke billowing from the gallery roof and instantly gave the alarm. The Kingston Fire Brigade attended immediately.

The firemen entered the building by forcing the pit exit doors to discover the seat of the fire originated in the gallery. The fire quickly spread to the whole of the roof at the front of the building. The firemen, fighting the flames from the ground floor auditorium, had to run for their lives as the burning roof suddenly collapsed causing more damage. Luckily they had time to run for shelter to a nearby concrete lined corridor. They emerged badly shaken, but returned to their duties and continued to fight the fire.

The large cupola, standing over seventy feet high, and used as a watch tower for the air raids, had toppled over and lodged on one of the iron girders balancing somehow on the wrecked roof. The Kingston Fire Brigade were assisted by units from Surbiton, Teddington, Wimbledon and Richmond. Finally, they had extinguished the fire by 3.30am.

From the outside of the theatre there appeared to be little damage but the interior showed a totally different picture. The gallery was burnt out and unrecognisable, the circle was a mass of burnt wood, with parts of the roof and the auditorium full of smouldering debris. Luckily the safety curtain had been lowered at the end of the evening's performance and the flames were prevented from reaching the stage, the prime location of the 1914 fire.

The performers during that week, included Talbot O'Farrell, Nora Delany, Willie Gardiner, Elsa Cowie and Reg King. One performer who was particularly appreciative of the bravery of the fire service was Miss Maud Allen and her animal act, as all her performing parrots, birds and her dog were rescued and taken to safety unharmed. The cause of the fire was never established, but it was thought that a smouldering cigarette or cigar had ignited the carpet and had probably smouldered for a while before bursting into flames.

It was reported that the cost of refurbishment would be in the region of £20,000. The theatre would be closed for a considerable period of time due to the extent of the damage. Strangely, in the previous fire in 1914, the stage area had been totally destroyed whereas in this fire, it was the only area escaping any damage.

## RE-OPENING

Six months later, on Monday 8 December 1919 the Empire re-opened to a sell-out audience, entertained by Eric Randolph, who opened the proceedings by singing the National Anthem. Frank Ellison & Co followed in a farce entitled 'Dear Old Bean'; Will Bland, magician; Peggy O'Hara,

*Marie Lloyd*

entertainer; Tommy Davis, comedian and Sam Barton, trick cyclist; all performing their acts to a delighted audience. The evening was concluded by a new Bioscope cinema projection feature.

Over the years many established stars appeared at the Empire including Marie Lloyd, Albert Chevalier and Harry Chapman, but the theatre had a tendency to present reviews alongside variety into the 1920s.

## 1920

Mr Harry Dean, was appointed manager of the Empire in 1920 having held a similar position with its sister theatre, the Aldershot Hippodrome. He remained at the Empire for thirty-five years, until it closed in 1955.

## 1931

In March 1931, the owners, Kingshot Syndicate Ltd, through their theatre director, Mr Stanley Watson, decided that the theatre, with its palatial structure, large external advertising spaces and its prime position in the town made it an ideal bedfellow for the inclusion of cinema facilities. Customers were highly critical of the internal condition of the theatre stating that it was badly lit, required decorating and cleaning, and in fact, was not generally welcoming.

In an effort to improve matters the management spent many thousands of pounds to make alterations to the entrance, total re-decoration, installed new sound and lighting, replaced all the carpets, and installed 'tip-up' seats. Equally as important, they provided attractive new uniforms for all the staff and ensured they were fully trained in all aspects of customer service. In future they would incorporate live entertainment and films in one programme therefore providing customers with more value for money

The Kingston Empire was regarded as a palatial building therefore in December 1931, the management decided to outline the external tower with Neon gas tubing in blue and red, making it visible for miles around. By day the tubing was practically invisible, by night the contour of the building would be outlined in glowing colours. An added benefit was that the cost of electricity consumption would be only 2p per unit per hour.

## 1934

On Monday 30 July 1934 the Empire closed once again whilst the latest sound and lighting was installed. Improvements were made to the auditorium and new technology installed in the stage area, in order to accommodate modern productions. The re-opening programme included Teddy Brown, xylophone; Elsie Bower & Billy Rutherford, singers; Duncan Grey, comedian; Leslie Weston, comedian and compere; and the Sharman-Fisher Girls. Further expensive modifications were carried out in November/December 1936 when the foyer was redesigned making it three times the size of the old one by removing one wall.

## 1939

As with all theatres, the Empire had to close its doors at the beginning of the war in 1939 but this national decision was quickly overturned and the Empire boasted it was the first theatre in the suburbs to re-open after the declaration of war. During 1939 and 1940, the Empire continued with variety bills of all descriptions including the famous Lord John Sanger's huge circus. However, the bombing became too regular and it closed its doors in September 1940 for three months. It re-opened in December when the pantomime, 'Mother Goose' started its three week run. It starred Ivy Luck, as the Principal Boy, Low & Webster as the Broker's Men, Fred Hale as Mother Goose, Joe Archer as the Golden Goose and Margherita Stanley as Jill.

During the war, the Empire had many periods of opening and closing during heavy bombing raids especially when the V1 flying bombs were at their most prevalent. In July 1944, the Empire closed again for a short while and the management took this opportunity to redecorate the auditorium.

## 1944

The Empire re-opened, at the end of hostilities on Monday 25 September 1944, with Lew and Leslie Grade's successful comedy show, 'Serenade to Fun' with a bill boasting nineteen acts. It was headed by Billy Thorburn and his Music, a BBC pianist: Marietta Dancers; Four Pagolas, dancers; Jackie Trevor, comedian; Nicol & Merrill, trick cyclists and Maudie Edwards, vocalist.

During the late 1940s and early 1950s stars such as Gracie Fields, Max Miller, Frankie Vaughan, Flanagan & Allen, George Formby, Frankie

Howard, Old Mother Riley, Louis Armstrong and the Four Aces and many, many others graced the stage to great success.

The management strived to provide the highest quality of entertainment possible and they presented diverse acts such as a circus, musicals, ice shows, classical music concerts and even provided a home for the local Kingston Amateur Dramatic Society. The circus took to the stage twice per year, the elephants were stabled in the warehouse of nearby Bentalls Department Store and wore red lights attached to their tails when being walked to and from the Empire.

In the mid 1950s variety was distinctly tired and jaded as nothing new was being presented to attract audiences, especially as television and other forms of entertainment were becoming more and more popular. On one occasion, Billy Cotton and his Band, who were popular performers at the Empire, failed to attract sizeable audiences as Billy was taken ill and a replacement conductor appointed.

## 1954

The Empire was entering a very difficult period. On Saturday 28 August, 1954, it offered the theatre for sale, and it was eventually bought by an investment company, headed by Mr W. L. Hodges of Kingshot Theatres Ltd. The owners stated *'business had not been what it used to be, it is the same story all over the country'*.

Top class acts were becoming difficult to attract as the newly opening 'theatre clubs' were able to pay more money and stars would not to commit to contracts due to other opportunities. The Empire was no different. As an example, the show commencing Monday 15 November 1954 was 'We Couldn't Wear Less', another boring 'girlie show' and lacked originality although there were some excellent variety acts, but lacking 'real', crowd pulling stars.

## 1955

In January 1955, the Empire presented the last of its famous pantomimes, 'Red Riding Hood' starring Shelagh Day as Principal Boy, Julia Rufford as 'Bo-Peep' and Eva Kenny and George Barnes as 'The Baddies'. The sound, of the music and laughter of pantomimes would no longer be heard as the closure of the grand old Empire was announced the following month, in February 1955.

The last ever show was presented on Saturday 26 March 1955. It featured the comedian Sonny Jenks in a new show called 'La Vie Parisienne' along with Billy Nelson, Chuck O'Neil, Stan Jay & Joan, Billy Morris and The Iris Long Trio. Maybe if the shows had been of this high standard, the Empire may have had a much longer life.

That was the end of Kingston Empire as a live entertainment venue.

## 1956

Throughout 1955 and 1956, the local inhabitants of Kingston Upon Thames tried desperately to reverse this decision and 2,000 people signed a petition. They handed it into the local Corporation hoping for support but to no avail and the building was offered for auction without success. However not all was totally lost, a retail chain, including Timothy Whites & Taylors and Premier Supermarkets leased the building in 1956 from developers who immediately removed the majority of the beautiful fixtures relating to its old use but, on a happy note, the Empire was not demolished similar to hundreds of other theatres.

## 1997

The building continued in various guises until 1997 when it was purchased by the pub chain, Wetherspoons, naming it 'Kings Tun', still with the name 'Empire' prominently displayed on the side of the building. Wetherspoons have the whole of the ground floor with some of the upper floor and thankfully, have revealed and restored much of the plasterwork in the foyer. The remainder of the upper floor is now occupied by Kingsgate Church and is used as a community centre.

No longer a theatre/cinema, the old Empire still attracts thousands of people every month therefore continuing to provide a service to the community.

## DID YOU KNOW…?

## 1912 – BUS CRASH

Late on Saturday 12 February 1912, a bus was turning the corner outside the Empire when it skidded, overturned onto its side, spilling many of the passengers onto the road whilst others were trapped in the wreckage. The majority were assisted by staff from the Empire, however fourteen passengers and the driver and conductor were injured and taken to the Surbiton Cottage Hospital for treatment.

Six were detained with concussion, spinal injuries, and severe cuts, but luckily, none were in a serious condition. The remaining ten were treated and allowed home that evening.

## 1914 – MR JACK WILLIAMS

Mr Jack Williams was co-starring in the pantomime, 'Sinbad the Sailor' at the Kingston Empire as lead comedian from Monday 5 January 1914.

On Friday 9 January he was travelling on his way to the Empire when he was arrested by police for failing to pay £2 per week to his wife which had previously been ordered by Manchester Magistrates Court.

This extraordinary case was brought before Judge Parry at Lambeth County Court on Monday 16 March 1914. Mr Jack Williams stated that he had regularly paid the money, but agreed he was £6 in arrears due to difficulty in locating his wife in view of her travelling theatre commitments. He had asked Manchester Magistrates Court if he could pay the money into the court to avoid problems, but they had refused this.

As a result, he was arrested on his way to appear in the pantomime and taken from London to Manchester Police Station by a police officer, where he explained the situation but was formally charged and detained in a cell.

Williams offered to leave the £6 with the Manchester police but this offer was refused. He was detained in his cell from Friday until Monday morning hence he could not appear in the pantomime on Friday and Saturday.

When the case was heard two months later, Judge Parry was highly critical of the way Williams had been dealt with. The Judge stated that it was the most monstrous miscarriage of justice brought about by Mrs Williams not communicating her changes of address to her husband on a regular basis. He also criticised the police for failing to assist Williams in helping to pay the outstanding money immediately he arrived in Manchester.

Judge Parry recommended that Mr and Mrs Williams should meet and make an agreement regarding future payments in order to avoid such a situation arising again.

Jack Williams also sued a theatrical agent for non-payment of his wages of £20 in respect of being unable to appear in the pantomime on Friday and Saturday due to being arrested. His absence was not his fault, but was due to a miscarriage of justice which placed him in an impossible situation.

Due to the extraordinary circumstances Judge Parry recommended that Williams and the theatrical agent should meet and mutually agree a settlement.

## 1914 – POLICE CONSTABLE JONES

On Wednesday 20 May 1914, PC 1020 Jones, at the commencement of the Kingston Magistrates Bench, was presented, by the Mayor, Mr C. H. Burne, with a bronze medal for his act of humanity awarded by the RSPCA for bravely rescuing a dog belonging to the theatre manager, from the burning Empire Theatre on Friday 17 April 1914. He was also handed a cheque for 50p from a 'lady from Streatham', and two further cheques, these were in addition to the Silver Medal of the Dumb Friend's League presented by the Lady Mayoress of London a few days earlier.

## 1914 – MR VERNON DARE

On Tuesday 19 May 1914, at the County Court of Kingston, Mr Vernon Dare, the musical director at the Empire since 1911, sued Mr Clarence Sounes, the owner of the Empire, for wrongful dismissal seeking £22.80p for loss of wages.

It was alleged that Dare approached Sounes for a reference to accompany his application for the position of musical director with Hastings Corporation. Soames refused to supply the reference. Dare eventually secured the position, which he accepted and duly informed Soames who dismissed him with two weeks notice.

Dare said to Soames that, in the meantime, he had agreed with Mr J. Gladwin, the theatre general manager, to remain as musical director at the Empire until the confirmation and commencement date for the Hastings position was in his possession which may take a number of weeks. Gladwin denied this discussion had taken place.

The jury retired and took four minutes to agree with Dare's submission that he was unfairly dismissed. The Judge awarded him £22.80p damages for loss of wages plus costs.

## 1918 – MR ALGERNON EDWARD CHATER

On Friday 1 March 1918, Mr Algernon Edward Chater, a musician, was charged at Kingston Borough Court with being an absentee under the Military Service Acts. He also failed to notify his change of address within 28 days to the local registration authority. The military prosecutor stated that Chater had lived at four different addresses within eighteen months and had not registered his most recent one, although he had resided there for nine months whilst performing at the Empire.

Chater had also ignored a 'call up demand' dated Saturday 5 January 1918. He was fined £3 for failing to report to the military, £2 for failing to register a change of address and was immediately handed over to the military.

## 1918 – POLICE PERFORMANCE

A unique performance took place on Saturday 21 December 1918 when the Metropolitan Police Entertainers performed their act at the Empire. This was to raise funds for the Metropolitan and City Police Orphanage whose financial needs had increased due to the first world war. The charity maintained and educated 250 orphans. Their orphanage also provided a financial allowance for a further 900 who could not be accommodated on their premises.

The guests of honour were the Mayor and Mayoress of Kingston, Sir Charles and Lady Burge who fully appreciated the singing, dancing, and the range of costumes and comedy routines of the police officers.

## 1919 – MISS KATHLEEN GLADWIN

On Wednesday 13 August 1919, the Mayor of Kingston presented Miss Kathleen Gladwin, the daughter of the Empire's general manager, with the Certificate of the Royal Humane Society for rescuing a little girl, Margaret Jones, from drowning in the Thames. Miss Gladwin was walking along the banks of the Thames on Sunday, 13 July 1919, when she saw the little girl in distress in the water, dived in fully clothed and brought the little girl to the embankment where she recovered after treatment.

## 1921 – MR VICTOR NIBLO

On Wednesday 20 April 1921, an amusing case took place in the Kingston Court. A parrot, called 'Polly', was brought into the court in connection with a summons for alleged cruelty to the bird by Mr Victor Niblo, a music hall artist. The parrot was very polite as it entered the court greeting the magistrates with the words 'Hello, how are you?'. The prosecution had been undertaken by the RSPCA alleging that Niblo compelled the bird to perform through fear. They produced evidence that when he banged the cage with a stick, the bird shrieked and appeared to be frightened by him.

Niblo said he had been appearing with his act for fourteen years and was allowed to demonstrate it in front of the magistrates proving he had no case to answer. The case was dismissed.

## 1921 – MR VAL WALKER

A further interesting incident occurred on Wednesday 19 October 1921 when Mr Val Walker, an escapologist, was appearing at the Empire. He announced that he could escape from any straight jacket presented to him and offered £50 to anyone who could provide such a challenge.

A local man, Mr John Bull, fitted his own designed garment to Walker and forty-five minutes elapsed before he could free himself. Clearly Walker was deeply embarrassed by this incident. He immediately destroyed the offending jacket and distributed the remains to the audience. Bull sued Walker for the cost of the jacket, approximately £10, but the Judge felt that there was always a risk of damage to the jacket and awarded him only minimal damages and costs.

Val Walker, born Valentine Augustus Walker, on Saturday 15 February 1890 was a leading escape artist and his most famous act was 'The Tank in the Thames' where he was bolted into a steel tank and lowered into the River Thames on Friday 20 August 1920. He escaped within twenty-seconds, he retired from the stage in 1924. Val died on Monday 17 March 1969, aged 79.

## 1921 – MR CLARENCE J. SOUNES

It was announced on Friday 21 October 1921 that Mr Clarence Sounes, aged 66, had died from a heart attack, at his home in Walpole Road, Surbiton. Sounes had a life long involvement with the theatre. At the age of 25 he made his first stage appearance at Drury Lane Imperial Theatre in 'La Fille de Madame Angot'. He continued his acting career by touring the provinces in dramas and pantomimes before joining the D'Oyly Carte Opera Company where he played in 'The Pirates of Penzance' and 'Iolanthe'.

Being a sound businessman, he formed and toured with his own company in 'Uncle Tom's Cabin' but he was quickly disillusioned as mishaps were prominent. His cast included live bloodhounds, one of which severely bit the leading man on the arm, another performer stole a watch, a chain and other valuables from another actor.

In the early 1890s, Sounes acquired the lease of the Victory Theatre in Aldershot, which burned down in 1898. Building the new Royal Theatre, in later years he became proprietor/lessee of the Lyceum in Newport (Monmouthshire), the Grand in Cardiff, the Grand in Woolwich, the Theatre Royal and Hippodrome in Aldershot and the Prince's in Poplar.

He built the Kingston Empire in 1910. Unfortunately he began to suffer heart trouble in the weeks shortly after opening the Empire and was troubled with its two serious fires. He eventually left the running of his theatre and other business interests to Mr J. Gladwin, General Manager of the Kingston Empire after the second fire.

Mr Clarence J. Sounes's funeral took place on Tuesday 25 October 1921, at Surbiton Cemetery. He was survived by his wife, there were no children,

## 1928 – MR GEORGE CHALLIS

Mr George Challis, an ex-policeman and a gallery attendant at the Empire, was a victim of a mysterious attack on Monday 11 September 1928. An unknown person telephoned the ambulance service at 11pm, in a disguised voice, stating that a person had been injured, and was lying on the side of the road by his undamaged cycle and urgently requiring an ambulance. The ambulance team found him to be unconscious, bleeding heavily from wounds to his face and head, taking him to hospital in a serious condition.

Challis regained consciousness the next day, the police investigated the incident but could not come to any satisfactory conclusion.

## 1931 – MESSRS HARRY PHILIP, SYDNEY HATCHWELL & VICTOR HUNTINGFORD

At Kingston Borough Court on Tuesday, 10 March 1931, Messrs Harry Philip, Sydney Hatchwell and Victor Huntingford were charged with using insulting words and behaviour the previous evening during the second performance at the Empire. It was reported that when one of the men was asked to leave because of his behaviour, around thirty of his friends began swearing and shouting. A glass panel in a door was broken and the attendants were threatened. Hatchwell was fined £2, Philip and Huntingford each fined £1.

## 1937 – MISS BETTY JUMEL

Betty Jumel, spent her life touring theatres with her comedy act and supported many of the top stars of the day including Nat Jackley, Will Hay, Sandy Powell and Norman Evans, mainly due to her excellent comic timing and versatility.

Betty Jumel, with her husband, Victor Arnley, one of the Arnley Brothers, toured the theatres with their comedy act, being booked to appear at the Empire for week commencing Monday 18 October 1937. Also topping the bill was comedian, Ronald Frankau. They were supported by Ken Johnson and his orchestra, the Kafta Sisters and Charles Judge with his chimpanzees. Betty Jumel and Victor Arnley stole the show with their hilarious act which included comedy songs, general fooling around and a comical burlesque ballet based on Swan Lake.

However, upon returning home on Sunday, they found their house had been burgled with many items stolen including money and clothing. Victor's international certificates and medals for skating were found dumped in the garden.

Betty Jumel, was born on Sunday 5 May 1901 as Miss Amy Ada Beatrice Grimshaw, in Lytham St Annes. She first appeared on stage at the age of ten making her way to the top of the bill before other performers persuaded her to join forces with them due to her perfect comedy timing.

She died in Hove, Sussex, aged 89, on Saturday 14 October 1990, one of the last famous survivors of the old music hall.

## 1938 – MR FREDERICK CARRE

There was another case of cruelty to animals heard at the Kingston Magistrates Court on Wednesday 29 June 1938 which involved Mr Frederick Carre, a Dutchman, who was accused of animal cruelty during his performance at the Empire. It was alleged that Carre, dressed as a clown, was seen to jab his mule in its hindquarters in order to make it buck and rear.

Carre denied the allegation, however the bench found him guilty fining him £5.

## 1938 – MR CHARLES WILSON

Mr Charles Wilson, aged 23, was given the chance to realise his lifelong ambition of being a stage performer and joined the Empire pantomime, 'Cinderella', commencing on Boxing Day Monday 26 December 1938. Prior to this, he took a temporary job as a waiter in the nearby Kingston Hotel in November 1938. Whilst working in the Kingston Hotel, he met Miss Adrienne Lamb, aged 43, who was employed there as a barmaid. They became engaged the following day, married one month later on Monday 19 December 1938 at the Kingston Register Office once the hotel had closed for the day and both returned in time to work the evening shift.

Wilson retired from the stage after the pantomime to live happily ever after with his new wife.

## 1944 – MR GEORGE BOLTON

The multi-talented singer, comedian, and 'Dame', George Bolton appeared many times at the Empire and was a great favourite especially when he starred alongside Big Bill Campbell in his popular Rocky Mountain Rhythm Show. They appeared at the Empire week commencing Monday 28 February 1944 with Bolton billed as 'The New Gagster'.

*George Bolton*

Bolton was born on Friday 12 June 1896 in Portsmouth and started his theatre career in 1919 when he left the Armed Forces, struggling to find suitable work in the early years. Working hard to learn his craft as a singer/comedian he quickly gained a reputation as one of the UK's leading and most talented performers reaching the top of the bill status in the mid 1920s, a position which he held for the rest of his life.

Bolton appeared regularly on radio in its early days, also co-starring with Albert Modley in the successful war film 'Bob's Your Uncle'. He made dozens of television appearances in programmes such as Dixon of Dock Green, Mrs Thursday, George & the Dragon etc. He was also a regular performer on the famous BBC television entertainment show, 'The Good Old Days'.

Regarded as one of the finest pantomime 'Dames' ever, he co-starred as the dame with many of the great comedians each year for over thirty years.

One particular pantomime was memorable, for all the wrong reasons.

Commencing on Saturday 23 December 1961, George Bolton co-starred with Tommy Cooper, Diana Day and Gordon & Bunny Jay in 'Puss in Boots' at the Bradford Alhambra. What could possibly go wrong, went wrong.

Tommy Cooper slipped a disc and had to wear an uncomfortable, heavy and cumbersome body cast but was in severe pain for the whole run. Tommy then disagreed with the show director and the show director was replaced.

One member of the The Three Kims, an acrobatic act, suffered a snapped achilles tendon during the first week, and had to withdraw from the pantomime.

A few weeks later, early in 1962, there was a severe outbreak of smallpox in Bradford. 285,000 people were vaccinated but crowded places had to be avoided at all costs. This seriously affected audiences, often only 100 people attended the performances and it was an absolute financial disaster.

There was one last sting in the tail, a member of the front of house staff was knocked down by a bus outside the Alhambra and died within hours.

That was the last straw. After five weeks of a ten week run the show was cancelled and it went into the record books as the shortest and most unsuccessful and unluckiest ever pantomime at the Alhambra.

Away from his first love of pantomime, George often chaired the show "Ye Good Olde Days" based on the BBC programme 'The Good Old Days' (which ran for thirty years, 1953 to 1983) and he was able to make an early impact due to his booming voice. He also appeared in 'Fol de Rols', 'Holiday Hayride' and 'Star-nite Spectacular' shows at many seaside resorts during the summer seasons and, in winter, was committed to pantomime, and he was the most sought-after Dame in the UK.

Bolton's last ever performance was at the Marine Theatre in Morecambe on Thursday 17 August 1978 in the summer show, 'The Good Old Days' at the age of 82. He died at Ewell, Surrey on Friday 16 October 1981 at the age of 85. What a great music hall legend who had succeeded in this tough and challenging profession and remained at the pinnacle for all of sixty years, seeing many changes in his lifetime. Well done George.

## MR GEORGE BOLTON'S NIECE – AUDREY JEANS

Clearly showbiz talent ran in the Bolton family as George's niece, Audrey Jeans, became a star in her own right topping the bill in the 1960s and 1970s. Audrey, was born as Audrey Jennings on Saturday 27 July 1929 in Portsmouth. She started her show business career as a dancer but was spotted by Sid Field, the famous comedian, who chose her from the chorus, for his show 'Piccadilly Hayride', putting her in the leading role as a comedienne.

*Audrey Jeans*

Her outstanding comic talent was spotted and she toured with Tommy Cooper, had four seasons at the London Palladium, two at the Prince of Wales Theatre, five at the Savoy Hotel and toured Hong Kong, South Africa and Australia. She was excellent in pantomime and played in principal roles for seventeen consecutive seasons supporting the huge stars of the day.

Audrey married her first husband, accountant Harry Frank, at the age of 24 but due to her nomadic lifestyle appearing in theatres around the country, her marriage failed.

Audrey was an excellent actress. In the Spring of 1976 she was undertaking a UK tour of the famous comedy, 'The Mating Season' starring Sid James and herself, scheduled to appear at the Sunderland Empire for week commencing Monday 26 April 1976. The opening night's performance opened on time, as Sid James was rising from the stage settee to greet Audrey Jeans as she entered the stage, he staggered and fell. On her knees, she cradled him in her arms, called for the curtain to be closed and summoned medical help. Sid was pronounced dead in Sunderland Hospital later that evening.

Audrey found love again, at the age of 49, she married Cyril Giddy, a director of Thompson Publishing in early August 1980. They married and went on honeymoon to the beautiful French city of La Rochelle planning to return to the UK the following month to continue her successful career.

This was not to happen. Whilst on honeymoon, returning from a restaurant, they crossed the road and they were both knocked down by a hit and run driver who was never apprehended. Sadly, Audrey died within minutes and her husband, Cyril received many broken bones, remaining in hospital in France for two months to fully recover, before being able to return to the UK.

Audrey's funeral was held at Portchester Crematorium, Portsmouth in late August, without Cyril, as he was too ill to attend. Many of her show business friends were mourners, including Jimmy Tarbuck, Jack Douglas, Mike Yarwood etc all paying their final respects to one of Britain's finest comediennes and a very talented actress.

## 1950 MR MICHAEL HOWARD

A summons was issued at Brentford County Court on Wednesday 25 January 1950 against Mr Michael Howard, an actor residing in Ealing, for a debt of over £100 owed to San Clu Hotels Ltd. It was alleged that Howard had appeared in a pantomime at the Empire in 1948, and had not paid his hotel bill. Howard, through his solicitor, asked for an adjournment as he was unable to be present due to illness. It was alleged that Howard had appeared at the Empire the previous evening, therefore he was not ill. His appearance could not be substantiated as the solicitor's clerk had failed to attend the theatre for verification.

The case was adjourned with the suggestion that it should be settled out of court.

## 1950 – MR FRANKIE VAUGHAN

Frankie Vaughan, born in Liverpool on Friday 3 February 1928, travelled to London in April 1950, after borrowing money from his father. He bulldozed his way into an audition in April 1950 with a noted theatre agent, who promised him a trial at the Empire during week commencing Monday 8 May 1950.

*Frankie Vaughan*

Frankie Vaughan would be unpaid for his performance, not billed and told he would be dismissed if the audience didn't like him. He was an outstanding success leading to a £100 per week variety tour, commencing immediately. He rocketed to record fame in 1955 with his best selling song 'Give Me the Moonlight, Give Me the Girl', followed by such hits as 'Garden of Eden' and 'The Green Door'.

Frankie Vaughan topped the bill at practically every theatre in the UK and appeared on the London stage in musicals. He featured in nine films and was a regular performer on television. He died of heart failure at his High Wycombe home on Friday 17 September 1999, aged 71.

## 1952 – MR BOBBY DENNIS

Bobby Dennis a twenty-six year old singing comedian was progressing in the theatre world and appeared at the Empire during week commencing Monday 20 October 1952. He supported the comedian, Gladys Morgan. During the week he was taken ill with acute fibrositis but insisted in completing all his twelve shows during the week, although in severe pain. Immediately after his last performance on Saturday evening he was taken by ambulance to hospital where he remained for a few days. He did, on strict doctors orders, cancel his following week's engagement.

Bobby Dennis was born in Hull in 1926, left school at the age of thirteen to join a theatre touring show 'We're in the Army Now,' giving a false name and age before the police found him and returned him to Hull to complete his education. Upon officially leaving school at the age of fifteen he returned to the theatre and performed in many theatres before being called up as a paratrooper during the second world war. He was seriously injured in an explosion in Palestine and spent a year in hospital overcoming his injuries.

Returning to the UK after making a full recovery, he re-started his music hall career, marrying Miss Jean Bradford, another performer in 1952, His career developed in the 1950s and 60s. principally as a comedian but also an excellent singer and piano player regularly touring Australia and South Africa. In the UK Bobby Dennis appeared in numerous television shows with stars such as Dave Allen, The Bachelors, Shirley Bassey and featured in the hit comedy shows 'It Ain't Half Hot Mum' in 1975 and 'Hi De Hi' in 1981. He enjoyed almost continuous employment during the later years performing in pantomime, summer shows, revues and on cruise ships.

Bobby Dennis's last ever performance was at the Royal Hippodrome Theatre in Eastbourne with Roy Hudd and Anita Harris in 2019 at the ripe old age of 93! He died in November 2020 at the age of 94. A real show business trouper.

# ROTHERHITHE HIPPODROME

*Rotherhithe Hippodrome*

## 1897 – THE TERRISS

Probably one of England's finest actors, William Terriss, born William Charles James Lewin, had taken a leading interest in a syndicate planning to build a theatre in Rotherhithe. He had already commenced negotiations to purchase a plot of land, on the corner of Lower Road and Culling Road, hoping to finalise the details of the contract on behalf of the syndicate, on Friday 17 December 1897.

Unfortunately, he was brutally murdered the evening before, by Mr Richard Arthur Prince. Terriss was about to enter the Adelphi Theatre, London, for his evening performance in Mr William Gillette's drama, 'Secret Service', when he was fatally stabbed by Prince.

The plans for the theatre progressed after Mr Terriss's death, the syndicate partners, headed by chairman, Mr S. Marler, were also involved in the Coronet and Brixton theatres and a further one, under construction, in New Camden. They appointed Mr W. G. R. Sprague, the famous theatre architect, to design their new building, constructed by Mr Walter Wallis of Balham, costing £35,000 and able to seat to 3,000. It was decided to name the theatre after William Terriss.

The classic design of the exterior was in red brick faced with York stone and was regarded as one of Sprague's finest designs in line with his belief that the exteriors of a theatre should be beautiful, prominent, imposing and be an architectural beauty. This was clearly illustrated with his design of The Terriss.

The interior was equally breathtaking, generally in a Louis Quatorze style, it had tints of cream and gold giving it a bright and cheerful appearance. There were two tiers, no pillars to obstruct the view of the stage and the auditorium measured 75ft square. The stage 68ft by 28ft, was completed by a double asbestos fire-proof curtain and a red plush stage curtain fringed in gold tassels. The ceiling was truly magnificent with a painted centrepiece and matching side panels with beautiful mouldings.

## 1899 – OPENING

On Saturday afternoon 16 October 1899, Mr Richard Mansell, general manager, welcomed a number of specially invited dignitaries and guests to hear Mr E. G. Saunders, the theatre's managing director, and Sprague, the architect, thanking everyone for attending and wishing the theatre every success in the future. He assured all residents of Rotherhithe that his theatre would satisfy their needs as admittance prices would be 2p for the gallery and 4p for the pit, the presentations would be fit for all ages with variety, drama and musicals.

Dr. Hopkins, vicar of St John's, Notting Hill, said in his speech that he believed drama and entertainment to be a social necessity. He followed his speech with a blessing saying he hoped churches would be as popular as the theatre. He closed his address by wishing the Terriss Theatre every success in the future. The guests of honour, Miss Ellaline Terriss, William Terriss's daughter, accompanied by her famous actor husband, Mr Seymour Hicks, thanked the audience for their kind words, especially those immediately following her father's tragic death. The reception they received was tremendous, they were called to the stage to receive a standing ovation from the enthusiastic audience. The evening concluded with selections from Carmen, Faust, The Belle of New York and the Festival March specially composed by Mr Louis La Rondelle, the orchestra leader.

At 7pm on the following Monday 18 October 1899, The Terriss officially opened to the public, with the orchestra playing the National Anthem to a capacity audience. The performance was 'The White Heather', direct from Drury Lane, London and starred Miss Susie Vaughan as Lady Janet MacLintock, Mr Julian Royce as Lord Angus Cameron and Dick Beach as Mr Wilfred Taylor. The music again was provided by Mr Louis La Rondelle. The following week's attraction was the drama 'Thou Shalt Not Kill'.

## 1900

Lessees changed a number of times in the early 1900s. The first one, on Monday 20 August 1900, was Messrs George Conquest Jnr and Herbert Leonard. They opened with Leonard's drama 'On Active Service'. It starred Mr Harry Powell as the Hero, Dick Foster; Frank Litchfield as Jim Thornbury; Mr Fred W. Leonard as Count Frisson; Mr Arthur Conquest as Horatio Nelson and Miss Ethel Rayner as Winifred.

## 1904 – FIRE

On Friday 2 December 1904, the theatre was almost destroyed by fire. The drama, 'A Dangerous Woman' was being played and the theatre, cleared around 10.30pm was duly locked and bolted. Around 2.00am the following morning a fire broke out filling the theatre with smoke. It started in an indoor skip, used for the removal of unwanted scenery and other general rubbish. The night-shift theatre fireman immediately used one of the fire hoses to control the blaze until the Fire Brigade arrived and quickly extinguished it. Some damage was done to the theatre through heat, smoke and water, but the performances were able to continue that evening.

## 1907 – THE HIPPODROME THEATRE

On Friday 15 November 1907, Mr Walter Gibbons, on behalf of the new owners, London Theatre of Varieties Ltd, (LTV), who owned theatres such as the Standard Theatre in Shoreditch, the Grand in Islington, Prince's in Poplar, and of course The Terriss; applied to the London County Council to change the licence. He wanted to change from nightly legitimate drama to two houses per night of variety/music hall in order to improve audience figures. This was granted on the condition that intoxicating liquor must not be sold. Gibbons decided that The Terriss Theatre would now be called the Hippodrome Theatre.

Being part of the powerful LTV Group enabled them to present more varied shows and therefore attracting larger audiences after struggling financially over the past few years. The opening variety act in December 1907 was the famous strongman and wrestler from Estonia, George Hackenschmidt, billed as 'The Russian Lion'.

*George Hackenschmidt*

Success followed during the first world war with a mixture of variety and revues with many different types of entertainment presented. This ranged from dramas such as 'Colonel Cobb', 'The Hairdresser', 'All Stop Here' to variety with artistes such as Walter Emerson, Wilson Hallett and the Carina Sisters. From 1918 to 1921, Mr Wallis Rice, the lessee, introduced revue in addition to variety, which proved very successful.

## 1927 – CHANGE OF USE

In January 1927, Mr C. Gulliver, managing director of London Theatres of Varieties Ltd, the owners of the Hippodrome since 1907, although leasing it to numerous people, some successful and some not, were approached by Mr A. E. Abrahams, the millionaire bill-poster and theatre owner with an offer to purchase their beloved Hippodrome.

This would result in the theatre being converted into a cinema, as would the other theatres Mr Abrahams had included in the deal, Kilburn Empire, Grand Clapham, Palace Hammersmith, Hippodrome Lewisham, Hippodrome Ilford, Empire Islington, Olympia Shoreditch, Hippodrome Willesden and Poplar Hippodrome. They would be in addition to Abrahams' numerous other theatres in Greater London, Liverpool, Glasgow and Margate The total deal for these eleven theatres was in excess of £1million. These theatres would be converted into cinemas over a period of a few months but it was felt to be a serious blow to the fortunes of theatre performers who would have their earning opportunities reduced.

The Hippodrome closed in August 1927. The new owners embarked on an extensive refurbishment and improvement programme. The hall was throughly cleaned, redecorated, and re-upholstered. Crimson tip-up seating was fitted and many other improvements made. From a technical point of view, a new operating box was installed and fitted with two Simplex projectors, a Jupiter Bulman screen, a Mustel organ and new, modern lighting.

## RE-OPENING

On Monday 5 September 1927, the famous film and stage actresses, Miss Fannie Ward, an American and Miss Gladys Jennings from London, officially opened the Hippodrome.

*Fannie Ward*      *Gladys Jennings*

The films presented were Tom Mix in 'The Last Trial' and 'Derby's Reward' followed by a live performance of the revue, 'The Whirlwind'. The management agreed to continue presenting films and live variety as that format was attracting huge audiences.

To celebrate their first birthday as a cinema, on Wednesday 5 September 1928, the management presented a 'carnival night' where the Mayor and Mayoress of Bermondsey and the local MP accepted an invitation to celebrate the event.

## 1929

Cinema sound was expanding rapidly and many cinemas were installing sophisticated equipment. The Hippodrome followed suit on Sunday 23 June 1929 with the showing of the talking and singing film, 'Weary River'. This 86 minute hybrid film, part speaking and part silent, starred Richard Barthelmess and Betty Compson making it one of the first films to feature the change-over.

*Film Poster 'Weary River'*

## 1930

On Thursday 14 August 1930, it was announced that Mr A. E. Abrahams had disposed of all his cinemas to the new Associated British Cinemas (ABC) Group. It was formed in 1928 by Mr John Maxwell to show films made at the famous Elstree Studios. The ABC cinema group would become a familiar sight on the British high street for many years. This business deal included the Hippodrome, and the management of the ABC group closed it for refurbishment on Thursday 11 June 1931.

## 1932

The Hippodrome received a 'make-over' in November 1932. A secondary lighting system was fitted, the provision of a new waiting room, separate entrances to different parts of the cinema were established, refurbishment of the orchestra pit and completed with the painting of the interior and exterior.

## 1941

The Hippodrome was leased by the ABC Group to an independent operator on Sunday 31 August 1941. Unfortunately, the outbreak of the Second World War put a halt to the entertainment offered by the Hippodrome. It was forced to close its doors in June 1943 due to the continuous bombing of the London Docklands.

## 1943

Mr A. A. Shenburn of Suburban Century Cinemas Ltd. took the lease in June 1943 and decided to concentrate on live entertainment again after a refurbishment of the theatre. It was re-opened on Monday 20 September 1943 by the Mayor of Bermondsey, who welcomed the return of continuous live entertainment at the Hippodrome. Topping the bill that night was Billy Reid and his Accordion Band, supported by Dorothy Squires, singer; Joe Young, comedian; Avon & Hall, jugglers; Claude Lester, comedian; Arthur Knott, comedy dancer and the Panama Dancing group. After a few weeks of variety, in December 1943, it was followed by number of plays and melodramas presented by the Benson Repertory Company.

## 1944/48 – THE END

The play, 'Rebecca' by Daphne du Maurier, was being performed by the Benson Repertory Company with Harley Walter, Marie Hast, Bernard J. Benson, Leon Reeves and Edwina Howell in the cast. The following week's Benson production would have been 'While Parents Sleep' billed as London's 'Naughtiest Comedy'!

The bombing during 1944 in the Docklands area was intense. In June the nearby Town Hall was severely damaged by one of the V1 'Doodlebugs', a form of ballistic missile, and was finally destroyed by a direct hit in November 1944. In the same bombing raid, the Hippodrome was left as a burnt out shell, but fortunately the theatre was closed and no one was injured.

Attempts were made to sell the damaged theatre. On Wednesday 12 December 1945 it was offered for auction, along with twelve other theatres owned by Loughborough Playhouses Ltd, at Goddard & Smith Auctioneers of St James's, London.

There were no offers. It was placed for auction once again in April 1948 but again there no takers and the wrecked building continued to deteriorate. What a sad end to a theatre which was little known outside of Rotherhithe, it had lasted less than fifty years before suffering such a painful, lingering and undignified demise.

**1955**

The Hippodrome stood for over ten years in its badly damaged condition, neglected and forlorn with the advertisement covered safety curtain still hanging ghostly from what remained of the stage. Now, in an even worse dilapidated state, no attempts had been made to effect any repairs, weather-proofing or rebuilding, and so the only answer was complete demolition. The ruins of the Hippodrome were demolished in June and July 1955 to be replaced by the Rotherhithe Free Church buildings.

The Terriss/Hippodrome lasted less than fifty years as a theatre and, latterly as a cinema and many famous artistes had appeared there over the years. The growth of easy transport to the more palatial and superior theatres of the West End of London was of growing concern. It had been unlikely to continue much longer. If the bombing had not intervened, it would have probably been one of the first ones to be closed in the 1950s due to falling audience numbers.

A real shame for such a beautiful building.

## DID YOU KNOW...?

### 1897 – MR WILLIAM TERRISS

Mr William Terriss made his first stage appearance at the Prince of Wales Theatre, Birmingham in 1868 at the age of 21, appearing in the West End at the old Prince of Wales Theatre, two years later. He married Jessie Millward in 1870, eventually having a son, Tom and a daughter, Ellaline who was invited to open The Terriss Theatre in 1899. His

*William Terriss*

outstanding acting skills, voice, demeanour and good looks made him one of Britain's most popular actors, in demand at every theatre.

On Thursday 16 December 1897 Terriss was starring in 'Secret Service' at the Adelphi Theatre, in the Strand, London, when he was stabbed to death by Mr Richard Arthur Prince who had a long hatred of Terriss.

Prince had often appeared in his plays, latterly 'The Harbour Lights'. Eventually, he was dismissed due to his dependancy on alcohol and his mental problems. Feeling sorry for him, Terriss regularly gave him money and tried to find him acting work. Prince was desperate for paid work, but found it impossible because of his reputation of being unreliable and irresponsible.

Prince had approached Terriss earlier in the morning of the murder, asking as usual, for more money and they were seen arguing. This request for money was refused but Terriss said he would try to help him.

Terriss entered the Adelphi through the Royal door, which he used as his own personal entrance. Prince had concealed himself in a nearby doorway waiting for Terriss to approach the theatre. As Terriss was walking through his stage entrance, Price stabbed him in the back at least twice and once in the heart, causing him to collapse onto the floor.

Terriss was carried into the theatre by fellow actors and stage staff but died within minutes from the amount of blood lost from the wound to his heart. Prince did not try to leave the Adelphi, he stood in the stage door entrance until arrested, was taken to Bow Street Police Station, and was charged with murder.

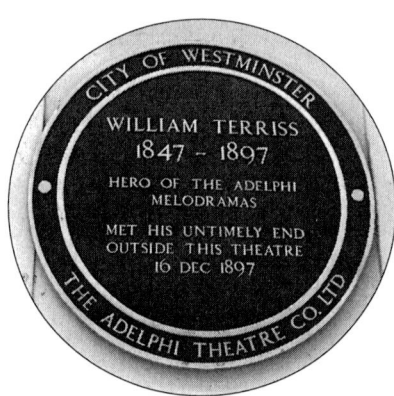

*William Terriss Memorial Plaque*

Court proceedings commenced on Monday 10 January 1898 and four days later on Friday 14 January the Jury returned a guilty verdict but the Judge spared him from hanging by deciding that Prince must be detained as a 'criminal lunatic' in Broadmoor Prison for the Criminally Insane, where he remained until he died in 1936. He was apparently a model prisoner organising a wide range of entertainment for other inmates such as choirs, plays, concerts etc.

Mr William Terriss's body was taken to Brompton Cemetery on Tuesday 21 December 1897. It was reported that over 50,000 people lined the streets to witness the funeral procession of over 100 carriages. Two hearses were required to specially carry the flowers. He left his fortune of £20,000 to his two children as his wife was independently wealthy. On the centenary of his death, Sir Donald Sinden, unveiled a memorial plaque to him at the Adelphi Theatre. The ghost of William Terriss is rumoured to haunt the theatre to this very day!

## 1905 – MR ALFRED RUSSELL

Describing himself as a comedian, fifteen year old, Mr Alfred Russell from Blackpool, was charged at the Tower Bridge Police Court on Tuesday 26 December 1905, with stealing two silver watches, a gold neck chain and locket and £1 in silver, belonging to Mrs Lewis, a landlady, of Rotherhithe.

Russell, who had a fascination for the stage, obtained employment in the summer of 1905 at a local Blackpool theatre as a programme seller and call-boy. In November 1905, desperate for a stage career, he travelled to London, was promised a 'trial' at the Star Music Hall, Bermondsey and at The Terriss but with no guarantees.

On the strength of these two trials, Russell secured lodgings with Mrs Lewis, by lying to her that he had been engaged at The Terriss at a salary of £5 per week. Mrs Lewis was suspicious, accompanied Russell to the theatre for verification, where he absconded through the stage door, and was arrested in another property some hours later. He was later accused of also stealing £10 from those premises.

Russell when found guilty on the first charge, wept bitterly, and he was sent to a reformatory.

## 1907 – MR ROBERT WOOD

Murder associated with the Rotherhithe Hippodrome reared its head again when Mr Robert Wood was charged in the Old Bailey of murdering Miss Phyllis Dimmock on Friday 13 December 1907. It was one of the most remarkable criminal trials for 50 years, due to the confusion and complexity of the case as witnesses differed in their account of the situation. The accused, Wood, a skilled sketching artist, was unfazed by the proceedings, and continued with his calm, relaxed and casual attitude during the six day trial.

The jury retired at 7.45pm on Wednesday 18 December 1907. Wood walked casually around the Court and commenced sketching the Judge, Mr Justice Grantham, and other members of the Court. A short while later, the Foreman of the Jury announced a 'Not Guilty' verdict and the Judge immediately discharged Wood. Outside the Old Bailey were thousands of fans all chanting his name and, when he appeared, they gave him three cheers and a standing ovation.

Mr Walter Gibbons who also controlled The Standard Theatre in Shoreditch, the Hippodrome in Woolwich as well as the Hippodrome in Rotherhithe, engaged Wood to perform twice nightly at those three theatres for one week, causing aggravation in the London theatre world. It was planned that during the following week he would be engaged at the Clapham, Balham and Holborn Empires.

It was alleged that his fee would be £50 per week per theatre, for a 'turn' of fifteen minutes, for presenting his thoughts of the outcome of the Court case, often illustrated by his sketches using a black crayon on white paper.

Gibbons's proposals caused outrage. Professional variety artistes objected most strongly to Wood's 'turn'. They demanded that the theatre organisation, 'The Grand Order of Water Rats' send a letter of protest to Gibbons expressing their feelings. Such was the level of disgust, that many genuine artistes said they would refuse to appear at any of the theatres where Wood had performed. At that point Wood was persuaded to abandon his plans of a theatre career, his act did not take place as planned, and the proposal was shelved.

## 1909 – MR JOHN ABRAMS

On Friday, 30 April 1909, after completing his performance at the Hippodrome, gymnast Mr John Abrams, was issued with a warrant for his arrest. He was charged with neglecting his daughter by failing to pay Southwark Guardians (the local Workhouse) the sum of 36p per week for looking after her whilst appearing at theatres in the North of England. The total debt outstanding was £28, In his defence, he said that he had only worked for six weeks in the last year and had no money to pay the Guardians.

It was agreed that Abrams would remove his daughter from the workhouse, make arrangements for repaying the £28 as he was currently earning a regular £3 per week from theatre work and could now meet his financial obligations.

## 1910 – SIX BROTHERS LUCK

On Thursday 1 September 1910, the 'Six Brothers Luck', a popular group of musical performers, were assaulted on their way through Bermondsey. They were appearing for the week at the Rotherhithe Hippodrome and the Peckham Hippodrome, in a double engagement.

After first performing at the Peckham Hippodrome, their bus was attacked by a gang of youths who threw large pieces of stone and granite towards the bus, the larger pieces entered the vehicle, injuring three of them. Mr Dan Wetherall, their leader, was knocked unconscious and suffered cuts to his ear. Mr William Britton received a serious wound on his head and a third member of the group, Mr Bernard Hall, also had deep cuts to his head and hand. All three were taken to Guy's Hospital for attention. Wetherall was detained overnight, the other two were released after treatment. They were unable to perform at either venue for the remainder of the week.

## 1914 – LES MARCELLIS

A large number of acts performing at the Hippodrome involved animals and every care was taken with them. However, there were occasions when the artistes may have overlooked the rules. On Tuesday 21 July 1914, at the Tower Bridge Police Court, London, Mr Ross Bassi Marcellis and his wife Mrs Sansowa Marcellis of the acrobatic act 'Les Marcellis' were each fined 50p for cruelty to a dog.

The National Canine Defence League (NCDL) brought the case against 'Les Marcellis' for excess cruelty. They reported that, as the dog entered the stage, it looked terrified, was thrown 3ft into the air, twisted, landing on Mr Marcellis's left hand with its forefeet. He turned the dog over, made it stand on one paw on his thumb followed by making it climb a ladder, having to use its lower jaw to enable it to do so and was made to stand on Mr Marcellis's head.

Mr Walter Betts, superintendent of the Animal Hospital Institute, Knightsbridge, stated that, in his opinion, the performance was un-natural, the training must have been cruel as the dog was clearly distressed. Mr Marcellis said he had been presenting his act for over six years without complaint, he assured the Court that his act would never perform in England again and they would return home to France.

The Magistrates found the case to be very distasteful and agreed it was cruel to treat a dog in such a manner, making an order for the dog to be handed over to the NCDL and not be returned to Mr & Mrs Marcellis.

## 1920 – MR HARRY WOODS

An accident took place at the Hippodrome in May 1920, resulting in a Court case on Friday 6 May 1921. Mr Harry Woods, a professional dancer and teacher, sued the Hippodrome for compensation. Woods, dancing on stage with his troupe, 'The Four Evening Stars', allegedly caught his foot on a bolt protruding two inches from the stage floor, badly wrenching his knee. He completed his performance, although in acute pain, and had to be assisted to his lodgings and then to his home. Following a medical examination it was found that Woods had severely damaged the ligaments in his knee and had to use a walking stick. He would never be able to perform or teach dance again, after a thirty year career, therefore losing his livelihood.

The proprietor of the Hippodrome, Mr Wallis Rice, said that a bolt was not visible on the stage and the accident could not have taken place as described, producing witnesses to that effect. Mr Justice McCardie awarded Woods £600 for damages and costs as he was satisfied the accident had occurred as alleged.

## 1922 – MISS RUTH HEMMING

On Thursday 26 October 1922, Miss Ruth Hemming appeared before His Honour Judge Sir Thomas Granger at the Southwark County Court. She was bringing an action against Mr J. Zussman and Mr H. Eckstein, proprietors of the Rotherhithe Hippodrome, seeking £18 for alleged breach of contract.

Miss Hemming stated that she was engaged to take the part of singer and dancer in the revue, 'Chic Chic 1922' at a weekly salary of £6 plus extra payment for matinees. Prior to the Hippodrome engagement, the revue had been appearing in Leicester but the remainder of the tour was cancelled, the cast receiving their notices but was asked to 'keep in touch' with the producers office in London should it be opened again. She failed to contact them on one occasion, found that all the remainder members of the cast had been re-engaged except herself.

Judge Granger agreed with Miss Hemming that there had been a breach of contract and awarded her £12 with costs.

## 1922 – MISS KATERINA BOCCA

Another sad event associated with the Hippodrome was on Sunday 19 November 1922. 'Bandmaster Guy' a musician, appearing at the theatre, witnessed the tragic event from his hotel bedroom. Miss Katerina Bocca fell 65ft to her death from a fourth floor window directly opposite him.

At the Westminster Coroners inquest on Saturday 25 November 1922 it was reported that there had been a dispute between Miss Bocca's fiancé and her father over the dinner table, where six people were present. This resulted in the fiancé being ordered to leave the house. The fiancé returned to his own nearby flat, but decided to re-visit Miss Bocca's flat. Whilst walking along the street he saw her fall from the window landing on the pavement at his feet. She died a few hours later.

The Coroner heard all the evidence but stated he was perplexed at the statements made as the other five people in attendance had not witnessed Miss Bocca falling through a window measuring nineteen inches and guarded by two iron rails. A doctor stated that there were no marks on the body suggesting foul play. The Coroner returned an open verdict.

## 1923 – MR 'KID' LEWIS

On Tuesday 20 February 1923, Messrs Alexander Share, Nathan Clear and Hyman Eckstein, proprietors of the Hippodrome, appeared before Mr Justice Aston at the Kings Bench Division. They were seeking damages against Mr 'Kid' Lewis, the well known boxer, for breach of contract. Lewis had entered into a contract to perform at the theatre for week commencing Monday 28 June 1922 where maximum audiences were expected, as he had previously filled other theatres. Mr Lewis refused to appear unless he received more money, this was refused as a contract had been signed. As a result, another less popular

Kid Lewis

boxer had been engaged resulting in the theatre losing considerable income and they were seeking damages of £341, the estimated loss in profits.

On Thursday 22 February 1922, the matter was settled out of Court with Lewis agreeing to pay the sum of £341. Mr Justice Acton said it was a very satisfactory conclusion of the action and Lewis should be congratulated for his gesture.

Lewis was born in London on Saturday 28 October 1893, became the World Welterweight Champion and was ranked in the top fifty of the top hundred fighters. He was the seventeenth best welterweight of all time and the seventh best UK boxer. He fought 303 fights and won 232 of them, 80 by a knock-out, had 23 draws and 46 losses. Following his retirement he had an active business life, becoming a bookmaker, travel agent, boxing referee and organising charity events using his name to raise funds. He died in London on Tuesday, 20 October 1970, aged 77.

## 1926 – MISS DOROTHY MULLORD

On Saturday 2 January 1926, Miss Dorothy Mullord, the famous theatre playwright and actor, and Mr C. A. Baker, also an actor, were travelling from Collin's Music Hall in London to the Hippodrome. They were involved in a serious car accident. They both suffered deep cuts to the head and face, and were taken to Guy's Hospital where their wounds were treated. Unfortunately Miss Mullord's injuries were so severe she required an operation the following day.

## 1942 – MR CHARLES MAHONEY

On Sunday 6 December 1942, Mr Charles Mahoney, the cinema manager, was counting the takings in his office at the side of the pay-box, and was approached by two soldiers who appeared at a window. One of them pushed a rifle through the window and said, *'this is a stick-up, give us the money, we need it'*. Mahoney, told them the money had been banked and telephoned the police, who eventually arrested the two soldiers.

# SHEFFIELD EMPIRE

*Sheffield Empire*

## 1869 – THE ALHAMBRA

In May 1867, the Union Billiard Saloon was opened in Union Street, Sheffield only operating for a short time. On Sunday 26 September 1869, Mr Edward Gascoigne acquired the property, and after significant conversion it was opened as the Alhambra Music Hall.

## 1874

On Saturday 30 May 1874, he was sued by his close neighbours, Messrs Foxon & Robinson, for carrying out further alterations by building a high wall which obliterated all light entering their engineering premises. They insisted that they had to use artificial lighting during the day time due to the lack of natural light and therefore, insufficient fresh air was entering their building.

At the same time, Gascoigne, in conjunction with his partner, Mr Walker, entered into discussions with Mr William Cooper who wished to purchase the theatre, and a deal was completed. Cooper immediately commenced refurbishing the Alhambra. He also purchased adjoining shops to enlarge the theatre, enabling it to seat upwards of 2,000 people. He opened two further entrances in Charles Street, enlarged the stage area and re-decorated it throughout. He hung several large and costly mirrors along the walls costing between eighty and ninety pounds each. A bar was installed under the circle. Four shops were built within the complex in order to generate further income.

## 1881

In November/December 1881 the owners of the Alhambra had to install enhanced fire safety as instructed by The Lord Chamberlain especially the building of a fire proof division between the stage and the auditorium. Whilst doing so, they took advantage of the six week closure by widening the proscenium arch and lifting the floor level of the seats on the ground floor to ensure a better view of the stage. In addition they re-decorated the interior, enlarged the majority of staircases and embellished the entrance foyer.

## 1882 – FIRE No 1

On Monday 29 May 1882, it was the opening night for the cast for that coming week's performance. They were Miss Franzini, a trick cyclist; Harry Dale, musician; Miss Lizzie Villers, Miss Rosa Blonde, Dick Wadeson, and the Brothers Ash.

Two days later on Wednesday 31 May 1882 at 10:30 pm the Brothers Ash had completed their act, and the audience and performers left the theatre after an excellent show enjoyed by all. At 11pm, one of the performers, Mr Harry Dale, in addition to the theatre manager, departed the building after a final inspection, leaving Miss Adkin, an employee, and her sister asleep in the sleeping quarters adjacent to the bar. Making a second inspection, the stage manager, Mr J. H. Glossop, ensured that all the gas jets were turned off, he locked the theatre and returned to his home.

At 3.35am the following morning, Thursday 1 June 1882, a young man passing the theatre noticed a cloud of smoke bellowing from the stage area of the theatre. He smelled burning and heard the crackle of fire, and immediately notified the local police and fire brigade. They attended within minutes. Their first task was to warn the two girls sleeping in the theatre of their potential danger and they were quickly escorted to safety.

Their second task was to inform local residents of the gravity of the fire, asking them to leave their properties and go to a place of safety. By this time the theatre was ablaze from end to end, they could see the flames advancing along the windows as each minute passed until the whole structure was one mass of flames.

Many firemen had lucky escapes, Two of them, Mr Sisson and Mr Scarfield were fighting the fire in the gallery when the roof collapsed burying them in burning timbers, slates and other debris. Fortunately both of them were able to extricate themselves and rush to safety without serious injury other than shock. By 4.30am nothing remained of the Alhambra, it was in ruins.

At daybreak, the owner, Cooper, was able to inspect the remains of the theatre. Everything was soaked in water, the once beautiful interior was full of charred beams. The seating and roof timbers were just a pile of smouldering debris. The very expensive mirrors had melted, due to the intense heat; all that remained of them were their twisted metal frames. The bar was wrecked, the ladies bedroom was destroyed and the dressing rooms, where the fire was thought to have started, unrecognisable. All the artistes' property was destroyed. Miss Franzini lost her silver plated cycle, and Harry Dale lost a set of thirteen, expensive silver bells, but luckily, he had taken his other instruments home.

Cooper, the theatre owner, had a permanent bedroom under the stage. However on that night he was visiting friends in Nottingham and rushed back to Sheffield upon hearing the terrible news. The theatre takings, documents and valuables were stored in a fire proof safe situated in the office and were saved. The majority of the artistes and musicians lost many personal possessions, and as a very kind gesture, local circus owner, Mr E. S. Drake placed his premises in Tudor Street at their disposal. Benefit performances were organised for the following Monday and Tuesday afternoons.

The total damage was estimated at between £10,000 and £18,000. Unfortunately the theatre was only insured for half of that amount as Cooper was awaiting a re-valuation in view of the improvements to the surrounding areas. A financial disaster for him.

## 1894 – THE EMPIRE

After acquiring the old Alhambra site, a new company, Sheffield Empire Palace Company (Ltd) was formed, on Friday 12 October 1894, by the famous theatre owner, Mr Horace Edward Moss. He appointed Mr Frank Matcham to design a new theatre on the site of the old Alhambra. The estimated cost would be £65,000; it would be able to accommodate an audience of 3,000 and be ready for opening in one year's time.

The end result was truly magnificent. Matcham had excelled himself. The Empire was a structure of pure beauty. The main frontage was situated in Charles Street and the central facade consisted of three arched openings which were flanked by a colonnade symbolic of 'Music and Art'. Situated on each of the two front corners were copper towers, one of which would play, or not, a large part in the theatre's future. The name 'Empire Palace' was emblazoned across the front of the building and included a figure of a boy carrying a 'flambeau' which lit up the night sky. As with the majority of Matcham's designs, an iron and glass verandah was installed along the front of the building. All the main entrances were beautifully decorated with glass ornaments, the floor was of marble, all the doors were of polished wood with coloured glass and the walls and stairwells were covered in rich leather paper.

Matcham ensured that all seats had an uninterrupted view of the stage. The first three rows of the circle formed the dress circle and the back six rows were the upper circle. Above that was a comfortable gallery with a promenade above that, reaching 60ft from the floor level. The auditorium was divided into the orchestra stalls with eight private boxes situated on the side walls.

The draperies and seating were in a green and bronze colour and the general scheme of decoration was in a Flemish design. The ceiling was beautifully designed with central artwork, "A Dream of a Carnival' and with twenty-five expensive brass electric light fittings. Over the proscenium was a painting representing 'Music and Dancing'.

The stage opening was 30ft wide, the depth 33ft, the height from the stage to the grid was 50ft. The finest stage facilities were provided including the latest traps, bridges, separate paint room and, importantly, quality dressing rooms containing every comfort. Safety was paramount. There were seven emergency exits from the ground floor, five from the circle and four from the gallery, all leading via fireproof stairwells to the streets. Numerous fire hydrants were conveniently placed around the theatre. Iron doors were fitted behind the stage and the obligatory asbestos fire curtain was provided.

Matcham ensured that the audience were comfortable and installed a ventilation system providing fresh air from pipes fed into the building by tubes and there were inlet ventilators via shafts formed in the ceiling. He also fitted a large sliding roof in the centre of the ceiling to ensure a regular temperature at all times. As a safety measure, all energy was provided by electricity as gas was not permitted in the building.

## 1895 – OPENING

On the opening night of Monday 4 November 1895, at 7.30pm, Mr Frank Allen, general manager, appeared on the stage and thanked everyone involved in the construction of the Empire, especially Matcham for his outstanding design. He welcomed onto the stage, the managing director, Mr H. E. Moss who had been instrumental in every aspect of the theatre from the original site inspection to planning the opening evening. He recommended that a debt of gratitude be given to Moss for providing Sheffield with one of the finest theatres in the world. This was received with a standing ovation from the audience.

Allen promised only the most popular acts would appear on its stage, as indicated by that evening's performers. Leading them were Cora Stuart and her Company in her sketch 'The Fair Equestrienne', with Douglas Cox as Charles Kinghorn and Mr S. Dark as Lord Loftus. This act was followed by Salerno, juggler; Lottie Lynn, singer; Will Evans, musician; F. W. Millis, ventriloquist; Oakland & Thompson, operatic duettist; Franz Family, acrobats; Miss Nellie Christie, singer and Spry & Austin, comedians.

All the acts were accompanied by the Empire Grand Orchestra under the leadership of Mr Ralph Booth. The admission prices were £1.55p for a private box, 10p for the stalls, 7p for the grand circle, 5p for the upper circle and 2p for the gallery.

On Friday 27 September 1895, the management applied for a full public licence for their new premises to the Sheffield Court which provoked a great deal of opposition. Letters were received by the Court from the Chief Constables of Edinburgh and Birmingham in support of the licence, stating that the Empire management were very suitable people to possess a drinks licence. Mr W. Thompson and Mr H. E. Moss from the Empire Palace Company were called, but it was in vain.

There was a great deal of resistance to the licence. It was alleged that large amounts of money were paid to some artistes, as much as £200 per week which was obscene and should not be permitted. The opposition was supported by a letter signed by thirty-three clergymen of all faiths. The licence application was refused.

## 1901

However this decision was over-ruled six years later on Thursday 10 October 1901. As a result of this reversal, the management had to make a number of structural alterations to the fabric of the building. The stalls bar had to be rebuilt with steel columns, requiring the floor to be lowered. The other locations in the circle and gallery were altered, coffee machines and refreshments were removed, replaced with bars selling all types of alcohol. New seating and lighting was fitted. This decision was overturned yet again by the Licensing Committee within a few years and the Empire remained dry once again.

## 1902

On Saturday 20 December 1902, the directors of the Empire made a strategic decision to change the direction in which they managed the theatre, and this had a serious effect on its future. With effect from Monday 22 December 1902, there were to be two identical performances each evening, rather than the traditional one. Each show would last just short of two hours, starting at 7pm and 9pm with no interval, allowing 10/15 minutes for the audience change-over. All possible reasons for delays in the presentation were eliminated, the number of 'turns' would be the same but their acts would be shortened by a few minutes. As one act finished, the music for the next one would be played.

The doors would open at 6.15pm for the first performance, (7pm start) and 8.30pm for the second, (9pm start). Admission into the theatre was made easier as additional waiting rooms and seating areas were to be made available within the building for patrons to use whilst the existing show was either being prepared or concluded.

In addition, the directors changed the configuration of the seating, and the pricing structure, to make it easier to understand and be more convenient for patrons. The demarkations between the seats in the stalls and pit were removed, as was the one between the grand circle and the upper circle. All seating would be replaced with the new 'tip-up' type. The gallery and amphitheatre areas would also be merged and new upholstered seats with backs, replacing the old, uncomfortable wooden structures. As a result of this change there would only be five admission prices instead of the existing eight.

All these alterations, new fittings etc would take place during the next two days, the theatre would re-open on Monday 22 December 1902. The theatre opened as planned to two full houses, all the new arrangements worked to perfection and the audiences seemed well satisfied.

A special meeting of the Stage Plays Licensing Committee of the Sheffield City Council was held on Friday 2 January 1903 to consider reports from the Fire Brigade. This followed their review of the safety implications on the change to two performances per evening. A detailed discussion took place and the Committee felt that the theatre was built with two performances in mind, there were seventeen exits allowing people to vacate the theatre in two minutes in the case of an emergency. The committee agreed to allow the waiting audience to converge in the theatre bars whilst awaiting entrance to their seats rather than wait outside in the streets in the cold and rain and in danger of nearby passing trams.

## 1907

The Empire nearly did not have a future. On Wednesday 21 March 1907, a passing policeman in the early hours of the morning noticed smoke bellowing from what he thought was the Empire. He raised the alarm, the fire brigade arrived and established that the fire was not at the Empire but located in an adjoining ballroom, which was ruined, but the Empire escaped damage.

## 1927

During the early 1900s, the Empire attracted the top stars of the day such as George Robey, Will Hay, Robb Wilton, both George Formby Snr, & Jnr,

Gracie Fields. Wee Georgie Wood, etc., but decided on a change of direction in the late 1920s. George Formby Jnr had commenced with his revue, 'Formby Seeing Life' on Monday 20 June 1927, a comedy of a Wigan man winning £5,000 in a lottery and purchasing a greyhound.

He was assisted by The Olracs, gymnasts; Jennie Howard, singer; The Grainger Girls, dancers and the Four Conchords, singers, the show ending on Saturday 25 June 1927. This was to be the last variety show.

The management decided to announce a ten week closure of the theatre in order to carry out a full refurbishment and modernisation programme, due to the change of policy by Moss Empire Ltd, reversing the December 1902 decision. Plays and drama would now take priority over variety and revert back to the one show per evening formula, leaving two shows per evening of variety to the nearby Lyceum Theatre.

There would be a number of significant changes. The public would not be permitted to queue outside and would be allowed to enter the various waiting rooms one hour prior to the start of the performance. The Union Street entrance to the pit stalls was sealed off, the area converted to a waiting area with new carpets, chairs and settees and magazines along with tea, coffee and other refreshments being available.

The auditorium was fully re-decorated, the ground floor and balcony were re-seated and re-carpeted. The orchestra pit was enlarged to accommodate thirty musicians. The ground floor was raised by 4 cm, the stage floor floodlights were hidden in a trough to avoid being seen in front of the performers. The ventilation system was improved to ensure all year round comfortable temperatures and new lighting was installed, The stage itself saw many improvements. A new oak floor, new curtains, and two and a half miles of new ropes were fitted for raising and lowering the 'cloths'.

Perhaps the most significant improvement concerned the dressing rooms. Previously cold, dark and drab, they were replaced by seventeen new ones. The 'star' one having a private toilet, bathroom, wardrobes, easy chairs and fitted curtains. Finally an instruction was issued that every morning at 9.30am they should be cleaned, dusted, disinfected and on Mondays, a box containing sewing thread, thimble, a pair of scissors and a tape measure would be placed in every room.

The re-opening performance was on Monday 29 August 1927 at 7pm, when the audience enjoyed Captain H. M. Harwood's new four act play, 'The

Golden Calf' starring Margaret Bannerman, Nicholas Hannen, Mabel Terry-Lewis and Raymond Massey. The prices of admission on that evening were 26p in the dress circle, 24p in the grand circle and stalls, 17p in the pit stalls and 12p for the front row of the balcony. The following week that production would transfer to the Globe Theatre in London.

It quickly reverted back to variety!

## 1930s

The theatre's success continued into the 1930s when established stars such as Gracie Fields, Naughton & Gold, Wee Georgie Wood, Max Miller, Albert Modley, Old Mother Riley with her 'daughter' Kitty, Billy Cotton and his Band, Elsie & Doris Waters, Louis Armstrong, Flanagan & Allen etc. all performed. Many hundreds of performers appeared on this famous stage in these very successful and profitable years often attracting full houses. The commencement of the second world war in 1939 witnessed the leading stars of the time appearing at the Empire including Frank Randle, Ted Ray, Max Wall, Lupino Lane, Wilson, Kepple and Betty.

*Lupino Lane*

*Wilson, Kepple & Betty*

## 1940 – BOMB DAMAGE

The Empire was a very popular theatre and attracted enormous crowds all through the Blitz, even though Sheffield experienced dozens of air raids with seventy-two barrage balloons flying over the city. However on the night of Thursday 12 December 1940, Henry Hall and his Orchestra topped the bill and were playing their popular hits of the day. As they began to play 'Six Lessons', a tremendous explosion from a nearby bomb rocked the Empire to its foundations.

The Manager, Mr Fred Neate, entered the stage and asked the audience to vacate the theatre, but they were prevented from doing so as many fires were raging in the nearby buildings and streets. Unable to leave safely, they descended into the theatre's boiler house, situated in the cellar, enjoying an impromptu performance from Henry Hall and his Orchestra until it was safe to leave.

The Theatre suffered very extensive damage to its right elevation, especially to one of the two copper towers, which was destroyed, along with adjacent shop properties and buildings on either side. Battered, but unbowed, the Empire survived many other air raids and reopened a few weeks later but the copper tower was never replaced, giving the building a lop sided appearance.

## 1942 – FIRE No 2

Disaster struck again during the war but not as a result of bombing. On Monday 3 August 1942, at 9am, the stage door keeper, upon entering the theatre at the start of his shift, discovered a fire in the stage area and immediately called the Fire Brigade.

Fortunately the safety curtain and the brick built proscenium prevented the fire from spreading to the auditorium and other parts of the theatre, but the curtain was witnessed by firemen as 'bulging and twisting' under the intense heat. Fortunately it stayed intact and prevented the Empire from being totally destroyed. At the peak of the blaze, six fire engines with pumps worked feverishly to extinguish the fire. By sheer professionalism they managed to gain access to the fiercely blazing stage area and used a platform ladder to help extinguish the fire.

There was some damage to adjoining buildings caused by flying slates and sparks from the now destroyed roof above the stage, but these outbreaks were easily extinguished by the firemen. There was only one casualty of the fire when Company Officer Jeffcott, overcome by smoke whilst fighting the fire from inside the building, staggered outside, only to collapse in the street. He was taken to the local Royal Hospital where he recovered quickly.

Ernie Lotinga's new production 'The Gestapo' was due to open at the Empire the following Monday 10 August 1942 and the scenery costing £3,000 had been destroyed. Some costumes and wigs had also been badly damaged by smoke and water. The performance was booked for the Empire, Liverpool the following week, Monday 17 May 1942, and every possible carpenter, electrician, seamstress, scenic artist etc were summoned to re-make the damaged scenery and clothing. The show successfully fulfilled its engagement at Liverpool Empire.

There was a major problem associated with the re-building programme which could have run into many thousands of pounds. The Government had imposed a £100 spending limit on any repairs not associated with 'essential repairs' which would have resulted in complete closure of the Empire until the end of the war. Sheffield was left with only one operational theatre, the Lyceum. In 1930 there had been five, but within a short period of time the Government relented and gave special permission for the repair work on the stage area to be carried out.

## 1943

The Empire re-opened on Monday 6 September 1943, after a closure of eighteen months. The opening show was 'Dorchester Follies', starring Johnny Worthy and Bertie Jarrett as the main attraction. Also included on the bill were Maurice Winnick's band; Darita, gymnast; Jack Haig, comedian; Gladys Sewell, comedienne and Gray, Austin & Worth, jugglers.

## 1950s

Over the next ten years or so many famous acts were seen on the stage such as Jewel & Warriss, Harry Secombe, Florrie Desmond, Norman Evans, Charlie Chester, Max Bygraves, Donald Peers, Lupino Lane, Ruby Murray, The Mudlarks, Leslie Randall, Arthur Haynes plus many from the pre-war years.

The famous film comedians, Laurel & Hardy, appeared at the Empire in week commencing Monday 30 June 1952 as part of a thirty week theatre

*Stan Laurel*

tour which started in Peterborough on Monday 25 February 1952 and concluded in Cardiff on Saturday 4 October 1952. They returned for a further week's performance on Monday, 15 March 1954, part of their last ever tour due to Oliver Hardy's ill health.

The management attempted to attract audiences in the mid 1950s by presenting a series of American musicals, also many from London, including 'The King and I', 'Carousel', 'South Pacific', 'Guys and Dolls' etc but the lure of television was too much and the Empire suffered more years of dwindling audiences. The building was now in a poor structural state and it continued to deteriorate as there was insufficient finance to carry out essential repairs. Many of the needed repairs were as a result of the continuing effects of the war damage, therefore many people doubted its long term future.

**1959**

Mr Emile Littler's final pantomime, 'Babes in the Wood' commenced on Christmas Eve, Wednesday 24 December 1958, continuing until Saturday 21 February 1959. Heading the bill were two recording stars, Edna Savage and Laurie London who played the two babes, and were supported by Billy Burdon as Simple Simon, Roy Barbour as the Nurse, Hackford & Doyle as the Robbers, Wally Thomas as the Sheriff, Eugene's Flying Ballet and the Tiller Girls added skill and glamour to the show.

It was an unlucky final pantomime and probably summed up the plight of the Empire in the late 1950s. Edna Savage, was rushed into hospital on Monday 26 January 1959 for an abdominal operation and twelve year old Linda Breeze had to take over the part with little rehearsal. To make matters worse, at the same time, Edna's husband, pop star, Terry Dene was admitted into a Military Hospital suffering from exhaustion. It was to become more problematic as, at the end of the pantomime, Hackford & Doyle announced they were splitting their long standing partnership and would follow separate theatre careers.

## 1959 – THE END

Immediately following the pantomime, on Thursday 26 February 1959, the management announced that the Empire would close in a few week's time as it had been sold for £300,000 to Murrayfield Real Estate, with the site being developed into nineteen shops. This statement did not come as a surprise to anyone as audiences had been dwindling for a number of years due, probably, to unattractive programmes and lack of modern facilities in the theatre.

The Empire could not have had a better send off. On Saturday 2 May 1959, 'Smedley's Foods' had sponsored the final week of a variety show. They arranged for the audience to be allowed in 'free of charge' provided they pre-booked tickets by presenting a label from a tin of Smedley's Peas. This final show starred the famous northern comedian Albert Modley who gave the sell out audience a wonderful and unforgettable evening of entertainment befitting such a theatre.

Albert Modley was accompanied by Earl & Elgar, musical clowns; Big Chief Eagle Eye, knife thrower; Reggie Dennis, comedian and the J. W.

*Albert Modley sat in the auditorium*

Jackson dancers. After the show ended and the audience had long departed it is said that Albert Modley sat as a lonely figure in a stalls seat, and cried at the thought of the loss of yet another beautiful theatre. Music Hall was collapsing around him.

That was the end of the Empire, never to hear or see the comedians, vocalists, speciality acts, ventriloquists, dancers, animal acts, drama, musicians etc again. One good thing is that it did not sit deteriorating for years as many other theatres had, as an early demise was planned. It was demolished the following month in July 1959 and the building of the shops commenced immediately. The Empire had entertained the people of Sheffield in their thousands for almost 64 years. It was a sad blow to Sheffield as only two theatres remained, the Lyceum and the Playhouse, to serve a population of approaching half a million people.

As is traditional with old theatres, the Empire was reputedly haunted by two ghosts, one man who met his death by falling from the tower on the night of the bombing and the second being a performer who hanged himself in the theatre.

Goodbye and farewell to a wonderful centre of entertainment.

## DID YOU KNOW...?

## 1897 – MISS MOULARD

The musical director of the Empire, Mr Moulard, had enjoyed a successful opening of the Empire in November 1895 but he received devastating news just over a year later. On Saturday, 6 February 1897 his wife and daughter were travelling by train when it was involved in a train crash at Brinningham Junction, near Stockport. His daughter died instantly, and his wife was taken to Stockport Infirmary in a critical condition.

At the inquest in Stockport on Friday 12 February 1897, it was reported that a train from Hull and another from Derby had collided. The signalman, Mr William Schofield, accepted that he had made an unfortunate error. He stated he had been over-worked on that day and had to handle too many trains at the same time. He had mistakenly given the line as 'clear' resulting in the crash. Mr Charlton, assistant manager of the Cheshire Railway Co, said that Schofield had eleven 'points' to look after, a number he thought was not excessive. Schofield was found guilty of manslaughter and was remanded on bail, there was a certain amount of sympathy for him as he had served twenty-one years in the Bradbury signal box without any complaints.

Miss Moulard's body was taken by train from Stockport to Liverpool for the funeral on Saturday 13 February 1897, the coffin covered by wreaths from her family and friends.

## 1906 – FIRE SUPERINTENDENT FROST

On Monday 28 May 1906, the famous Lillie Langtry was appearing at the Empire, supported by Garrett's Monkeys, Walter Stanley and Alexandra Dagmar. The show closed around 10.30pm. During the nightly fire inspection, the night watchman noticed a strong smell, definitely saw clouds of smoke, and the fire brigade was called, headed by Superintendent Frost. He commenced an immediate inspection. His crew visited the back stage area, cellars, offices, auditorium, circle, gallery etc but, wherever they inspected, the smell and sight of smoke always seemed to be behind them!

Superintendent Frost and his team spent over three hours searching for the fire as the smell and sight of smoke continued into the middle of the night. Everyone finally agreed there wasn't a fire. The crew stood down and returned to their station completely confused by the events of the exercise. In the end the presence of a ghost was blamed, after all the original theatre on the site, the Alhambra, burnt down in June 1882. Strangely, upon the staff arriving at 8am, there was no smell or sight of smoke and it never occurred again!

## 1908 – MR THOMAS HEADLEAND

On Monday 24 February 1908, at the Sheffield Stipendiary Court, Mr Thomas Headleand, an employee of the theatre was sentenced to three months imprisonment for stealing £10 from an office at the Empire owned by Moss Empires Ltd.

On Saturday 22 February 1908, Mr William Marriott, supervisor of the pit pay box, left his office, returning a few minutes later to find that two bags containing £10 in silver had disappeared. The police were called, and they interviewed Headleand along with a number of other employees, but noticed he had left the theatre at 10pm and returned at 11pm. He admitted visiting a nearby pawn shop, had bought a raincoat for 65p and changed money for gold. Inspector Hollis asked Headleand to empty his pockets where he produced £8 worth of gold, £1.40 in silver and 1p in copper. At that point, he ran across the stage, through the exit door into Hereford Street where he was apprehended.

Headleand's only excuse was that he had 'taken a drop of beer' and regretted his actions.

## 1910 – MISS LIANE d'EVE

On Monday 11 April 1910, French actress, Miss Liane d'Eve, from the Casino De Paris carried out her act, which received criticism from the local paper. They believed it had not been approved by the Watch Committee. Apparently she changed costumes in full view of the audience, which was not 'humorous or pleasing' and was at the limit of suggestiveness.

The newspaper also printed that the show was not worthy of a second visit! Miss d'Eve's supporting acts were given first rate reviews and included Jack Pleasants, comedian; Nelson Jackson, singer; Papifax & Paulo, eccentric dancers; Harry Friskey, comedy juggler; Tom Moore, comedian; Rhoda Paul, male impersonator and the Two St Johns, comedians and dancers.

This critical review by the newspaper, brought a formal letter of complaint from Miss d'Eve, a few days later. It came via a firm based in London requesting 'adequate' compensation for the mental injury she sustained and demanded a printed apology. The newspaper asked readers for their comments on her act before replying, also pointing out that the alleged dates of when the newspaper article appeared were wrong.

## 1912 – MR G MAREK

On Monday 1 April 1912, a full variety show was engaged for the Empire with Violet Romaine, vocalist; Dare's Minstrels, singers; Mendal, blind pianist; Frank Powell, comedian; Sisters Reeve, vocalists; Harry Leybourne, comedian and Guy & Grahame, comedians. The show was headed by Mr G. Marek in his thrilling drama, 'a Terrible Dream' where three live forest lions appeared on the stage and performed tricks.

On Thursday 4 April 1912, Marek was midway through his act when one of the lions clawed his hand causing it to bleed quite profusely, creating consternation amongst the audience. He left the stage for bandaging and returned, badly shaken, to complete his act to a standing ovation.

## 1912 – SIR HORACE EDWARD MOSS

Sir Horace Edward Moss, chairman of Moss Empires Ltd, one of the greatest music hall entrepreneurs, died at his Scottish home on Monday 25 November 1912, aged just 60. He was knighted in 1905 for his services to charity. He had revolutionised music hall entertainment by organising the circuit system, arranging two shows per night and opening an Empire in most major cities and towns.

Sir Edward Moss was born in Newcastle and followed in his father's footsteps as an entertainments manager, at the age of fourteen, taking over the Gaiety Theatre in Edinburgh whilst in his mid 20s. He rapidly expanded the Empire Group throughout the UK but never forgot his roots in Scotland. He had major disappointments over his short lifetime. His eldest son, James Edwin died of typhoid fever at the age of 24 on Tuesday 19 January 1904 after a short illness; suffering further sadness when the Great Lafayette, died with many others, in the fire in his Edinburgh Empire on Tuesday 9 May 1911.

The King was to have honoured Sir Edward Moss by holding the 'Command Performance' at the Edinburgh Empire in 1911, but this had to be abandoned and eventually took place in London a year later.

## AUDIENCE DEATH 1

### 1917 – Miss Nellie Gladys Brett

During week commencing Monday 12 November 1917, the musical comedy review, 'Carry On' appeared with Harry Renee, Angers Reel, Lowe & Loman, Yvonne Mehro, Bert Escott, the Six Martell Girls and the Bonnie Bunch of British Beauties. During the opening performance of the first house on Monday, Miss Nellie Brett, aged 29, sitting in the stalls, was seen laughing and enjoying the entertainment when she suddenly collapsed only to be pronounced dead by Dr Matthews a few hours later.

## AUDIENCE DEATH 2

### 1917 – Miss Kate Fletcher

Two weeks later on Monday 26 November 1917, Harry Weldon, the famous comedian, was commencing the week's entertainment supported by Miss Elsie Evans, singer; Frank Whitman, dancing fiddler; Nora Delany, singer; Kiddie

Kennedy, child comedienne; O'Wray & O'Dare, comedians and the Sisters Urma, gymnasts. In the middle of the show, on Tuesday 27 November 1917, Miss Kate Fletcher, aged 19, was taken ill with a heart attack, transported to Sheffield Royal Hospital where she died later in the evening.

Two sad deaths of two young women within two weeks.

## 1922 – MR ATTILIO FRANZONI

The strong man act, the Apollo Trio, were in full display on Friday 17 November 1922 when one of the senior members, Mr Attilio Franzoni, completed his skill of strength by lifting two large members of the audience, he walked to the side of the stage to collect a further piece of personal lifting equipment whilst his two partners continued to entertain with their particular skills.

Upon returning to the centre of the stage, Franzoni stepped onto a raised platform to perform another of his immense strength abilities to close the show, when he suddenly collapsed, fell backwards onto the stage floor holding his head. Stage hands thought he had collapsed due to exhaustion, lowered the curtain, but then realised he had died instantly. The manager ordered the National Anthem to be played as a mark of respect.

## 1933 – MR ERNEST GEORGE DALTON

During the morning of Friday 1 December 1933 a unique event took place when Chapman's Circus was appearing at the Empire. A tiger by the name of Rajah attacked its handler, Mr Ernest George Dalton, by leaping onto his back when he was cleaning its cage. His screams of agony brought other stage hands to his assistance who managed to beat Rajah off with shovels and iron bars. The animal escaped from the cage by running down a flight of stairs into the cellar below the stage.

There was mayhem in the theatre as numerous cleaners, tradesmen, stage hands etc ran for their lives and a gas inspector fell down a flight of stairs. Rajah took refuge in the offices, damaging fittings, musical instruments and furniture in the meantime. The head trainer was summoned, Mr De Kok, along with Mr Yesserick, theatre manager, the police and fire brigade who creatively erected a sturdy tunnel made of wooden boards and strong boxes. The fire brigade played their high powered hoses onto Rajah persuading him to enter the tunnel until he was guided back into his cage.

Apparently the tiger was in training and inexperienced, but, the afternoon and evening performances went ahead as planned. Dalton was rushed to the Sheffield Royal Hospital where he was detained with severe injuries to his face, back and shoulders.

## 1936/37 – MISS MARION WILSON

The pantomime, 'Cinderella', was being performed at the Empire during the winter of 1936/1937 and starred Jay Laurier as Buttons, Gene Durham as the Baron, Jack Shepherd & Lawrence Barclay as the Ugly Sisters and Miss Marion Wilson in the lead role of Cinderella. On Monday afternoon 9 January 1937 the last week of the run, Miss Marion Wilson was travelling back to the Empire from nearby Firbeck Hall for the evening show when her car was in a collision with another on the outskirts of Sheffield.

In the accident, Miss Wilson's car door flew open and she was catapulted through it and landed in a flooded ditch. Luckily she escaped with cuts, scratches and severe bruising. She continued her journey to the Empire. Having had her injuries treated by the theatre doctor, she was able to appear for the remainder of the shows with bandage on her ankle, plaster on her left knee and make-up on her bruises. Luck was with her on that day.

## 1940 – MR FREDERICK PARKES SPENCER & MR STANLEY SLACK

The blitz in Sheffield on Thursday 12 December 1940 was horrendous and many people were killed, injured, or had their property damaged as the city centre received a major bombing. The Empire was badly hit, people were injured, luckily, no-one in the audience was killed, however the bombing of the Empire caused severe heartache for two Sheffield families.

Mr Frederick Parkes Spencer, a full time police fireman, and an auxiliary fireman Mr Stanley Slack, were on duty in the city centre on that fateful night. They witnessed the damage to the Empire, rushing to assist any injured or trapped people. Unfortunately they were both killed in the Empire whilst carrying out their duties.

## 1947 – MR ALBERT HORTON

Animal acts proved very popular at the Empire and there were a number of serious incidents involving them. One in particular was horrendous and caused life long disabilities to an unfortunate person. A 4ft 5in clown, Mr Albert Horton, was employed by the Chipperfield Circus to perform in their 'Big Top Circus' presentation at the Empire during week commencing Monday 17 November 1947. He would act as stooge to the leading clown, Fiery Jack, but would carryout other duties, such as looking after the animals when not performing.

During the afternoon prior to the evening opening, Horton was feeding two tigers, Rajah aged six and Ricky aged four, when one of them knocked down the feeding tube. Horton tried to re-fix the tube instead of calling for help from Mr Frank Carlos, the lion and bear trainer. Carlos heard a shout from Horton *'they have got me'*. He rushed to the cage, picked up an iron bar to hit the tigers on their paws making them release Horton but, by this point, they had torn his arm off from the shoulder joint. Rajah, one of the tigers, weighed in excess of three and a half cwt making him one of the largest in the country. The theatre was empty at the time of the accident, Rajah, Ricky and four other tigers performed their act that evening without any problems.

Carlos said Horton was very brave, he sat having a cigarette and a cup of tea whilst waiting for the ambulance. The following day, the hospital reported that Horton was comfortable and out of danger.

## 1949 – MR FRANK BREAN

On Monday 21 November 1949 another animal act was booked for the Empire, 'Circus Royale' which would be the first ever appearance of five zebras trained for stage performances. This was felt to be unique for Chipperfield's Circus as zebras are naturally nervous animals and hide at a moment's notice. In addition to the zebras, there would be elephants, lions, horses, performing dogs, grizzly bears and the famous Blackpool Tower clowns, The Cairoli's.

It did not work out as planned. On Thursday 24 November 1949 during the zebras performance, one of them kicked a clown Mr Frank Brean so severely, he had to attend hospital for treatment.

## 1950 – MR JOE O'GORMAN & MR DAVE O'GORMAN

Joe & Dave O'Gorman, originally from Ireland, were two brothers from a theatre family. They were extremely successful in all areas of variety, especially comedy and pantomimes, topping the bill wherever they appeared.

They were starring in the pantomime, 'Little Bo Peep in the 1949/1950 season at the Empire. They were playing the parts of 'Gertrude and Simple Simon' along with Jean Colin as "Blue Boy". Accompanying them were Alec Halls, Teddy Brogden, and Pamela Carr, plus many others, but particularly Eugene's Flying Ballet who 'flew' over the audience!

On Wednesday 1 March 1950, Dave and Joe O'Gorman were each fined £5 for acting parts which were not approved by the Lord Chamberlain's Department, during the 'Little Bo Peep' performances on Monday 9 January and Tuesday 10 January 1950. The theatre licence owner, Mr Charles Parnell and the theatre manager, Mr Lewis Edward Pierpoint were each fined £10. The production manager, Mr Hastings Mann, was fined £30 and ordered to pay £10.75p in costs.

The O'Gorman Brothers said that the original pantomime performed in Northampton in 1948 had been slightly altered for the Sheffield stage with new scenes and characters being added. The original script had been mislaid, a new one drafted and the errors had not been fully realised until the complaint. The O'Gormans had been performing for over 30 years without a single complaint and felt the case was harsh.

Joe O'Gorman, born Thursday 24 July 1890, formed a song and dance act in 1907 with his brother Dave, who was born on Thursday 14 June 1892. Their father was the famous comedian, Joe O'Gorman (Snr).

The brothers became world famous and had considerable success in such countries as South Africa, Italy and the USA, as well as appearing on radio. They appeared in the 1936 film, 'Variety Parade', based on a number of variety artiste's rooming at a hotel managed by Harry Tate. Also in this were Teddy Brown, xylophone player; Nat Gonella, jazz trumpeter and Mrs Jack Hylton and her orchestra.

Joe became King Rat of the Grand Order of Water Rats in 1956, following his father into that prestigious role. Dave died in Birmingham on Thursday 19 November 1964, Joe died in Weybridge on Monday 26 August 1974.

Rather uniquely, both the O'Gorman brothers played cricket for the Surrey second eleven. In May 1927, Joe was selected to play three matches for the first eleven taking four wickets and scoring 106 runs. He 'retired' from the game to concentrate on their very successful theatre career.

# SHEFFIELD THEATRE ROYAL

*Sheffield Theatre Royal*

## 1763 – THE PLAYHOUSE THEATRE

Sheffield has had various theatres, many built in the late 1700s, and probably the most famous one of them all, the Theatre Royal, situated at the junction of Tudor Street, Norfolk Street and Arundel Street.

Built on the site of the old Playhouse Theatre and Assembly Rooms, it opened in 1763 as an entertainment centre, it was different to other entertainment buildings at the time. The new Playhouse Theatre could seat 800, opening with a performance of 'The Provoked Wife' by William Congrave.

## 1773

In 1773 it was proposed that the whole building should be demolished and replaced by a theatre resulting in the loss of the multi-purpose Assembly Rooms, a rather unpopular decision at the time.

## 1777/78 – THE THEATRE ROYAL

Work commenced and the foundation stone for the new building was laid on Wednesday 6 August 1777. Opening in 1778, the building, named The Theatre Royal, was very impressive in its looks, but received a great deal of criticism for its poor internal design and bad acoustics. The theatre did not have a successful start as Sheffield was experiencing a great depression at the time which seriously affected audiences. It was acquired by a number of different owners over the years who tried to make it succeed. Gradually business improved and the Theatre Royal had some success by continuing to present a wide range of plays starring many famous actors of the period.

## 1855

In June 1855, the management, headed by Mr Charles Dillon, decided to close the theatre and undertake a major refurbishment costing around £30,000. Upon entering the auditorium, patrons had sight of the changes which would benefit everyone attending the performances. The pit area had been increased in size, additional seating had been installed under the boxes, each seat had been refurbished and allocated a number. The ceiling was new and of improved construction, complemented by new lighting illuminating the theatre with a warm and pleasant glow.

The new stage was fitted with the most modern equipment and machinery enabling the Theatre Royal to accept the larger touring attractions. A new green room and additional, vastly improved, dressing rooms were built, ensuring the actors had a comfortable and lasting experience of the theatre. The architects were Messrs Flockton & Sons of Sheffield; the builder was Alderman Mycock of London; decorations by Mr Anderton and Messrs Hankins & Eccles of Manchester and the upholstery by Mr Johnson of Sheffield.

The grand opening on Monday 15 October 1855 at 7pm had the curtain rising for Shakespeare's 'Much Ado About Nothing' starring the favourites,

Mr Diddear, playing Capt. Dudley Smooth, and Mr J. G. Neville as Benjamin Stout. Other performers were Mr Pritchard, Mr F. Younge, Mr Charles Dillon, Mrs Charles Dillon and Mrs Vickery. The Mayor, William Fisher was guest of honour and Mr Charles Dillon addressed the audience to rousing cheers followed by the entire company and audience singing 'God Save the Queen' and ' Rule Britannia'.

## 1880

In August 1880, Mr Romaine Callender acquired the leasehold of the Theatre Royal. He requested Mr J. C. Phipps, the experienced theatre architect, to create designs for the total refurbishment, carried out by the Foxton Brothers of Sheffield with an estimated cost of £8,000. This would require the closure of the theatre for a number of weeks whilst the roof was raised 20ft. A further alteration was to the stage area and the new one would be significantly larger than the original one.

In addition to the pit and gallery, a new upper circle was created, fitted with 'tip-up' comfortable seats and, on the new fourth floor, were six private boxes. The decorations, in white and gold, were carried out by Messrs E. Bell & Co from London, a new 'sun-burner' lighting system installed by Strobe & Co and new gas fittings by Mr J. B. Corrie of Sheffield. Finally a glass and iron veranda was erected, covering two sides of the entrance areas sheltering customers against Sheffield weather.

The re-opening took place on Monday 1 November 1880 when Callender, in his opening address, stated that his plan was to stage dramatic productions rather than variety.

The Theatre Royal continued to present high quality plays for the population of Sheffield with a great deal of success, performed by the leading actors of the day. The list is endless with such artistes as Sir Henry Irving, Joseph Grimaldi, Dan Leno, Bransby Williams etc. The first presentation was Shakespeare's Henry V where Callender took the lead followed by productions of 'Le Voyage en Suisse' and 'Le Cloches de Corneville'.

## 1883

On Saturday 17 March 1883, Callender addressed the audience once again stating that he would present only the best in dramatic entertainment over the next twelve months as his contract was due to expire in June 1884 and he was eager to continue beyond that date.

## 1884

In June 1884, the owners did not grant Callender a further extension to his lease therefore he had no alternative but to leave the theatre. As a final gesture a benefit concert was arranged for Mr & Mrs Callender on Friday 27 June 1884. Mr and Mrs Callender would star in the comedy, 'Megs Diversion' when the Right Hon Earl Fitzwilliam would be guest of honour.

At the conclusion of their performance, Callender took centre stage to say 'a few parting words'. He launched into a tirade of abuse at the owners and said he had been treated in an unprofessional manner resulting in a financial loss for himself and his wife due to their poor financial assessment of his assets. The evening terminated with the orchestra playing 'Auld Lang Syne'

The incoming lessee in July 1884, Mr W. H. Dawe, struggled during his first few months. He was unable to engage sufficiently high quality acts as they were committed for the summer and autumn that year, but he gave a commitment that shows would improve in the following years. On the positive side he had resolved much of the criticism concerning the facilities in the theatre and making it one of the most comfortable theatres in the North of England.

## 1889

On Friday 14 June 1889, Dawe said he was retiring from theatre life, a benefit concert was arranged for the following Friday where Mr Charles Collette would sing his new song 'Skibbereen'.

It was announced on Wednesday 31 July 1889 that Mr Edmund Tearle, one of the foremost actors of the day, was to be appointed lessee and would undertake a major refurbishment of the theatre.

The theatre had a sombre appearance. Therefore Tearle's initial task was to change the colour of the walls by fitting light blue wallpaper with a darker shade of blue for the woodwork, using Messrs Johnson and Appleyard of Sheffield.

The fronts of the circles, boxes and proscenium were also decorated in shades of blue and the centre of the ceiling painted in a sky blue colour with stars. All the doors would have heavy duty crimson coloured curtains which excluded all draughts. This had been a criticism of previous management for not providing such protection. A further improvement was the re-positioning of the seating in the stalls as it was regarded as an unpopular area due to the closeness of the old cramped seats.

A new asbestos safety curtain was installed at a cost of £100, cutting off the stage from the remainder of the theatre. A new act drop of a Venetian scene, painted by Mr W. H. Drury, was fitted along with beautiful blue and white damask front curtains edged with gold trimmings.

Most popular of all, Tearle reduced the prices of admission in all areas.

The re-opening took place on Saturday 3 August 1889 with Mr Horace Guy's new romantic comedy, 'Delia'. This was performed by Miss Fanny Wentworth, Miss Clare Harrington, Miss Adelaide Newton, Miss Nelly Cozens and Mr Lytton Grey. At the close of the first act, Tearle appeared on the stage and admitted he was nervous as the Theatre Royal was his first venture into theatre management and thanked the owners for having confidence in him to run a successful theatre. In closing, he assured the public of Sheffield of the very best and emphasised that there would be no deterioration in the quality of the entertainment.

## 1893

The theatre continued in Tearle's management until 1893 when the lease was acquired by Mr Wallace Revill who continued with its success.

## 1898

In May 1898, Revill purchased the freehold of the Theatre Royal, appointed Mr Frank Matcham to re-design the theatre with the object of upgrading all the facilities. The majority of the colours were replaced with brighter ones such as rich rose red curtains, upholstery and wallpapers harmonising with the cream and gold of the boxes, circle and balcony fronts. New scenery was obtained from the local studio of Messrs W. Maugham & Sons.

Matcham paid a great deal of attention to safety. A new lighting system was installed, he had staircases and waiting areas widened, installed new exits, and refurbished the old entrance veranda.

The re-opening took place on Monday 1 August 1898 when Revill welcomed everyone, initially apologising to them for certain areas of the refurbished theatre not having its final piece of decoration in place, but assurances were given that all would be completed by Wednesday at the latest.

He thanked Matcham and all the contractors for the help and assistance in completing the majority of work within the tight schedule. Revill introduced the star of the evening, world famous comedienne, Louie Freear in the farcical comedy in three acts, 'Julia'. The following week's performance would be 'The Bell Ringer'.

Revill, had a tremendous interest in theatres, in addition to owning the Theatre Royal in Sheffield, he also owned the Royal in St Helens, the Royal in Leicester, was the lessee of the Grand in Derby. He was also in partnership with his brother in law, Mr F. W. Purcell at a theatre in Bury.

There was to be great sadness within a few months, as the death of Mr Wallace Revill was announced early on Tuesday 20 December 1898 due to typhoid fever.

This followed the death of his teenage son, Mr William Revill, the previous Thursday 15 December 1898 due to the identical illness. It was felt that Revill (Snr) caught the fever from his son whilst helping to nurse him during his illness. Revill (Snr) was 46 years of age, his funeral was held in St Helens on Thursday 22 December 1898, he left a wife, who took control of Revill's theatre businesses, leaving her with their three young children aged from 3 years to 12 years.

There was worse to come. Mrs Revill never overcame her double bereavement of December 1898, and her health deteriorated quite rapidly. The doctor suggested that she move to Blackpool where it should improve with sea air and new surroundings. Unfortunately there was no improvement in Mrs Revill's condition, she died, aged 38, five months later on Monday 1 May 1899, thus leaving her children without a father and mother.

Mr Frederick William Purcell, Revill's brother in law, purchased all of the theatres from Mrs Revill's estate shortly after her death. He planned to make numerous improvements to them, including the Theatre Royal. He also owned the Alexandra in Stoke Newington and was in the process of building a new theatre in Parkhurst, London. He arrived in Sheffield with a tremendous amount of experience in theatre management and was hopeful of success.

## 1901

On Saturday 15 June 1901, Mr Purcell appointed Mr Frank Matcham to prepare designs and plans for alterations and improvements to the Theatre Royal resulting in its temporary closure for five weeks.

Matcham's clear objective was to improve the experience of both the audiences and the performers by providing the maximum amount of comfort. He had the interior totally re-decorated in white and gold, but wisely retained the tasteful, previous choice of colours as he felt that they could not be improved by a colour change.

The re-decoration extended to the mouldings on the walls, balconies and ceilings. New curtains were fitted to the exit doors to prevent draughts and he also insisted upon high quality drapes fitted between the Grand Circle and the refreshment bars to reduce noise.

A new system of heating by water pipes was introduced which guaranteed a consistent temperature inside the building, irrespective of the outside weather conditions. A new electric lighting system was installed, far more powerful than the previous one and, combined with the new decorations, made the Theatre Royal look more comfortable and inviting. Another area for comfort improvement was obviously the seating, Matcham replaced the old, basic wooden seating in the pit and upper circle with fully upholstered ones which were as comfortable as those in the stalls.

However the most radical and equally important change was within the stage area. The depth of the stage was extended by 25ft making it 45ft deep by 66ft wide, sufficiently large enough to take the scenery and equipment of the larger touring production shows. Performers were not neglected as they had suffered sub-standard dressing rooms for many years, therefore Matcham totally re-built them and included the most modern bathing and toilet facilities available. These improvements made the Theatre Royal one of the finest theatres in the UK and Mr Purcell was able to use his connections to attract the best possible acts.

The Theatre Royal re-opened for business on Monday 5 August 1901 with a 2pm matinee performance of Mr J. F. Ellington's American sporting comedy drama, 'In Old Kentucky' direct from the Royal Princess Theatre in London. The audience were delighted at this opening attraction, the drama included burning stables, drunken jockeys, guardian angels, excellent vocalists and performers with genuine musical talents.

## 1906

On Tuesday 6 February 1906, the Sheffield Lyceum Company announced it had purchased the Theatre Royal including all the fixtures, fittings, scenery etc with the exception of the alcoholic beverages. The new owners committed to honour all the existing contracts with artistes and theatrical companies.

The theatre closed in early June 1906, and the management carried out a major refurbishment. The theatre was full of painters, joiners, plumbers and decorators for quite a few weeks. New, modern toilets were fitted in all areas, a new bar installed in the stalls and circle areas, even ash trays were screwed to the rear of the seats for the convenience of cigarette smokers. The electric lighting was extended to the gallery therefore gas, along with its fumes, was virtually eliminated within the theatre making the whole theatre more comfortable. To assist this improvement a new ventilation system was fitted along with numerous electric fans.

Specific attention was paid to the stage area, the now drab dressing rooms were re-furbished, an additional layer of asbestos was fitted to the safety curtain whilst all its operating machinery was overhauled and serviced.

The Theatre Royal re-opened for business under its new owners on Monday 6 August 1906 with the musical comedy drama, 'The Dandy Doctor' starring Miss Elfie Vincent as Ivy, Miss Florence Smithers as Jane and Mr Edward Marriss as the millionaire.

## 1920s

The management of the theatre were receiving numerous requests for the presentation of twice nightly plays during the early 1920s,

The pantomime staged during December 1923 and February 1924 was 'Aladdin' starring Kit Keen as 'Wun Lang'; J. H. Wakefield as 'Abanazar'; Daisy Wood as 'Aladdin'; Tatton Hall as 'Widow Twankey' and Jenny Dean as 'Princess'. After a very successful run of performances, it closed on Saturday 16 February 1924 and the management made an announcement which was quite a surprise. With immediate effect, all future presentations would be twice per evening, they had secured a number of leading London productions to open the season.

The evening shows would commence at 6.30pm and 8.40pm. All intervals would be eliminated and the shows would be 'speeded up' wherever possible.

The opening performance would be the Criterion Theatre, London success of 'A Little Bit of Fluff'.

Many thousands of performers appeared on the famous stage during the early 1900s and it continued with its reputation of excellence by presenting a wide variety of first class dramatic plays, including the famous actor, Ivor Novello appearing in his production of 'The Rat' in 1927. The most popular event was the annual pantomime which attracted thousands of people from all regions of South Yorkshire. The production teams successfully made each one more spectacular than the previous year.

## 1933 – FIRE No 1

On Sunday morning 30 April 1933 Sheffield was hit by a tremendous thunder and lightning storm which caused a fire at the Theatre Royal. Electric cables under the stage fused during the storm, the flames setting fire to adjacent flammable material. They burst through the stage floor putting the whole theatre in serious danger. Fortunately, the theatre caretaker, Mr Bell, heard the crackling of the flames, immediately investigated the source, found the stage to be well alight, and called the fire brigade.

By the time the fire brigade arrived, the 'flies' over the stage and a piece of scenery had formed a type of chimney which was assisting the spread of the fire. The firemen quickly extinguished the flames, however the main board, which controlled the stage lighting, was destroyed.

The manager of the Sheffield Corporation Electric Supply Department, Mr F. Morgan, immediately called for a team of electricians to repair the damage to the switchboard and cabling, thus enabling the evening's performance of the revue, 'On The Council', to be performed.

## 1934

In the spring of 1934, the management decided to introduce live variety rather than the established plays. The building was designed for straight plays therefore the facilities were lacking in a number of areas, particularly back stage.

A full programme of re-furbishment was planned with the principle object of providing maximum comfort for the audiences. The stalls and circle seating were replaced with modern 'tub' shaped ones, complete with tip-up seats, new carpeting was fitted in all areas. There were considerable improvements back stage. A new switch board was installed which could give more impressive stage lighting effects and speeded up the presentation of the variety artistes.

The new theatre manager, Mr Will Dalton, from the Prince of Wales Theatre in London, introduced a policy of 'variety shows at cinema prices'. Nine 'turns' would be presented, the maximum price of admission would be 15p.

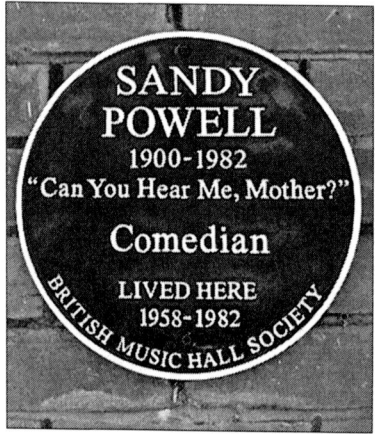

*Sandy Powell blue plaque*

It re-opened on Monday, 5 August 1934 with the De Guise Seymours, musicians; Judd & Hale, silent comedians; Billy Fray, comedian; Clifford Guest, impressionist; Holmes & Edwards, comedians; Revene & Norval, tap dancers; Boy Foy, juggler and Edward Victor, hand shadows.

A number of the leading music hall stars made regular appearances at the Theatre Royal including Frank Randle, Robb Wilton, Sandy Powell, Reg Bolton, Albert Modley etc until the next fateful fire.

### 1935 – FIRE No 2

The Theatre Royal enjoyed overwhelming success in the 1920s and 1930s until the night of Saturday 29 December 1935. The performers were Castelli and his Gypsy Accordion Band

Also appearing were Girda Vallee, Elenora, Risden & Vedale, Jack Payne & His Orchestra, Stamford & Taylor, Joe Kerr and Max Hoffman supported by Mr J. W. Daley & his orchestra. They completed their acts around 10.30pm, the audience and performers departed, and the theatre was secured by the stage staff.

At 3.30am the following morning, Sunday 30 December 1935, the Sheffield Fire Brigade received an alarm call that the Theatre Royal was on fire and thirty firemen on three fire engines rushed to the scene. They entered the theatre but were beaten back by the flames, smoke and fumes, despite their protective clothing. The flames had already spread through the whole of the four storeys of the 80ft high building.

Flames were appearing out of every window and shortly afterwards the roof came crashing down to the ground floor with a terrific roar which was heard many streets away. When the roof fell, flames leapt 50ft into the sky and the glare could be seen throughout the city. As a result of the roof collapse, burning embers, tiles and charred wood fell into the street but fortunately no one was injured.

A 100ft water tower was erected by the firemen, brought into action where it poured thousands of gallons of water into the theatre from the powerful high level hoses, but with little effect. Some firemen bravely entered the stage area through a back door for a second time but met a roaring furnace in front of them. They had no alternative but to make an immediate retreat to the safety of the street. It was obvious at this point that the theatre was lost.

Witnesses stated that it was probably Sheffield's fiercest blaze for many, many years. Every available fireman from the brigades of miles around were utilised to fight the blaze. It took the firemen over two hours for them to take control of the fire. It was 9am before they could stand down, some remained to dampen the smouldering debris. They were expected to stay on site for a further two or three days to totally extinguish the fire and search through the wreckage.

In the meantime there was a great danger of two of the theatre's outer walls in Tudor Street and Arundel Street collapsing, so severe was the damage to the whole building. The Police and Local Council had no alternative but to close these streets until those remaining walls were demolished.

The origin of the fire was unknown. The discovery was made by the licensee of the nearby Adelphi Hotel, who saw flames in the upper windows from his bedroom window. The licensee, his wife and their three year old son, together with three staff, left the hotel in their night clothes to stay with neighbours until the hotel was declared safe for them to return. Hundreds of people dashed to the theatre to watch the blaze including the performing artistes, staff and members of the orchestra who all witnessed their costumes, musical instruments, documents etc destroyed in the flaming mass.

The damage was estimated at £40,000 and the value of the instruments alone was nearly £500. The loss of costumes, fixtures, scenery etc would run into many thousands of pounds. The Managing Director and Licensee, Mr J. E. B. Beaumont and the theatre manager, Mr Arthur Holland joined them and watched as their favourite theatre was destroyed within a few short hours.

The blaze may have been even more serious for its neighbours but an adjoining warehouse had previously been demolished, leaving an open space which halted the fire from spreading to other buildings. As the Theatre Royal had a large frontage onto three streets, the firemen feared that its sister theatre, the Lyceum, on the opposite side of the road and the nearby Sheffield Central Art Gallery and Library may be affected. Due to the heroic efforts of the firemen, they were undamaged and the only reported fire was a small one on the roof of the Lyceum which was quickly extinguished.

That was the end of the Sheffield Theatre Royal within days of its 157th birthday, one of Sheffield's oldest and most famous landmarks. Luckily, Shakespeare's monument was salvaged from the fire and placed in the nearby Lyceum Theatre. The remaining walls however, were in a dangerous condition and had to be demolished within a few weeks. On Thursday 9 January 1936, BBC Radio had an outside broadcast planned to present a variety bill from the theatre, which would have been a first in Sheffield's history.

A subscription fund was formed to raise money for Mr Castelli's band and also for the theatre's musicians and artistes for the loss of instruments, wardrobes etc. A large amount of money was collected. A newspaper advertisement for the appeal placed by the Chesterfield Hippodrome in week commencing Monday 20 January 1936 actually stated *'Castelli and his Gypsy Accordion Band, all instruments and dresses destroyed in Sheffield Theatre Royal Fire'*.

A strange incident occurred which was to remain with the theatre manager, Mr Arthur Holland, for the rest of his life, the family crest, for many years sitting on top of the office safe, survived the fire and was safely recovered, and not damaged in any way. That motto was 'The Cross Rules the World'.

## 1936 – FIRE No 3

That was not the end of fires at the Theatre Royal. Six months later on Saturday evening 6 June 1936, the remains of the previous fire ignited once more, spreading to the hoardings surrounding the partly demolished site. The City Fire Brigade attended and quickly extinguished the blaze.

## THE END

After months of discussion and many failed plans, the re-building of the Theatre Royal did not materialise and it was announced on Thursday 18 June 1936 that Sheffield Corporation had purchased the site for £1,700. They made immediate arrangements for it to be cleared.

Mr Arthur E. Holland, the last manager of the Theatre Royal, now manager of the Lyceum, was presented on Thursday 18 June 1936, with a canteen of cutlery by Mr E. Innocent, the managing director of the Lyceum Group *'as a token of regard by his friends of the old Theatre Royal'*. It was accompanied by a coloured photograph of the Theatre Royal in flames. There was not a dry eye in the house that evening at the loss of this fantastic theatre.

The site was never redeveloped, it remained as a car park for many years. In 1970, it was partly excavated for the construction of the new Crucible Theatre and parts of the old Theatre Royal cellars were revealed. The site became the paved Crucible forecourt with grassed area adjoining and adjacent to, the Lyceum Theatre.

A tragic end to a famous historic theatre which was at the heart of Sheffield's entertainment.

## DID YOU KNOW...?

### 1860/1868 – MR CHAS PITT

Mr Chas Pitt, an actor, became the lessee of the theatre in the early 1860s, and died in 1868, Mrs Pitt then became the lessee. Such was the poor financial position on his death, she had to borrow £500 from Mr Crowther, a local grocer, for her to finance the 1868/69 pantomime. She gave certain securities to Crowther for furniture, gas fittings and scenery located in the theatre, which he allowed her to use during future productions.

Mrs Pitt was declared bankrupt in April 1869. She obtained her discharge the following month and hoped the new lessee would acquire her security agreement upon take-over. Arguments followed concerning the official ownership of these securities, and after a great deal of consideration the Judge decided that Crowther should receive damages of £50.

## 1881 – MR ROMAINE CALLENDER – INCIDENT No 1

Mr Romaine Callender acquired the lease of the Theatre Royal in August 1880. In December 1881 he decided to advertise for one hundred ladies who must be 'young, attractive and have good figures' for his forthcoming pantomime, 'Dick Whittington'. The response to the advertisement became a theatre farce as the stage door was inundated with hundreds and hundreds of ladies of every shape, size, age, including experienced and non experienced dancers. They were large, small, short, tall etc. and all saying they were seeking the glamour of the footlights, fame and maybe a husband!

Mrs Callender attempted to control the mass of women but almost a riot ensued. Mr Callender was asked to assist, and he managed somehow to control the mob of screaming women. The majority were refused an audition and they left the theatre abusing those who remained, as well as the management. It was doubtful If he advertised again the following year!

## 1882 – MR ROMAINE CALLENDER – INCIDENT No 2

The theatre life for Callender continued to be challenging as, in February 1882, he refused to engage the famous music hall artiste, Lillie Langtry, for a week's engagement at the Theatre Royal. He also refused her request for sixty percent of the box office takings, new furniture in her dressing room and new scenery to be painted, as she said the existing pieces were unacceptable. This caused quite a stir as Lillie Langtry was one of the leading music hall stars of the day and her appearance in Sheffield would have guaranteed sell out audiences for every performance.

## 1884 – MR ROMAINE CALLENDER – INCIDENT No 3

Mr Alfred Derkara and his wife were engaged to perform, for £5 per week, their specialist juggling act in the 1884 pantomime, 'Beauty and the Beast'. On Thursday 14 February 1884, Callender asked Derkara and his wife to appear in an additional comedy scene. They agreed to do so, but discarded their normal, expensive stage clothes and appeared in some older ones.

Callender was most unhappy at their decision. He immediately dismissed the pair from the pantomime, the Derkara's sued him for £50 for wrongful dismissal and the resulting loss of earnings. The Judge said there had been no complaints from the audience and awarded the Derkara's damages of £50.

## 1905 – MR PITT HARDACRE

On Thursday 12 January 1905, Mr Justice Wills, in the Kings Bench Division heard Mr Pitt Hardacre, a well known actor, requesting an injunction and damages against Mr F. W. Purcell, owner of the Theatre Royal, Sheffield and Miss Haldie Wright, a theatre touring manager. The injunction concerned a demand that Purcell and Wright refrained from performing their 'Bullock' version of 'East Lynne' as Hardacre alleged that he had purchased the copyright from the author, Mr Chute and had exclusive rights. No one was allowed to alter the original script.

Purcell and Miss Wright agreed they had introduced Bullock, a comic policeman, into the play at their cost, in order to lighten what was a sad and depressing play, he was not a very important character and little was seen of his name on the advertising material.

The Judge found that Purcell and Miss Wright were guilty and awarded damages of £14 each against them.

## 1925 – MR FRANK MILNER

On Tuesday 6 January 1925, Mr Frank Milner, musical director at the Theatre Royal appeared at the Sheffield Police Court following a request from his wife for an increase in the existing maintenance order. Mrs Milner said that in June 1923 she obtained an order on the grounds of desertion for £1.75p per week for one child based on her husbands wage of £4.50 per week from the theatre. He also owned a musical instrument business which he alleged was a hobby and made no profits.

Mrs Milner said her husband now earned 79p for each performance, plus additional payments for matinees. She produced evidence stating that there were five additional performances the previous week and three the week before that. This related to a weekly wage of £8.71p and £7.13p respectively.

The Judge increased the maintenance order to £2 per week.

## 1926 – GRENVILLE COLLINS COMPANY

The life of entertainers was always perceived as glamorous and exciting. The Grenville Collins Company thought otherwise after a recent attempt to reach the Theatre Royal for a weekly appearance in the drama 'The House of Glass'. On Sunday 9 May 1926 they left their home in Maidstone, Kent at 6am taking a coach to London to catch the 9.30am train to Sheffield, due to arrive on Sunday afternoon.

For a number of reasons, including the train getting 'lost', it suffered delay after delay. Talking to the train driver at a stop in Leicester, the Grenville Collins Company established that the driver used to be an opera singer and the guard a revue comedian. This did not help as the train arrived in Sheffield at 6,30pm on the Monday evening, just one hour prior to the start of their performance.

## 1930 – MISS GWENDOLEN VERSCHOYLE

One of the most popular plays of the 1930s was Miss Elinor Glyn's play 'Three Weeks' by Mr Frank Cariello's Company, who were engaged to appear at the Theatre Royal during week commencing Monday 15 December 1930.

The first night attracted a sell out audience, and another maximum crowd gathered for the Tuesday evening performance. The play commenced but Miss Verschoyle was clearly struggling with her part and, after fifteen minutes, the curtain was suddenly lowered. Cariello entered the stage and announced that Miss Verschoyle, the leading lady, had been taken ill and could not continue with her performance, no understudy was available at such short notice.

Mr Arthur Holland, theatre manager, apologised for her sudden illness and announced to the audience that Cariello was in a position to present another play, hoping they would accept this gesture in these difficult circumstances and apologised for any delay.

## 1931 – 'TRAFFIC'

Mr Arthur Holland, theatre manger, was sitting in his office on Tuesday 3 March 1931 when two policeman entered and demanded that he immediately withdraw the bills advertising that week's performance of Noel Scott's play, 'Traffic'.

This request had been issued by the British Poster Advertising Association via its own censorship committee. It concerned an image of one of the actors tying a scarf around one of the actresses, gagging her. Holland organised an army of helpers to patrol the streets of Sheffield and retrieve the bills, paste them over or obliterate the offending picture.

Mr Reginald Faher, producer and manager of the play said he was confused as identical bills had been posted in London, Norwich and Chatham without any complaints The British Poster Advertising Association said a decision had been made that the poster was unacceptable and should be withdrawn.

## 1932 – MR & MRS THOMPSON

The marriage took place on Thursday 22 September 1932 at 10.30am between Mr Rafe Thompson and Miss Joan Ingram, two of the leading members of the Denville Players who were appearing at the Theatre Royal for the summer season. They met for the first time in July when they were rehearsing their summer plays and embarked on a lightning romance.

## 1933 – MR ALBERT WOOLLEN

On Tuesday 1 August 1933, Mr Albert Woollen was working from a ladder at the Theatre Royal, when it came into contact with an electrical wire making it 'live'. He was unable to free himself until electricians cut off the electricity supply at the mains switchboard. When they did so, he fell to the floor injuring his head and had to be taken to the Sheffield Hospital for treatment.

## 1935 – MR JIM NOLAN

Mr Jim Nolan, a comedian, was booked to appear at the Theatre Royal during week commencing Monday 14 January 1935, but failed to appear on the first morning for rehearsals. The manager made numerous telephone calls, sending telegrams, contacting agents etc and finally traced Nolan to Glasgow the following day.

Nolan apologised most profusely, stating that there had been a serious fire in his home, all his contracts had been destroyed and he had to rely on his memory, which had failed him on this occasion. Nolan motored to Sheffield on Wednesday morning and completed the remainder of his contract.

## MR JIMMY JEWEL

Jimmy Jewel, born on Monday 4 December 1909 as James Arthur Thomas Jewel Marsh in Sheffield. He became one of the UK's most popular comedians over a 32 year period, in partnership with his cousin, Ben Warriss. They regularly appeared at the Theatre Royal, his most favourite theatre, as he was given his first chance on that stage when he was serving his apprenticeship as a scenic artist in the theatre.

*Jimmy Jewel blue plaque*

Jimmy Jewel was standing in the wings watching the play 'From Cross to the Crown'. Mr Edmund Tearle, the manager, said that one of the actors had been taken ill and could he take over the part as he would know the lines. After a brief rehearsal with Tearle he played the part and he was hooked on a stage career. Jimmy Jewel died in London on Sunday 3 December 1995, just one day before his ninetieth birthday, after a lifetime in show business.

## 1936 – MR ALEXANDER MORPHY

Actor, Mr Alexander Morphy, became an integral part of the fund raising scheme for re-building the Theatre Royal after the disastrous fire in December 1935. However, on Monday 10 June 1936, he appeared at the Marlborough Police Court, London charged with stealing £11 from Mr Ellis Rimmer, a Sheffield Wednesday footballer and Mr A. M. Colbert, a Sheffield journalist, whilst they were staying at the Regent Palace Hotel, London. Both Rimmer and Colbert outlined the details of the thefts by Morphy including the dates, circumstances etc and there was no doubt that the money was taken when both of them were out of the room.

The police were called, arrested Morphy who admitted the offence and said he was 'hard up'. Morphy apologised to the Court for the theft, asked for leniency stating that he had to leave the Navy as a cadet due to an injury, then becoming an actor but with little success. The magistrates said Morphy had been bound over for a similar offence in Torquay in 1929, therefore they had no alternative but to sentence him to three months imprisonment.

# SOUTHPORT PALLADIUM

*Southport Palladium*

## 1913

Cinema in the early 1900s was rapidly gaining interest from the public. The decision was made in 1913 to build one on Lord Street with a two month build plan. It would overlook the beautiful, recently built gardens. Named the Palladium, and costing £6,000, it would seat 1,070 in the auditorium, 333 in the circle and 8 in the two private boxes located at each end of the circle.

Mr Leonard Williamson, the proposed owner, requested Mr George Edward Tonge, a Southport architect, to design a multi-purpose theatre/cinema with the intended prime use as a cinema although it had to have all the necessary stage equipment installed behind the 37ft wide proscenium.

This very attractive building with a 16ft high frontage in the Italian Renaissance Design had 16ft high turrets at either end. The interior design in the style of the English eighteenth century had a colour scheme consisting of soft shades of grey, cream, gold and white, with all draperies and carpets in an old rose colour.

There were clusters of French style lamps installed on each side of the auditorium and on the front of the circle. Adjoining the auditorium was the main entrance foyer with a vaulted ceiling, and leading from it was a marble staircase to the circle, lounge and refreshment rooms. The outstanding feature of the building was the first floor tea lounge decorated in the style of the Adam brothers with copies of their originals strategically placed around the room. It was painted a pale greyish-blue colour in the Wedgwood style.

The centre of attraction in the auditorium was the £6,000 Aeolian organ which had been specifically adapted for the Palladium as it differed significantly from the traditional church organ. It had features which could give the effect of many different instruments to offer the impression of a full orchestra. A professional organist had been appointed to accompany the films. The individual morning organ recitals that were proposed, would also attract large audiences. The organ pipes were situated in the centre of the side walls, significantly enhancing the acoustics.

The interior structural work, lighting, sanitation, interior design and furnishings were carried out by Hampton & Sons Pall Mall East, London.

## 1914

The planned opening on Thursday 1 January 1914 could not be achieved due to construction delays, and so it was re-scheduled for the following Saturday, 3 January 1914 at 1pm. It was opened by the Director of Music, Mr Kenneth Burns who played an overture on the new organ, followed by the showing of a number of films, 'The Note in the Shirt', 'The Death Stone of India', 'Mabel's New Hero', 'Where's the Baby' and 'Lieutenant Pimple on Secret Service'.

The building was planned as a dedicated cinema but the management were swift to recognise the advantages of providing live entertainment as well as moving pictures. Therefore, they altered the Palladium to a dual entertainment centre catering for both audiences. This change took effect from Monday 13 April 1914, Miss Hetty King, the male impersonator, regarded at the time as the highest paid entertainer in the United Kingdom, had the honour of cutting the ribbon.

The plan would be to have an organ recital and films during the afternoon, live entertainment and a film during the evening and children's shows on Saturday mornings.

The management of the Palladium concentrated more and more on live entertainment attracting the majority of the stars at the time, Harry Lauder, George Formby Snr, Little Tich etc plus top London revues such as 'Zig Zag' and 'Smile'. It boasted in its publicity that it was the only theatre in the Kingdom possessing a 'Splendid Organ'.

## 1920 – FIRE No 1

At 4am on Saturday 1 May 1920, PC Russell, patrolling the centre of Southport, noticed a smell of smoke, at the same time Mr Cave and Mr Hopkinson, local neighbours, also noticed smoke and raised the alarm. The fire brigade attended, the caretaker arriving at the same time, opened the stage door, the firemen saw a number of seats in the stalls blazing, also the carpet and the wooden floor boards were also well alight. Fortunately the concrete base beneath the floor boards prevented the fire from spreading to other areas.

The fire was quickly extinguished but the damage to sixty seats and the flooring needed repair, therefore all performances on the Saturday were cancelled. The theatre staff worked throughout Saturday and Sunday, replacing the damaged seats with ones from the circle and replacement carpet was obtained from other parts of the theatre. The Palladium re-opened for business on the Monday evening 3 May 1920.

## 1921

On Thursday 27 January 1921, the chairman of the directors, Mr Leonard Williamson stated that he planned to retire at the end of the year, move to Surrey, and so he offered the theatre for sale. A local syndicate, Southport Amusements Ltd, purchased the Palladium in February but would not make any announcements of their intentions until later in the year. In August, Mr J. Leslie Greene, a syndicate member, said that they would formally acquire the Palladium from Sunday 2 January 1922 and it would be business as usual.

## 1925

On Thursday 19 February 1925 the management announced that the Palladium would close in two months time when all the present contracts had been fulfilled and re-open as a cinema. There would no longer be live entertainment. The cinema re-opened on Thursday 9 April 1925, with three film showings per day all accompanied by Mr Herbert Steele on the famous Palladium organ. The opening film was Louis B. Meyer's 'Husbands and Lovers', made in 1924, and released by First National Pictures.

The Southport Watch Committee banned a film, 'Foolish Wives', in May 1925.

Foolish Wives was a 1922 erotic silent film drama being shown at the Palladium and had previously been shown in cinemas in Oldham and Bolton. Mr L. Dixon, cinema manager, had obtained a copy of the film the previous week, from a cinema in Liverpool, offering the Watch Committee the opportunity of a private viewing. They did not attend the viewing. Mr Dixon received confirmation from the Chief Constable confirming the decision to ban the showing. The 1922 film, 'Rose of Paris', starring Mary Philbin and Robert Cain, planned for the showing at the week-end, was brought forward by a few days as a replacement.

## 1925 – FIRE No 2

The Palladium successfully featured films for the next six months when a another fire seriously interrupted proceedings.

At 1am on Tuesday 20 October 1925, a passing policeman, PC Clarke, on his way to the Central Police Station, noticed smoke rising above the roof of the Palladium and called the fire brigade. They forcibly entered the building through locked doors and found the seat of the fire in the circle and roof which would be difficult to extinguish. Firemen entered the circle whilst others bravely entered the roof space, crawling between the actual roof joists and the ceiling, but parts of the ceiling were collapsing into the auditorium, endangering firemen operating at ground level.

By early morning the fire had been extinguished. Luckily, the ground floor was largely untouched by the fire, especially the famous organ. The majority of the damage was caused by smoke, heat and water. The circle and gallery and the adjoining corridors were totally wrecked, full of smouldering debris, the seats were unrecognisable, except for the ironwork. The floor had been burnt through in places and the ground floor could be seen. The first floor cafe situated over the entrance was untouched, the outer roof was left intact, however the decorated ceiling suffered serious damage.

It was presumed by Mr L. Dixon, that the outbreak originated in the corridor leading to the circle or in the circle itself, probably caused by one of the audience dropping a lighted cigar or cigarette when leaving around 10.30pm the previous night. The building was fully covered by insurance, the repairs would commence as soon as possible, but he thought it would be many months before the Palladium could be re-opened.

During the enforced closure to effect the repairs, the Palladium received a total makeover, the entrance lobby and cafe were decorated with soft blue panels in the ceiling. The wall panels were blended from a rich light brown colour to a full cream tint with gilded plaster ornamentation. In the auditorium, the ceilings were re-panelled in a soft blue colour embellished with gold stars.

The draperies, seating and carpeting were in a purple colour with silk shades fitted to the chandeliers. An electrically operated velour stage curtain, costing £160, was installed and the stage had been widened by around 13ft. The orchestra pit had also been increased to accommodate additional members, particularly in the string section. The famous Palladium organ received a full repair and overhaul.

## 1926

The re-opening date was Saturday 3 April 1926. The feature film 'Siege' starring Virginia Valli and Eugene O'Brien attracted a sell-out audience who were very impressed with their refurbished cinema. The highest price of the seats would be 6p, hoping to attract huge audiences.

## 1928

On Thursday 1 March 1928 it was announced that the Palladium had been acquired by Sir Walter Gibbons and Mr F. A. Szarvasy of the Gaumont British Picture Corporation and its associated company, the General Theatres Corporation. The purchase price was not disclosed but it was rumoured to be in the region of £100,000 as the Palladium was one of the finest cinemas and theatres in the country.

## 1929 – FIRE No 3

History was to repeat itself at 4.30am on the morning of Tuesday 26 March 1929. A passer-by, Mr Lee, on his way to work, noticed that part of the roof was alight and instantly called the fire brigade who ordered three fire engines to the site. Unfortunately the fire was out of control and, within half an hour, the roof fell into the auditorium with flames and sparks shooting hundreds of feet into the air, lighting up the sky as though it was daytime.

The outbreak appeared to have started in the roof area above the stage and spread rapidly to all areas destroying everything in its path. The firemen attacked the fire from all possible entrances but, in reality, it was a worthless exercise and it was obvious that the Palladium would be totally destroyed.

Nothing remained of the auditorium but bare walls and a mass of twisted iron and steel roof girders. Mr A. W. Hughes, the manager, arrived, dressed in his pyjamas, and, with some of the firemen entered the fireproof brick and lead lined projection box to rescue a large number of films. He returned to enter his smoke damaged office above the entrance lobby, carried the books and money to safety, before having his badly cut hand treated.

Mr J. Rimmer, the caretaker, had carried out a full inspection of the Palladium at 11.30pm the previous evening, reported that all was safe and secure and was shocked at the devastation when he arrived at 4.45am. He was surprised to hear that the roof had collapsed into the auditorium half an hour after the initial alarm. The interior was a complete wreck, everything was destroyed except the cafe and the offices above, all the four remaining walls were badly damaged and they would have to be demolished immediately. The fire destroyed most of the orchestra's musical instruments, valued at £500, and the famous £10,000 organ was beyond repair.

The previous evening was a variety/cinema presentation. The film shown was a melodramatic thriller entitled 'Paying the Penalty'. The live performance was provided by Mr Fred Lewis, a novelty impressionist in a sketch entitled 'At the Variety Ball'. Lewis had cause to remember his appearance at the Palladium. He had been married a fortnight previously and their luggage had been stored in the theatre but the majority of it was destroyed. Fortunately, a piece of wedding cake, a number of signed autographs of fellow artistes and Mrs Lewis's jewellery were rescued from a suitcase buried in the debris.

British Gaumont Theatres appointed their in-house architects, Mr W. E. Trent and Mr E. F. Tulley, to re-design the Palladium. They chose to retain the original façade, including the two towers, but extend the auditorium into an area of the car park in order to increase the seating capacity to over 2,000. Detailed plans were submitted to the Southport Magistrates on Monday 18 November 1929 and they granted permission on the proviso that some construction work was offered to the unemployed of Southport.

## 1930

Building commenced by McLaughlin & Harvey on the Palladium early in 1930 to erect probably the finest cinema in the north of England. The 99ft long entrance and 30ft wide entrance foyer, with a marble mosaic floor and wood lined walls, greeted the patrons as they waited to enter.

The auditorium measuring 120ft wide, had its walls in a delicate grey colour with horizontal bands of blue, green and red separated by silver lines. These features led to a green, grey and silver painted ceiling complemented by Art Deco style chandeliers, Situated under the balcony were numerous concealed lighting fixtures, hidden from view in large plaster moulded fittings, also housing the modern air conditioning units.

The distance from the projection box to the screen was 140ft. There were about 1600 seats in the auditorium and 600 in the balcony. The architects installed twelve exits for immediate evacuation, placed numerous fire hydrants in strategic areas and had a sprinkler system fitted above the stage.

The well loved old organ, destroyed in the fire, was replaced by a Compton model. Sufficient space was allowed for an orchestra of around 20, the stage area was adequately fitted for live theatre shows. The cafe was totally refurbished in exactly the same design as before with the original Wedgwood colour scheme.

The fire had an effect on many people, some lost their jobs and performers had their on-going contracts cancelled. Randolph Sutton, the famous singer and comic entertainer, whose hit song, 'On Mother Kelly's Doorstep', is still popular today, was due to appear the following week Monday 6 May 1929.

The firemen of Southport had a very hectic time in 1929, as, on Friday 20 December, the prestigious Opera House, situated on the Winter Gardens Pier, suffered a major fire when the whole building was destroyed within a few hours.

## 1930 – THE RE-OPENING

On Monday 1 October 1930, the Mayor of Southport, Alderman Tomlinson; the Mayoress, Miss Tomlinson; Mr Will Evans, joint managing director of Gaumont-British; Mr W. E. Trent, architect; Mr J. E. Jarrett, Town Clerk, members of the Town Council plus local magistrates, officially opened the Palladium. The Mayor thanked the Gaumont British Picture Group for rebuilding the Palladium in such a delightful manner and hoped that it would continue with both cinema and variety as Southport needed a good mixture of entertainment to satisfy the residents and holiday visitors. He continued by commenting that 120 Southport residents had been employed in the build, all the bricks, marble, plumbing, drainage and plaster work had been supplied by local people.

A fanfare of trumpets introduced the programme. The opening film featured Janet Gaynor and Chas Farrell in 'High Society Blues' followed by entertainment from the Continental Dance Group, 'The Blue Slavonic Company'. The evening was concluded with an organ recital by Leslie James on the new 'mighty' organ, accompanied by the twenty-two piece, Lewis Baxter Symphony orchestra. The Palladium management were pleased to announce that seventeen of the twenty-two musicians and ninety per cent of the staff lived in Southport.

## 1950 – THE GAUMONT

The Palladium continued as a cinema/variety theatre for many years attracting many stars onto its famous stage, however, on Friday 24 July 1950 it changed its name to the Southport Gaumont continuing with films and only the occasional live show.

## 1959 – FIRE No 4

Fire, a regular feature of the building, happened again on Monday 8 June 1959 when smoke and flames were discovered in the foyer. The fire brigade arrived, found a settee burning, quickly extinguished it and no damage was caused except to the settee.

## 1962 – THE ODEON

The Gaumont was renamed the Odeon in 1962, with both films and live entertainment attracting large audiences. During week commencing, Monday 26 August 1963, for six nights, The Beatles topped the bill supported, along with others, by Gerry and the Pacemakers.

*Gerry and The Pacemakers*

## 1979 – THE END

In the early 1970s attitudes to cinema and theatre entertainment were changing with the introduction of television, night clubs, bingo and bowling alleys etc. The audiences at the Odeon were beginning to fall, causing the management some concern. The first indication of the owner's intention to close the Odeon was on Saturday 18 October 1975 when they stated that the Southport Odeon was suffering from falling audience numbers and they intended to carry out a full business review. A decision on its future would be made in due course.

A planning application was submitted to the Sefton Borough Council on Thursday 11 October 1979 to demolish the Odeon Cinema and develop a supermarket on the site. There was a very heated Council meeting, lasting well over an hour. Different opinions were expressed ranging from an allegation that a number of facts had been withheld from the planning committee, that it was situated in a conservation area, that there would be excessive traffic congestion in the town centre and forcing many local shops to close.

Sainsbury's Supermarket were seeking planning permission for a 27,500 sq ft building with parking for 110 cars.

Later that evening, planning permission for the new build was finally given, and the Odeon would close shortly. Its last screenings on Wednesday 28 November 1979 were the films 'Confessions of a Pop Performer' and 'The Day for Vultures' shown to a very small audience. The residents of Southport had organised a 'Save Our Cinema' campaign some weeks earlier. They were hoping for a bumper attendance but only a few hundred were in the audience that night, the rest probably stayed at home to watch television! This was quite surprising as over 1,000 had signed the petition but they obviously confirmed that their entertainment interests were elsewhere on that final night and not with the Odeon.

## 1980

The building was demolished in July/August 1980 along with its elegant facade, which, with a little element of thought, could have been incorporated in the newly built Sainsbury's supermarket, opening on Tuesday 12 October 1982. Unfortunately it wasn't and therefore was lost forever.

That was the end of the Palladium which had experienced almost everything since its opening in 1914 but it gave immense pleasure and entertainment to hundreds of thousands of people over its sixty-five years of existence.

Long may it be remembered.

## DID YOU KNOW...?

## 1915 – MISS NINA GORDON

In the early 1900s Miss Nina Gordon, a popular music hall artiste, who had appeared in a Royal Command Performance, was booked to appear at the Palladium. This was for week commencing Monday 8 March 1915 as part of her Moss Empire's contract. Her salary would be £45 per week for two performances each evening.

She was approached by the stage manager and asked to reduce the length of her act from around eighteen minutes to twelve minutes. As top of the bill she thought this unfair as such artistes normally performed a set piece and it should not be reduced. She agreed to cut out the song 'Just Her Way' as the stage manager threatened that he would lower the curtain on her performance.

However, ignoring his request, she performed for the full eighteen minutes. A discussion took place after the second performance between Miss Gordon, her mother Mrs Westall and the theatre manager, resulting in Miss Gordon packing her personal effects, make-up etc, leaving the theatre and being offered one night's salary. Miss Gordon sued the Palladium for breach of contract and damages for the remainder of her contract.

Judge Thomas at the Southport County Court on Tuesday 13 July 1915 heard the case and had to decide if Miss Gordon discharged herself from the contract or was dismissed for failing to reduce her performance. There was evidence submitted by both parties which was contradictory and may be down to interpretation by them, the Judge having to assess the position and make a decision.

Judgement was given to Miss Gordon for the payment of the remaining week's wages as it was not clear that she had voluntarily resigned, the theatre were wrong in terminating her contract without payment.

## 1917 – MR GEORGE FORMBY SENIOR (COURT CASE)

Mr George Formby Snr, signed a contract on Thursday 10 August 1916 to appear at the Palladium during week commencing Monday 4 September 1916 but he failed to appear.

He was therefore sued for damages by the owners of the Palladium, and the case was heard on Tuesday 3 April 1917, in the Kings Bench Division before Judge Mr Justice Ridley.

Mr Holman Gregory KC on behalf of the theatre, stated that George Formby agreed that a contract had been signed, but he stated that ill health in September 1916 had prevented him from performing.

*George Formby Senior*

He had alleged that he had been suffering from haemorrhaging from his lungs and consumption for at least fourteen years and was undergoing special treatment from a London hospital. In fact, an accident at the Theatre Royal, Drury Lane, London in June 1916 had made his condition worse.

The theatre believed it was a matter of money rather than Mr Formby's health which had influenced his decision not to perform. By failing to appear, the theatre had suffered a huge financial loss as they would have been guaranteed full houses at every performance, such was his popularity.

In defence, George Formby said he was forty one years of age, had seven children and there was no doubt he was a dying man, therefore he wished to earn as much money as he could before died or was forced to retire, In view of his London medical treatment, which would have precluded any travel especially as far as Southport, he agreed he had accepted £250 for the same week's work with the Moss Empire Group at the Empire Theatre in London.

Judge Ridley, in summing up, said that if George Formby, although suffering a serious illness, was well enough to perform in one theatre he could do so in another, therefore he had broken his contract. He awarded damages to the theatre for £175 plus costs. The Judge said that had he been unable to perform due to illness, he may have made a different decision.

## MR GEORGE FORMBY SENIOR (THE APPEAL)

On Thursday 1 November 1917, George Formby appealed against the decision made on Tuesday 3 April 1917 where the Palladium was awarded £175 in damages for his non-appearance. George Formby's Counsel argued that he could not leave London as he was receiving special treatment at a hospital therefore the contract with the Southport Palladium was invalid.

After lengthy discussion it was confirmed that George Formby had appeared the following week at a Newcastle theatre. Therefore if he was fit to appear in Newcastle, he was fit to appear at the Southport Palladium. The original decision was found to be correct.

There were no ill feelings as George Formby appeared at the Palladium during week commencing Monday 1 May 1918, but he only managed to perform his act at the first house on the opening evening, and was taken ill at the interval. He was confined to bed by his doctor and was unable to fulfil his contract.

George Formby died on Tuesday 8 February 1921, aged only 46, at his home in Stockton Heath, Warrington due to pulmonary tuberculosis. He had been appearing in the pantomime 'Jack and Jill' at the Newcastle Empire where he collapsed on stage following a severe coughing fit as the condition of his lungs deteriorated further and he was rushed to his home in a very serious condition. George Formby died a wealthy man, leaving almost £1m in today's monetary value. His son, George Formby Jnr, born in 1904, became the country's leading music hall and film star in the 1930s, 40s and 50s, and he died in March 1961 at the relatively young age of 57. Father and son are buried along side each other in a Warrington Cemetery.

## 1918 – BOGANNY ACROBATIC TROUPE

On Wednesday 1 May 1918, in the King's Bench Division, Mr Justice Shearman heard an action by the Boganny Acrobatic Troupe, against Mr Chris Marner manager, of the London Palladium, claiming damages for withholding their troupe's property. There had been a dispute between the two parties. Marner would not permit their property to be removed from his theatre on late Saturday evening 13 October, or Sunday morning, 14 October. As a result the Troupe were unable to fulfil their contract with the Southport Palladium, commencing Monday 15 October 1917, thus claiming £70 for lost salary and £70 for damages payable under the contract for non-appearance.

The London Palladium denied liability and said it had been a technical error, and if awarded, the damages should be nominal. Mr Justice Shearman said that Marner was not entitled to take the law into his own hands and awarded the Troupe a total of £140 plus costs.

## 1919 – MR GEORGE CATO

Commencing Monday 12 May 1919, Seymour Hicks and his wife Ellaline Terriss, were starring in the one act comedy, 'After the Honeymoon', supported by May Henderson, Harry Shirley, Peter Pariss and Cato's Comedy Circus. On Tuesday 13 May 1919, an inspector of the RSPCA witnessed one of Mr George Cato's donkeys limping and almost unable to walk. The Inspector presented his findings to Cato who said that a veterinary surgeon had examined the donkey and it was receiving treatment. The animal performed the following evening. The Inspector witnessed the donkey perform in an identical painful manner, and he ordered Cato to cancel the donkey part of his act and reported the matter to his manager.

On Wednesday 21 May 1919, the cruelty case was heard at the Southport Police Court. Cato said the donkey was only slightly lame, it merely walked onto the stage, laid down, got up and walked off which was not cruel. He was fined £1.

## 1921 – STAGE COLLAPSE

The Palladium was regularly used by numerous charity organisations. The Southport United Choir were raising money for the local infirmary and agreed to present a performance of the 'Messiah' on Sunday 23 January 1921. A six feet high temporary stage, hired from the Southport Corporation, was erected in the centre of the theatre's own stage.

The 250 choristers took their positions on the temporary stage in readiness for the performance to begin, when part of this stage began to subside and gradually collapse. They rushed from the crumbling stage, a number were injured in the panic and received treatment. The temporary stage was dismantled and removed allowing the performance to continue from the theatre's own flat stage. Upon investigation it was found that one of the iron supports had broken causing the stage to collapse.

## 1921 – MR ALEX ALLAN

Mr Alex Allan, formerly a manager of the Palladium, resided with his wife in a rented house in Post Office Avenue, Southport in 1919, until resigning to take up a managerial position at another theatre in Liverpool. Mrs Allan had not seen her husband for over a year and their landlord had applied, reluctantly, for an eviction order at Southport County Court on Tuesday 7 June 1921.

Since her husband's disappearance Mrs Allan had not received any money from him, she did not know his whereabouts, her son had died and the only money she earned was a small amount from dressmaking. Mrs Allan could not pay the rent from Friday 1 October 1920, the landlord said he would not seek an order for payment of the outstanding rent or any costs involved in the legal process. The Judge had an enormous amount of sympathy for Mrs Allan but said he had no alternative but to grant the eviction order.

## 1922 – MR PETER PARISH

Mr Peter Parish, a well known music hall comedian, was engaged to appear at the Palladium during week commencing Monday 23 January 1922. He was taken ill at his lodgings on Sunday 22 January, and was rushed to the Southport Hospital. Unfortunately he died in the hospital a few days later on Wednesday 1 February 1922.

## 1924 – MR NOR KIDDIE

Mr Nor (Norman) Kiddie, a leading music hall comedian in the early 1900s, was topping the bill at the Palladium in the comedy revue, 'The Globe Trot' commencing Monday 26 May 1924. He decided to park his car on the promenade during each performance. On Monday afternoon after the matinee show, Nor Kiddie realised his car had been stolen, notified the police immediately, who investigated the theft. They eventually arrested Mr Percival Johnson, in Warrington, for the theft of his vehicle.

At Southport Police Court on Wednesday 28 May 1924, Johnson was formally charged with the theft of Nor Kiddie's car. He agreed he had stolen it, but pleaded that he had taken the car on Monday evening, driven to Warrington Police Station and admitted the theft. He admitted to the theft of other cars on the same day. He had previously been convicted of motor car theft, stating that the crime was caused by him being unable to obtain employment and having no money whatsoever.

Johnson was sentenced to six months imprisonment.

## 1928 – LITTLE TICH

Little Tich

Little Tich, a regular at the Palladium, born Harry Relph on Sunday 21 July 1867, made his first appearance on stage at the age of twelve, adopting the name of Little Tich due to his small stature. He only grew to 4 feet 6 inches tall (137 cm) and it was rumoured he had five fingers and a thumb on each hand. He became world famous through his 'Big Boot Dance' where he carried out acrobatic dancing in his boots, which had soles 2 feet 4 inch long. (71 cm). He regularly toured the world topping the bill in major theatres, but the call of England, especially London, ensured he performed in his home country.

During his life he struggled with marriage, and had financial concerns as his wages fluctuated as his popularity began to wane. To make matters worse, in 1926, when performing his variety act at the Alhambra Theatre in London, he received a severe blow to his head from a mop which fell on him, causing a massive lump on his head followed by intense headaches for many weeks afterwards. Shortly afterwards, he suffered a stroke, probably caused by the accident. This left him unable to speak and losing the feeling in his right hand side.

Little Tich died on Thursday 10 February 1928, aged 61 and will be remembered for many decades as one of the finest and most novel comedians of his time, and for overcoming his physical problems.

## 1938 – MR CHARLES BROWN

On Saturday evening 16 April 1938, Mr Charles Brown, manager of the Palladium in the 1930s, was accompanied by Mr William Sutcliffe an attendant at the cinema. They were on their way to deposit £300, which were that evenings takings, to put into the night safe of the local bank, 200yds away. The money was contained in five wallets, two held by Brown and three by Sutcliffe. Suddenly, a masked man stepped out of the shadows and pushed a gun into Brown's stomach shouting 'Hand it over boys'.

Brown said 'Don't be a fool', the robber struck him on the jaw with his gloved fist, ran off leaving the gun on the floor which turned out to be a toy one. He chased after the robber and went into nearby Anchor Street, assisted by tramways inspector, Mr Bridger but the robber disappeared into the dark. The police were called. Brown gave the description of the robber as aged around 22, slim build, 5ft 7in or 5ft 8in, wearing a grey trilby hat, light coloured raincoat, kid gloves and gold rimmed spectacles. He added that the man did not seem to be an expert in the hold-up business! He was never apprehended.

## 1965 – MR JAMES JOHNSON

On Friday 5 March 1965, an elderly gentleman suffering from loss of memory, collapsed in the Odeon during the showing of a film, and was taken to Southport Infirmary. He was eventually identified as Mr James Johnson, address unknown, but a railway ticket was found in his pocket for a journey between Birkdale and Southport, a distance of less than two miles.

# ST ANNE'S ON SEA PIER PAVILION

*St Anne's Pavillion*

## 1880 – THE PIER

St Anne's-on-the-Sea is a seaside resort on the Fylde coast of Lancashire, situated at the mouth of the River Ribble. It is approximately four miles south of Blackpool. In the 1800s, pleasure piers were fast becoming a feature, and by 1870 Blackpool boasted two, the North Pier and the Central Pier.

Neighbouring Southport and Lytham already had one pier each. Therefore, to compete for the ever increasing number of holiday makers from the industrial areas of Lancashire, St Anne's commissioned a pier for themselves.

After much delay due to disagreements regarding where it should be located along the promenade, the building of the pier finally commenced in 1880. It was constructed by the St Anne's Land and Building Company at a cost of between £17,000 and £18,000. Designed by Mr A Dowson of Westminster, the pier was 914 feet long, 19 feet wide with columns sunk into the sea bed to a depth of 50 feet. The pier was built mainly of cast iron with lattice girders and wooden decking.

The pier had a three level extension jutting out from the pier-head. The designers of these landing stages were Messrs Garlick and Sykes, the contractors were Allsupp and Sons, both from the nearby town of Preston. This facility enabled visitors to enjoy short sea going excursions to Liverpool or Blackpool which proved to be a very popular attraction for the many holiday makers. Unfortunately, the enjoyment of these pleasure trips was short lived as the River Ribble channels were dredged to improve shipping access to Preston Docks and this work, effectively, left the pier isolated from the sea and unreachable by boat!

*The Ineterior of St Anne's Pavillion*

## 1885 – OPENING

The pier was opened on Monday 15 June 1885 by Colonel, the Right Honorable F..A. Stanley MP, who congratulated St Anne's for developing their seaside resort to be one of the most popular in the north-west. At regular intervals along the pier were numerous built-in recesses, furnished with comfortable seats to enable visitors to rest and view the magnificent coastline scenery. At the very end of the pier was a covered shelter and a band stand.

## 1901 – THE PAVILION THEATRE

The pier continued to grow as an entertainment centre and, in 1899, a Mock Tudor entrance was built which added style and glamour to its already impressive surroundings. At a meeting on Wednesday 18 September 1901, of the St Annes Land and Building Co, the management were authorised to plan and design an extension to the head of the pier and create a 1,000 seater self contained entertainment centre with an estimated budget of £30,000, this being raised by a new share issue.

Messrs Garlick and Sykes, the appointed architects, decided to build a number of different structures but, in order to do so, they had to double the width of the pier walkway from the promenade to 34ft. In addition they also had to create a totally new building at the pier head, by extending the width from 66ft to 221ft. This new 'T' shape extension would include the 1,000 seater theatre situated on the north-west side. On the south-east side an enclosed band stand, numerous shops and refreshment facilities were also built.

The centrepiece, the Pavilion Theatre, was designed in a Moorish style of architecture complete with two domes, one situated at the main entrance and the other positioned over the stage. A central chandelier, providing excellent lighting, was placed over the auditorium which measured 84ft by 56ft and there was final seating for 920 people. There were six fire exits, all fitted with instant opening 'panic bolts'. The lighting was provided by six, 1000 candle power gas lamps installed by Suggs of London.

The stage measured 30ft by 24ft and the floor of the theatre had a rake of two feet from front to back to ensure everyone had a perfect view of the stage. The roof was one single span, the ceiling had fibrous plaster panels, all with floral designs, designed by Mr Bookbinder. The principal contractor was Messrs J. Butler and sub-contractors included Messrs W. A. Peters of Rochdale for the joinery and Messrs A. Higginbotham & Sons for the plumbing.

## 1904 – THE OPENING

On Saturday 2 April 1904, Mr Harold Porritt, a director of the St Annes Land and Building Co., officially opened The Pavilion before retiring with the guests to the Grand Hotel for luncheon. This was a lavish affair and, as a new lifeboat station had been built at the end of the promenade, the lifeboat crew were asked to be included by following the procession in their lifeboat, the 'Laura Janet', drawn by four horses.

They regarded this request as a great honour for the lifeboat service and they were proud to take part. After the luncheon, toasts for the success of the theatre were given, the Mayor of Bury, Mr G. Webb responded by stating that he had visited virtually every pier theatre in the country and he had not found one to be so beautifully designed as the Pavilion.

On Monday 4 April 1904, the Pavilion was opened to the public who were entertained by thirty-five performers including Miss Evangeline Florence, Mr Charles Saunders and Mr Robert Radford. Also performing were the Royal Windsor Quartet direct from His Majesty's Chapel Royal.

## 1910

Further improvements to the pier were planned and in June 1910, the Floral Hall was built at the left hand side and adjacent to the Pavilion Theatre. Typically that building was constructed of steel and plate glass and designed by Arnold England. It offered a venue for orchestral concerts, operas etc complementing the traditional variety/music hall acts presented at the Pavilion. The Pier itself had a period of almost fifty years as a tourist attraction and then suffered the first of three fires which would seriously disrupt its success over the next few years.

## 1959 – FIRE No 1

A newly built 50 seater children's theatre on the pier was damaged by fire on Friday 5 June 1959, a few days before it was scheduled to open. Fortunately the fire was contained within the building and did not spread to the other parts of the pier. This theatre, due to be opened on Monday 15 June 1959, by Uncle Leo of BBC fame, offered a Punch & Judy Show as the first attraction accompanied by other puppets. Painters were finishing their work when the blaze was first noticed and damage was limited to a piano and seating, the area was quickly repaired in readiness for the planned opening.

## 1962

St Anne's Pier changed ownership in 1962 when the Amalgamated Investment & Property Company bought it for £240,000 and commenced a refurbishment programme of the Floral Hall, the Pavilion entrance and the children's entertainment facilities. During the following years the Pavilion attracted many top stars of the day, including Ken Dodd, who appeared on that stage during the early years of his career.

## 1974

Following a further major refurbishment in May 1974, Princess Anne attended the Pavilion for a charity concert on Friday 7 June 1974, in aid of the Save the Children Fund, given by the world famous violinist, Yehudi Menuhin and his sister, Hephzibah.

## 1974 – FIRE No 2

Booked for the 1974 Summer Season in the Pavilion were Ken Platt and the cast of Comedy Playhouse who were performing a West-End comedy play, 'The Man Most Likely to…'.

Ken Platt had just completed his evening performance on Saturday 20 July 1974 at around 10.15pm. He was quietly relaxing in his dressing room around 11.15pm, having a drink, and discussing that night's performance, attendance figures etc with Impresario, Mr Duggie Chapman, producer of the show, together with Ken's manager, Mr Bryan Robinson.

Ken Platt said that they had almost finished their discussions and were preparing to leave, when Duggie Chapman said he smelled burning rubber. Suddenly all the lights fused, and they groped their way in the dark as best they could to find the nearest emergency exit. All three said they initially saw smoke coming from back-stage and then the whole area suddenly burst into flames.

They immediately left the pier whilst a member of the Tyrolean Bar staff called the fire brigade. Luckily the majority of the audience had already vacated the theatre and bars. Three engines were on the scene within minutes but after 30 minutes the fire had engulfed the whole of the stage area and was spreading rapidly to the remainder of the theatre.

By midnight the steel framework of the roof crashed into the auditorium and then into the sea. The beautiful onion shaped domed roof also collapsed into the sea shortly afterwards. The fire continued to rage and the flames reached the nearby stores of white spirit and the beer gas cylinders. The stored canisters exploded with great force making the firemen's task of controlling the fire even more difficult and dangerous.

The firemen fought heroically for over two hours to control the blaze but the Pavilion was completely destroyed. However, the remainder of the pier including the Floral Hall, although slightly damaged, was saved. The fire was so fierce it was seen in Preston, some 14 miles away. Ken Platt, who lived in Blackpool, confirmed he lost clothes and personal possessions to the value of £400. General opinions were offered as to the cause of the fire and it was assumed that a discarded cigarette remained burning on a seat or had been discarded onto the floor by a careless audience member.

The owners of the pier held an emergency meeting and hoped that a replacement Pavilion could be built. After six months consideration they decided that the level of incoming business could not meet the estimated replacement cost of £1m and the plan was shelved.

## 1976

Trading for the company became difficult and in December 1976, the pier was bought by the Webb family for £30,000 who had plans to reopen the Pavilion in all its previous glory. These plans were not to come to fruition however, as during the planning stage, the Floral Hall, now known as the Tyrolean Beer Garden, was destroyed by fire number 3 on Friday 23 July 1982.

That effectively ended any hope for the re-development of the seaside entertainment centre and a decision was made to demolish all that remained at the end of the pier. Many residents objected to this proposal hoping for a refurbishment, however the local council decided that the 150ft remnants of the original pier's landing jetty should be retained as a permanent reminder. The wooden remnants of the old pier still stand today pointing their bony finger-like frames towards the sky as a defiant gesture.

The shortened pier, now only 600ft long, was designated a Grade ll listed building on Friday 21 September 1973.

## 2010

The pier is still trading today with cafes, shops and an amusement arcade, The new owners, Fylde Council and the Lancashire & Blackpool Tourist Board have spent money on various refurbishments. In 2010 new lighting was installed making the pier and town centre more attractive at night time. In 2012 a new cafe, The Deckhouse, opened at the end of the shortened pier.

Both the Pavilion and the Floral Hall are now distant memories and whilst they both vanished in a mass of flames, they are well remembered by the thousands of visitors who were graciously entertained for so many years. The two sisters, the Pavilion and the Floral Hall, have often been regarded as two of the finest examples of seaside architecture ever built.

## DID YOU KNOW...?

## 1886 – 'THE LAURA JANET' LIFEBOAT

On Saturday 11 December 1886, just eighteen months after celebrating the opening, the 'Laura Janet' lifeboat was summoned, along with the Southport lifeboat, to the sinking of the ship 'Mexico' in the Irish Sea. Due to the

*Laura Janet Lifeboat*

treacherous sea conditions both lifeboats were overturned by huge waves, oars were either broken or lost and twenty-seven men perished in the heavy seas. Their funerals were conducted by The Bishop of Liverpool on Wednesday 15 December 1886.

The Coroner, Mr Brighouse, at the inquest on Saturday 18 December 1886, gave a verdict of 'death by misadventure' and the National Lifeboat Association presented a new, up-graded, lifeboat to each of the two life-boat stations. A committee consisting of Lord Derby, Lord Sefton, and the Mayor of Southport, plus many others, had been formed to administer the Lifeboat Disaster Fund which had now reached the staggering sum of £20,000.

*Laura Janet Memorial*

## 1961 GEORGE FORMBY

George Formby, the famous comedian, was born on Thursday 26 May 1904, the son of the famous George Formby Snr, who himself was a very successful music hall comedian in the late 1800s and early 1900s, George Snr died on Tuesday 8 February 1921 after collapsing on stage at the Newcastle Empire Theatre a few days earlier. He was 45 years old.

*George Formby with his wife Beryl in front of him, entertaining British Troops 1944*

Shortly afterwards, George followed in his father's footsteps, and began his own music hall career in 1921 at the age of 17. He became the UK's most famous comedian starring on stage, screen and television in the 1930s, 40s and 50s.

George was a regular performer at the Pier Pavilion in St Anne's and he and his wife Beryl, bought an impressive detached house there in 1953. It was purchased from the famous tenor Joseph Locke and situated on the main sea front promenade a few hundred yards from the Pier Pavilion. The renamed it 'Beryldene'.

Beryl had a heart attack and died suddenly at Christmas 1960. George passed away just over two months later on Monday 6 March 1961, at the young age of 56. He was buried alongside his father, George Formby Snr in Warrington Cemetery with 150,000 mourners watching the funeral procession pass by.

George's death was followed surprisingly quickly by the auction of his house, his Bentley car and all of his and Beryl's personal possessions in 1,007 auction lots. This took place at their home 'Beryldene', which was open to the general public for the auction on Tuesday, Wednesday and Thursday, 20 June, 21 June and 22 June 1961.

The listing in the catalogue was very succinct, particularly when listing his personal clothing, including his underwear. The auction lots ranged from household furniture, to much diamond jewellery and many fur coats. Quite

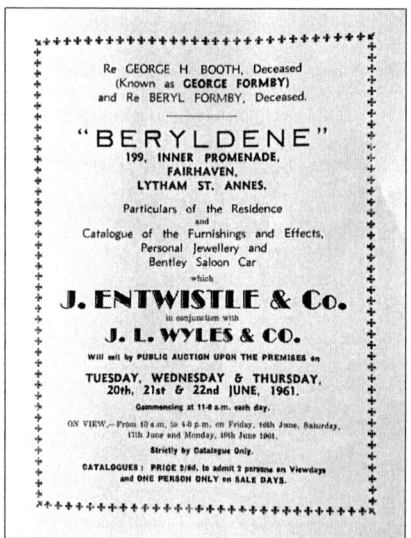

a number of George's ukuleles were in the auction. Also included were what was described as the contents of the 'Wash House' and also a box of spanners and tools! George's will was contested and not resolved until four years later in September 1965, when he left £1.9 million at today's value.

```
449  George Formby banjolele in case.
450  GEORGE FORMBY BANJOLELE IN CASE—SIGNED.
451  Banjolele in case—damaged.
452  WILL VAN ALLEN BANJOLELE IN CASE "MR. WOO'S A
     WINDOW CLEANER NOW".
453  "Melody Uke" banjolele in case.
454  GEORGE FORMBY BANJOLELE in CASE, signed 20th January 1952,
     "MR. WOO'S A WINDOW CLEANER NOW".
455  Ludwig banjolele in case.
456  Angelus miniature banjolele in case.
457  Gibson banjolele in case.
458  GEORGE FORMBY GOLDEN BANJOLELE IN CASE "WINDOW
     CLEANER".
459  GEORGE FORMBY GOLDEN BANJOLELE IN CASE—SIGNED.
     "CHINESE LAUNDRY BLUES".
```

George is remembered to this very day especially because of the 'George Formby Appreciation Society'. They meet over four weekends each year in Blackpool, to perform his famous songs, watch his films and show their appreciation of his marvellous talents. It's a great tribute to George, performed by outstanding musicians and many ukulele players both professional and amateur.

*George Formby's house 2017*

*Blue Plaque at George Formby's house*

## 1974 FIRE

In times of disaster, there are often lighter moments and there was one connected to the pier fire. Mrs Jean Brown, Manager of the Tyrolean Bar, was taking a well deserved weekend break. She watched the fire from the promenade and thought nothing could be saved from the bar as everything, including the floor, had collapsed into the sea. Mrs Brown then suddenly remembered that the weekly bar takings were stored in an office fire-proof safe.

By now, it was surely buried under the tangled metal, debris and mud beneath the pier. She persuaded a team of firemen to rescue the safe and drag it up the beach, out of harms way. It was then taken to the local Police Station. The lock was jammed and they called in experts to blow it open! Sadly, no record is available as to whether the bar takings survived the fire.

## 2008 – LES DAWSON'S STATUE

As a fitting memorial to the Pavilion and the hours of fun and enjoyment it brought to the many hundreds of thousands of visitors, Mr Graham Ibbeson, the Barnsley artist and sculptor, created a statue of the famous comedian Les Dawson, who was a long term resident of St Annes. Standing in a lovely ornamental garden setting next to the pier's entrance, it was unveiled by Les Dawson's widow Tracy and their daughter Charlotte, on Monday 23 October 2008.

Leslie Dawson Jnr, was born in Collyhurst, Manchester on Monday 2 February 1931 and, after trying a number of unsatisfactory jobs he entered the world of show business, initially playing the piano in a Parisian brothel. He later developed his comedy career into an act similar to that of Norman Evans, featuring a gossiping middle-aged woman. Les sometimes included another comedian, Roy Barraclough and they often performed as a double act.

A very talented pianist, Les developed this skill into an hilarious comedy routine where he played wrong notes with immense enthusiasm encouraging the audience to join him in a sing song. He also had a successful career on both radio and television as well as packing theatres wherever he appeared. He was in demand for his 'Dame' in pantomime and he wrote many books.

Les's first wife, Margaret, died from cancer on Tuesday, 15 April 1986. Les married Miss Tracy Roper on Saturday 6 May 1989, on Tracy's 30th birthday. Les died of a heart attack on Thursday 10 June 1993 aged 62 whilst undergoing a medical examination in a hospital in Manchester.

*Les Dawson Statue*